Cevamp, I

About the author

Jackie Williamson is a compulsive scribbler, whose earliest literary attempts were inscribed on the wooden headboard of her bed with the sharp end of a hairpin when she was seven. After that she went into print as a local newspaper journalist and later into media and public relations work with Thames Valley Police, where she also edited the force newspaper. This was followed by two years as national press officer for the charity Dogs for the Disabled. She is the editor of 'Best Friends: the story of Dogs for the Disabled', a book about the charity. The mother of Sarah, Claire and Alex by her first marriage, she married Michael, a police inspector, in 1990. They now live close to the sea in Pembrokeshire with their beagles, where she has recently become inspired to write poetry.

Cevamp, Mike and Me:

Tales of romance and adventure in the Irish Sea

Jackie Williamson

Acorns Publishing

Published in 2007
by Acorns Publishing

A catalogue record for this book is available from the British Library

Extracts from Cevamp, Mike and Me also appear in 'In Her Element',
an autobiographical anthology about women's experiences of the
Welsh landscape, published in 2008 by Honno Welsh Women's Press:
www.honno.co.uk

ISBN 978-0-9557375-0-3

Designed and set by Elaine Sharples

Printed and bound by CPI Antony Rowe, Eastbourne

Acorns Publishing
Pembrokeshire

www.acornspublishing.co.uk
email: acorns@acornspublishing.co.uk

This book is dedicated to the captain of my ship, Mike, and posthumously to my father-in-law Alex Williamson. Without them it could not have been written.

Acknowledgements

Everyone at Acorns Writers' Group, Royal Oak, Fishguard for
their interest, support, constructive criticism and good ideas
My grandson, Charles Douglas for his invaluable feedback
Vanessa Mellor for her objective analysis of the typescript
Sylvie Nickels of Deddington, for spurring me on
The mothers: Vera Williamson and Sylvia Fewery
Corrine Martin, friend and reader
Annette Ecuyeré Lee of Wordzwork Wales for advice and
encouragement
The BBC press office for information about the
great storm of 1987
Jean Williamson of Holyhead Sailing Club for checking the
length of the harbour wall
Ann Roberts of www.holyhead.com and John Cave, also from
Holyhead, for their willing answers to my questions
Brian Harris of www.cemaes-bay.co.uk for putting me back in
touch with Arthur
Captain Arthur V. Orchard for the bath
Lynn McKnight of Manx National Heritage
Paul Sayle and Dougie Davidson, Isle of Man Lifeboat Service
Lowri Jones, New Quay Tourist Information Centre
Sue Passmore, New Quay historian
Hugh Eaglesfield and Ron Billing for keeping me up to date
The Welsh Books Council
And all those people mentioned in the book who helped
make the story what it is

A wet sheet and a flowing sea,
A wind that follows fast
And fills the white and rustling sail
And bends the gallant mast

A Wet Sheet and a Flowing Sea
Allan Cunningham, 1784–1842

Contents

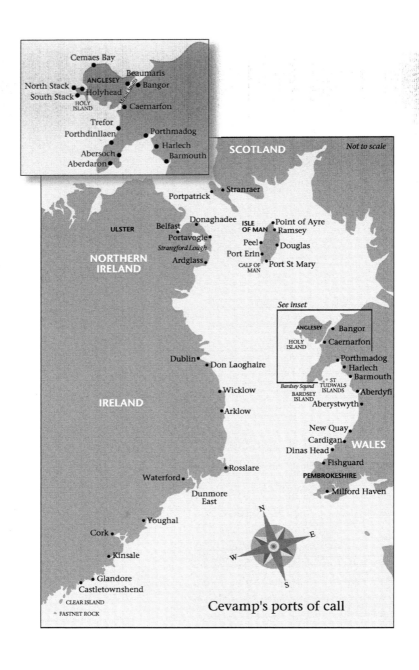

Cevamp's ports of call

Prologue

The owl and the pussycat

LIKE a small child who savours in her imagination the heady delights of Christmas through the slow, dark weeks after Bonfire Night, I'd lived through this weekend dozens of times in my mind.

I'd smelt the sea air, felt the wind whip my hair against my cheeks and felt our bodies lying warm together, sleepy and soothed by the gentle rocking of the boat.

And now, at last, the dream is reality.

We sit companionably on deck, enjoying the sound of wind in the sails as the sturdy wooden hull surges through the waves.

Our eyes meet – his green, flecked with amber, mine a murky grey – and we smile. For once I don't mind him seeing me without makeup, my unruly mop of curls tangled, unkempt and stringy with salt.

Suddenly a dolphin arches clear of the water to swim lazily around the boat, and we agree it just wants to take a look at us and let us know it's there.

Mid-afternoon: the sun breaks through the leaden sky and at last we can get out of our oilskins and woollies into shorts and tee-shirts, then nothing at all.

A swim in the clear but icy sea, then we tumble, gasping, in a shivering, dripping heap onto the deck. Getting warm again.

Back in harbour, we row ashore in the dark, his hands over mine as I try, and fail, to ply the oars as expertly as he does.

Starving now, we race hand in hand through the sleepy Welsh town, to catch the chip shop before it closes. And sitting on a roadside bench in our wellies in the rain, greasy fingers dipping into bags of over-battered cod and vinegar-soaked chips, we tuck into our feast, drinking a toast to each other in cola champagne.

1

Steer into the Wind

'Can you take the tiller for a bit while I go and reef the main?' Mike asked, giving me no time to refuse. I obediently slid into the driving seat as he lurched along the coach-roof to start getting the sail down. Sharp needles of rain mixed with stinging salt spray, the wind howled with vindictive ferocity, the boat was bucking like an unbroken bronco and my co-ordination went completely haywire. I had never found it easy to steer into the wind. This time it was impossible.

'Can't do it, can't do it,' I moaned miserably to myself, my stomach churning in terror at the sight and sound of the big white sail flapping crazily in all directions as the violent tossing of the boat caught every gust. Each time the wind snatched at the canvas the heavy boom slammed over the cockpit and cannoned across to the other side, stopping with a juddering crash that yanked on the rigging and made the yacht shudder. The main-sheet snapped free of its retaining cleat on Cevamp's stern and whipped at my head and ears before snaking away over the back of the boat. Mike wrapped one arm around the cold aluminium of the mast and struggled with his spare hand to release the main-halyard so that he could lower the sail. He is a strong man but I knew he wouldn't be able to hold on for long, before the wildly swinging boom sent him flying into

3

the raging water. The noise was deafening. Wind and waves conspired to shut out all other sound and as Cevamp heeled further and further over, the top of the mast threatened to dip into the waves. I hung on tight to the tiller, hugging it close against my body in a desperate bid to straighten the boat. Frantic, I looked up at Mike and saw his lips moving as he tried to communicate something to me.

'Pardon?' I yelled, polite in spite of my fear. His lips moved again, but the wind tore his words away almost before they left his mouth.

'What?' I yelled back, pitting my full strength against the force of the tiller. By now Cevamp was heeling at an impossible angle and the sea was tumbling over the gunwales, swamping the cockpit and gushing through the companionway into the cabin. I was glad Mike had insisted on me putting on my safety gear but he'd removed his harness to go up to the mast and now he was struggling to keep his footing. The power of the waves against his legs and ankles threatened to sweep his feet from under him and he was having real trouble holding on. The boat was no more than a fragile matchbox, crashing up, down and sideways into the huge foaming breakers which were coming at us from all directions. By now I was really frightened. I desperately wanted to do the right thing. I was terrified Mike would be swept overboard, and I would be to blame. My knees were weak and shaking and my heart was pounding so hard that I could almost hear it over the noise of the storm. Using a peculiar logic, and as much muscle power as I could muster, I pulled the tiller harder and harder towards me, hoping this would pull the boat back up and onto an even keel again. I was so frightened I couldn't think straight and I failed to realise that my actions were having the opposite effect, tipping the boat even further over onto her side. I was overwhelmed with panic. By now, not only Mike's lips were moving, he was also gesturing frantically with his free arm, still hanging on grimly to the mast with the other. I was incapable of understanding, powerless to act and convinced I was about to consign him to a watery grave. I'd be a widow before I even married him. My heart stopped pounding and sank altogether. I was pretty sure by now that I wasn't doing what I was supposed to be doing, but I didn't know what else to do.

'I still can't hear you,' I wailed, holding ever more tightly onto the tiller and wondering how long it would be before the mast actually went under the water.

'Steer into the wind,' yelled Mike over the slamming of the sea and the slapping of the sails. No response.

'Steer into the wind,' he yelled again. Still no response from me. I could only watch, frozen in fear, as the end of the boom dipped into the waves and Mike's booted feet began to slide from under him.

2

Berth pangs

Alex had always enjoyed building boats. Although he spent the first twenty years of his life living far from the sea in Slough and joined the Royal Air Force in preference to the navy, sea water coursed through his veins and sailing boats filled his dreams.

His first foray into the world of shipbuilding resulted in a modest boat for the family to use on the River Avon in Stratford while he was stationed in Warwickshire. Constructed in marine ply and powered by a small outboard engine, it was named the Christine, after Alex's eldest daughter. Later, while the children were young, growing up in north Norfolk and spending their school holidays in the Ransomesque idyll of Wells-next-the-Sea, he was forever building sailing boats for them, starting with a Mirror dinghy. At ten feet long or thereabouts, it was the perfect introduction to sailing for the children. Of the two boys, Mike was the more interested. His brother Phil, older by a little over a year, was less practical and although family photographs show him tanned and tousle-headed in the dinghy – with one arm in plaster – he often preferred to spend his time with his head in a book. The boys occasionally allowed their younger sister Chris to tag along when they went sailing together but at two and a half years younger than Mike she was never in any doubt that she was only there on sufferance.

The Mirror was probably the craft that triggered Mike's enduring passion for yachts and the sea. To this day he enjoys boyhood memories of being caught out by the fickle tides that drained the creeks and salt marshes, and suffering the indignity of plodding doggedly home along the flats dragging his boat behind him.

All the while, though, at the back of Alex's mind, lurked a plan to build a yacht. A proper boat. One for his retirement, when he would climb aboard with his wife Vera and his fishing tackle and sail off into the sunset, down to the Med and a life of perfect contentment.

Although he made several small boats he always dreamed of building a big one and while he was still in the RAF he bought a set of plans for a twenty six foot Yachting Monthly Eventide. This was a sailing yacht designed by the legendary Maurice Griffiths, whose Eventide, Golden Hind and Waterwitch designs were famous for their sea worthiness. They became popular among sailing self-builders and there are few British harbours that don't have a Griffiths design on one of their moorings. As well as designing yachts, Griffiths was a highly respected sailor and writer. Founder of The Little Ship Club, he died on 11th October 1997, aged 91.

Alex modified the plans slightly, to add an extra couple of feet to the boat's overall length, and then set to work. He built the frame of his Eventide in the garage of the family's home in Norfolk. This was a large detached bungalow, also built by Alex. Building the frame entailed a lot of work involving wet wood and clamps – the garage seemed always to be full of clamps and the bath full of wood, soaking in water to make it more pliable. Once the wood softened, Alex bent each piece the way he wanted it and then clamped it firmly so that it dried into the required shape. Having got off to such a good start with the frame, Alex then found he had no time to go any further and took it to pieces again, storing it all in the garage. Realising he couldn't construct the ocean-going yacht of his dreams while he was still in the RAF he settled for a smaller one to tide him over, a sixteen foot, two-berth Yachting Monthly Senior.

He named her the Lizbo, after his youngest child, Elizabeth. Over the years this play on names became something of a trademark for Alex: naming boats after members of the family, but usually by playing with words or family initials in such a way that only the family would get the joke.

By the early 1970s Alex had left the RAF and was working in Slough as a systems analyst with Plessey, the electronics giant. Alex and Vera's relocation to the Berkshire town with the girls was overshadowed by the still unbuilt Eventide. None of the properties the couple viewed was suitable for Alex's yacht-building scheme and, exasperated, Vera bought a tiny, terraced house in the interim. They left the embryonic Cevamp behind in Norfolk. The right house eventually came along but it still had to have the garage extended before another pantechnicon could be despatched to Norfolk to collect the yacht's frame and all the other bits and pieces that Alex had accumulated over the years. Even then there was no room for a car.

Twelve years had passed since Alex bought the plans for the Eventide and his precious yacht was still nothing more than a few skeletal limbs and a big pile of wood but he still cherished his dream.

'It started way back in the mid 1950s when I was a young officer in the RAF. We often flew down to the Med and I was transfixed at the sight of all the beautiful yachts gleaming in the sun and sailing the dappled waters below us. I dreamed of the day when mine would be among them,' he told us. 'I made up my mind that one day the dream would come true. If I'd known how long it would take, I would probably have given up in despair.'

It was to be another two decades before he finally stood at the harbour-side of a small town in north Wales and watched the launch of Cevamp – the jewel of his fleet and the best name of them all. Pronounced Sea Vamp, the letters of her name represented the initials of Alex's own family: Christine, Elizabeth, Vera, Alex, Michael and Philip.

Cevamp's story really began in the early 1970s, around the time that that native trees all over the country were falling victim to the voracious and deadly Dutch elm beetle.

'Vera wanted some garden furniture,' Alex recalled, 'and one sunny Sunday afternoon we decided to take Liz for a drive in the country. As we drove along a lane I heard a buzzing sound. "That sounds like a sawmill," I said to Vera. "I reckon I could get some timber for making your garden seats and table".'

Leaving Vera and Liz in the car at the top of the lane, he walked down to the sawmill and had a look round. One piece of timber caught his eye.

'The man came over. I told him I wanted some elm for garden furniture but I was also interested in this other piece...for making a boat. It turned out to be chestnut.

'I told him I really wanted English oak and told him how big the boat was. He pointed to a tree trunk that was just about ready. It'd been "in the stick" for quite a few years, but the longest lengths were only twelve feet. He said he couldn't help me to scarf – or join – them but said he would cut them as long as possible to keep joints to a minimum. We went over to have a look. It looked good, nothing rotten.'

There and then, completely forgetting about Liz and Vera who were sweltering in the car up the lane, Alex got the man to cut some pieces straight away so he could load them onto the roof rack and take them home with him. The rest would be cut to size and delivered later.

'It was a good hour later that I got back to the car. Vera was fuming. She asked me where the wood for her furniture was. I told her I hadn't got any...but I'd got wood for my boat!'

A few weeks later Alex was the proud owner of a rough-cut pile of wood. All from the one tree, it was just what he wanted and had cost the princely sum of £260. As far as we know, Vera never did get her table and chairs.

Buying the oak tree acted as a spur. Other bits and pieces for the Eventide gradually began to mount up...and so did the cobwebs that gathered upon them. Alex's father gave him some wood for the floor timbers, the rudder was crafted from an ancient piece of wood that had probably come from a boat and then been used in a building and the piece which was eventually to become a magnificent tiller was made out of driftwood.

It seemed there was a tale to tell about every piece of wood that went into Cevamp, but Alex reckoned that acquiring the skin, the marine ply, was the most bizarre. He needed twenty six sheets and knew how expensive it was. He scouted around and eventually someone gave him the phone number of an importer who was thought to have just had some brought in. Alex gave him a call. Yes, he had some, but not a lot. Just a few sheets of top quality BSI 1088, but if Alex phoned 'the guy at Bristol docks' he could probably 'work something out with him'.

The importer was right. The man at the docks did have some left and promised Alex that if he paid for the lorry to take it away he could have the ply for nothing.

'I had no idea what that would cost,' said Alex, 'but he wouldn't wait long for an answer. I asked Plessey Transport to give me an idea of the cost of a lorry from Bristol to Slough. The answer was that it would be about £100 and I knew that even if I could only get two or three sheets of ply that would be worth about the same, so I told the man in Bristol to go ahead.'

A few days later Alex drove home from work to find a very large, open sided truck parked in the road, and two men unloading a piece of wood.

'I would have been thrilled just to have received half a dozen sheets. That would have set me well on the way. So I was delighted and astonished in equal measure to find there were twenty seven sheets of eight-by-four marine ply stacked up against the side of the house. I'd got it for a give-away price and couldn't believe my luck.'

By 1978 Alex had retired from Plessey and he, Vera, Chris and Liz were doing the one thing they always said they would never do – running a pub – in a part of the world they said they'd never move to – Wales. It was a family business, with Alex and Chris in charge of the pub while Vera and Liz ran the hotel and restaurant. They did this with no little success: in 'The Hidden Places of Britain' the author Leslie Thomas describes his 'unerring nose for a good hostelry' and writes about being served 'a nice plate of roast goat and three veg' by Liz when he stayed there whilst researching the book.

The New Inn in Llangynog nestles in a peaceful valley at the foot of the Berwyn Mountains forty miles from the coast and is the last place you would expect to find a yacht being built. But the inn's centuries-old barns and outbuildings gave Alex the space he needed. At long last Cevamp began to take shape.

The mast was another of the lucky finds that often seemed to come Alex's way. Although Cevamp was a wooden boat he wanted an aluminium mast and after ringing around his many contacts he discovered some on Hayling Island. They were in six-inch by four-inch sections, which was roughly what he wanted. Blithely leaving Vera, Chris and Liz at home to run the pub, look after the overnight guests and cook for the restaurant, he drove south. The mast man told him about a shipment of masts he'd ordered from Holland that, on arrival, turned out to be the wrong shape. He added that his only option was to get rid of them, as it would cost him more to send them back. This got Alex thinking. Through his long-standing connections with the Eventide Owners' Association he knew there were a lot of people building Eventide 24s, which the surplus stock would be just right for, and he reckoned he could easily get rid of the unwanted masts. So he struck a deal with the man. Alex would arrange to offload the redundant poles and in return he would get the mast he wanted for £30. The deal was done. Alex cornered the market for Eventide 24 masts and returned home with a brand new 32 foot mast lashed to the roof of his Ford Cortina 1600E.

'That mast certainly startled a lot of people on the journey home and I got a lot of funny looks from other drivers,' he remembered.

He got a lot of funny looks when he got home too, from his wife and daughters.

'Wait till you hear what I've been doing,' he announced as he burst into the kitchen of the inn on his return, naively unaware of the anger they had been brewing at yet another of his absences on boat business. All they knew was that they'd been left holding an extremely demanding baby while he'd been off enjoying himself. The reception he got was considerably cooler than the enthusiastic welcome he was expecting.

Alex was genuinely surprised at his wife and daughters' wrath.

'I thought you were proud of what I'm doing. You're always telling people about it. I really thought you'd be pleased about the mast.'

'We are proud of you Dad, but can't you see how exhausted we get? While you're out there in the barn or chasing boat bits all over the country, we're left to do all the work. Surely you can see how frustrated it makes us. If you pulled your weight a bit more there'd be less for us to do and we wouldn't get so tired.'

It was a familiar scene, caused by a combination of resentment at Alex's absences, their tiredness and overwork but, as always it soon blew over.

Chris's memories of those bitter confrontations remain vivid, although, with the passing of years, she is able to look back on the noisy scenes with fond amusement rather in anger.

'As far as Dad building the boat was concerned, the words blood, sweat and tears always come to mind. Blood because of the times he hurt his hands or hit his head on something; sweat, because of how hard we all had to work, especially Dad doing continuous shifts (bar, boat, bar, boat) and tears, mainly Mum's, Liz's and mine because of how tired we got running the business. Yes, we grumbled at him and resented his absences but he was always a tower of strength, even though he must have been as tired as we were, if not more so.'

The iron keel was another challenge. Alex enjoyed working in wood: it was a material he felt at home with. But iron and lead and molten metals were alien elements and Alex wasn't sure how to do deal with them. He knew the keel would have to weigh about a ton and what's more he knew it was a job for an expert. Worse, he'd already made some enquiries at a foundry and discovered that to have a keel made amounted to a great deal of money.

'I'd had the idea of making a mould and then casting the keel out of pig iron in a reinforced box sort of thing,' he told us. 'But by this time word was getting round about what I was doing and because of this I got to hear about a man on the south coast. He was building a modified Eventide, which he was planning to launch in the near future. Tragically for him, his boatshed caught fire and everything was destroyed except the keel, which he said I could have. It cost me peanuts, about sixty-odd pounds.'

Problem solved.

Or was it? There was a snag. How do you get a one ton iron keel from Southampton to mid Wales? The answer is, you tow it on a trailer behind a borrowed Land-Rover. And when the promised Land-Rover fails to materialise? Well, what the hell. You tow it behind your own car – a game little Ford Fiesta, which was, amazingly, fully up to the job! Another good day for Ford and the Williamson yacht building project but, once again, Alex returned home to find three worn out women who were less than enamoured by his latest exploits.

Having got the keel home, he found that manoeuvring it was no easy job for one man working alone. But he was nothing if not ingenious and rigged up a system of blocks, tackles, pulleys and wedges, which worked fine except for one unforgettable day when the end of the keel rose a little too high, a little too fast, and smacked Alex on the nose.

From then on it was plain sailing all the way. Alex spent every spare minute and a good deal of borrowed time over the next few years in the barn behind the inn, sawing, planing and hammering. He covered the marine ply of the hull in layers of fibre-glass and epoxy resin to keep the boat dry at sea and coated the woodwork on the upper decks with layer upon layer of varnish. Although he frequently suffered injuries to himself during the building process and would have been a Health and Safety inspector's nightmare, the yacht's safety at sea was uppermost in his mind and he went way beyond all safety specifications as far as Cevamp was concerned.

The yacht was Alex's obsession and took priority over everything. Despite this, he still somehow found the time between boat building and running the bar to help with the building of a new house next door to the inn for him and Vera, and to attend evening classes in navigation and the theory of sailing. What's more, however battered and filthy he got while he was working on the boat, he was always clean, fresh and immaculately dressed behind the bar. Customers seemed not to notice the dreadful smell of epoxy resin hanging around the inn and were too polite to comment on the appearance of the monster pulling their pints, with his face and hands swollen from a ferocious reaction to the resin after he'd been applying it to Cevamp's hull.

'Can't you keep all this blooming boat stuff out in the barn?' Vera would grumble as, tired from working long hours at the inn she'd go upstairs to settle down with a book for half an hour, only to find the place draped in acres of sailcloth. 'I've come up here for a bit of peace and quiet and I can't even find a space to sit down.'

Alex, deaf to his wife's complaints, remained where he was, sitting hunched over her 1938 Singer sewing machine, passionately turning the handle and gradually converting the voluminous and unwieldy fabric into the mainsail for Cevamp. Liz's newer machine was also brought in on the act when, not satisfied just with making his own sails, Alex got stuck in to upholstery making, cutting and stitching the black vinyl cushion covers for the saloon and forward cabin.

By the time he had added a Yanmar 8hp marine diesel inboard engine for around £1,000 and £400 worth of bronze nails and screws, Alex calculated the total cost of the yacht prior to launching was around £3,500. He had known just what engine he wanted for a long time and Vera gave him the Yanmar for his fiftieth birthday. A VHF radio, electronic log, ship's compass, echo sounder, radar system and life raft, together with various other pieces of vital equipment such as a cooker, chemical toilet, oilskins, otherwise known as oilies, and life jackets, bumped up the final cost by about the same again but Cevamp was undoubtedly the best equipped, safest small yacht that would ever sail the potentially treacherous waters of the Irish Sea.

More than thirty years after Alex first had his dream of building his own yacht the day finally dawned when Cevamp was to be craned out of the barn and lowered onto the waiting keel in the yard. It was a tense time. Alex knew his calculations were as accurate as he could make them. But were they accurate enough? Would the hull fit the keel? Early in the morning on a damp, misty day in early July, a tall crane on a low loader drew up on the bend in the narrow road outside the New Inn.

Such was the excitement that a television crew turned out to record the event for that evening's news and Vera even promised on camera, to the rest of the family's astonishment, that she was going on a diet so that she would be fit for sailing. Up to that point she hadn't actually set foot on Cevamp. She shared the pride in Alex's achievement that was felt by her sons and daughters but she knew she wouldn't be able to sail because of severe sea sickness. For now, though, she was happy for her husband and enjoying the celebratory atmosphere of the occasion. The grandchildren were running around in a state of super-charged energy, the family was kitted out in smart new Cevamp sweatshirts, bought by Chris especially for the occasion and Alex was taking quiet satisfaction in overseeing the entire operation.

It was a heart-stopping moment for him when his pride and joy was lifted high into the air and swung over the tops of buildings onto the back of the lorry, to cheers from the assembled villagers and a muttered 'I hope that doesn't crash into my garage,' from Liz's husband Wayne, as the yacht lurched perilously close to the roof of the house he had recently finished building for the two of them, just over the wall from the inn.

The yacht was slowly lowered in her cradle and hovered for a few seconds before she finally settled onto the keel. Yes. It was a perfect fit.

There was a strong pulse of satisfaction in Llangynog that day. The building of Cevamp had given the locals, customers and visitors to the remote village something to talk about and everyone wanted to be part of what had almost become a community project.

A couple of weeks later it was time to take Cevamp on her journey over the mountains to the sea. Once again the lorry parked outside the inn and the yacht was strapped into position on the trailer. Mike climbed into the passenger seat of the lorry and, with Alex and the rest of the family following behind, the unlikely convoy wound its way out of the village, up the steep and twisting mountain roads, round the hairpin bends into Bala and across country to Porthmadog.

At 12 noon on Monday, 14 July 1986 Yacht Cevamp, sail number YM1202, was launched onto an incoming tide. It was the culmination of nearly half a lifetime's work for Alex and the realisation, at long last, of his dream.

3

Going for it

'I've met the man I'm going to marry,' I announced confidently to my mother on the phone.

'Oh,' she said. 'That's nice. How long have you known him?'

'Forty five minutes,' I told her. She went quiet. Unusual for her.

'Don't you think,' she asked delicately, 'you're jumping the gun a bit?'

Actually, no. I didn't. I had never been more certain of anything in my life.

It was Monday, March 31 1987. I had been divorced for nearly two years and was working as a reporter on the Bucks Free Press at High Wycombe. One of my jobs was police calls. This was a morning ritual in which reporters from all the newspapers in the area met for the daily press conference at the town's police station. We would gather in a cramped interview room that smelt of stale sweat and tobacco smoke, ready for the nine-thirty meeting with the duty inspector. He, and it was always a he, would then talk us through the crimes, accidents and other events worthy of local newspaper coverage from the previous twenty four hours or, on Mondays, the previous seventy two hours. Over the months we'd got to know each other, and the various police inspectors, pretty well. But on this particular morning we were greeted by a new man.

'I'm Inspector Michael Williamson,' he told us 'and it's my job to get rid of you lot as quickly as possible.' We paid scant attention to his brisk words of welcome, as we knew that not all police officers enjoyed this particular part of their early-turn duties. In fact, even the more co-operative of them did their best to go through the accident and incident books as quickly as they could so they could get back to their 'proper' police work with the minimum of disruption. We were an irritating intrusion, one that had to be kept reasonably sweet and one that sometimes had its uses, such as making appeals for witnesses or warning the public about bogus water-board officials. We were lucky if we could stretch the press conferences to fifteen minutes most days, even allowing for the 'couple of quick questions in private' that we all pestered for, to get our own slant on a story or to ask about an 'exclusive' that we didn't want the others to get wind of.

But this new man was different. Hadn't anyone told him that three quarters of an hour was a bit of a record, even for a Monday morning? He went painstakingly through every job, every stolen car radio, every minor damage accident and every break-in. I was impressed. Not, it has to be said, by his thoroughness or attention to detail. More by the breadth of shoulder under his crisp white shirt and the way the trousers of his police uniform sat on his hips. But what really finished me off was when he caught – and held – my eyes at some point during the meeting. His steady green-brown gaze locked into mine with such an electrical force that my stomach jolted. I was hooked. For me there was no-one else in the stuffy room and even though I knew nothing about him I knew this was the man I would marry.

At that time Thames Valley Police used to hold what they called press liaison evenings in the main towns in the force area and the other reporters and I were looking forward to going to one that Thursday. On the Thursday morning I asked Mike Williamson if he would be there.

'Not if I can help it,' came the terse reply. After just four days as an inspector, he had clearly had enough of the press.

That evening my colleagues and I duly turned up at the police station. There among the uniforms was a by now familiar figure.

'I thought you weren't coming,' I said to Mike.

'The superintendent decided I would,' he replied.

We spent the rest of the evening chatting together and neither of us did much liaising with any one else. He told me he was divorced, lived alone and was looking forward to going home that evening for 'a lonely pizza'. Just what I wanted to hear!

Afterwards, my friend Maureen and I went round the pub for a drink and a chat.

'What should I do now?' I asked her.

'Go for it,' was her unequivocal advice.

Easier said than done. How, exactly, do you 'go for it'? Until my divorce I had been married for nineteen years and was out of practice, to say the least, with chat-up lines.

'Go round the police station and ask to see him,' said Maureen. 'Ask him out.'

The next day I had to go to Thames Valley Police Headquarters in Kidlington, Oxfordshire for a job interview. I enjoyed journalism and the privileges that came with it, but was fed up with interminable council planning meetings, low pay and nil appreciation. In common with many local newspaper reporters of a certain age, I decided my future may well lie in public relations and when I saw an advertisement for assistant press officer with Thames Valley Police I decided to apply.

After the interview I headed back to the office. I had to pass, sort of, the police station so I plucked up the courage to go in and ask to speak to Mike. I didn't have a clue what I would say to him and just hoped I'd think of something. I needn't have worried. He was off duty on a long weekend, but the officer I spoke to said he'd leave him a message.

'When does he start back?' I asked.

'He's back on nights on Monday,' he said.

'Okay, tell him I'll ring him on Monday night,' I said.

Monday dawned. It was a long day, and I wondered if I'd have the courage to make the call. What on earth would I say? Maureen was more confident.

'You've got to go for it,' she kept saying. 'You'll think of something.'

By twenty past ten on the Monday night I was shaking with nerves, my mouth was dry and I nearly bottled out. Maureen's voice echoed in my mind. So I went for it. Mike answered the phone and I drummed up some cock and bull reason for ringing him – something to do with an under-age driver who had stolen a car, and had he been arrested yet? Then I ran out of things to say. Silence. More silence.

'Did you have a nice weekend?' I managed. Hardly original but it kept the conversation going. Mike said something about doing a bit of horse riding and playing a game of squash and I made some noises in reply. More silence.

'Oh well,' I managed to blurt out, before hanging up. 'Perhaps we could go for a drink sometime.'

That was it. I'd done it. I knew I would never hear from him again, but at least I'd gone for it.

Two weeks later, at eleven o'clock on a Thursday morning, I was working on that week's page one lead. I was in a bit of a panic as it was press day and I'd only just started researching it. In fact, I'd forgotten all about it until the news editor asked where was the lead, so I was working flat out. The phone rang on my desk. I answered it irritably.

'Michael Williamson here,' said the voice.

'Who?' I snapped back.

'Mike Williamson.' I still didn't get it.

'Who?' I repeated.

'Inspector Williamson,' he persisted. 'I wondered if you'd like to come out for that drink.'

4

Early days

I got the job and our romance progressed, slowly but surely. Mike is not an easy person to get to know well, but as far as I was concerned he was worth the effort. He talked a lot about his father's sailing yacht, which was moored in Porthmadog harbour in north Wales, and although I didn't say much, for fear of seeming pushy, I inwardly hoped I would be around long enough to see it. We had known each other for nearly four months when Mike said to me diffidently one day in July: 'I'm going up to the boat for the weekend. You're welcome to join me if you'd like to.' Would I like to? I'd love to. I'd always been attracted to the sea and to boats, and what's more, we watched Howard's Way on television every Sunday so I knew all about sailing.

I packed carefully for the weekend. My choice of clothes rather gave me away: white shorts, blue and white stripy tee-shirt, tight white jeans, summery little moccasins, skimpy swimming costume, sexy nightie, make-up, perfume, hair dryer…Thanks to Howard's Way I knew exactly what you wear to go sailing. It wasn't long before I found out, from bitter experience, what genuine yachties really wear – several layers of warm clothing, thermal vests, thermal long-johns, wellies, thick socks, thicker sweaters, waterproof sailing suits, warm gloves, bobble hats, nothing white and track suits in bed to keep out the cold!

It was Mike's long weekend off work and I managed to get a couple of days off in lieu of some extra days I'd worked so we were able to set off late on the Thursday afternoon. Mike picked me up from my terraced cottage next to the old slaughterhouse in Banbury and we were in high spirits as we set off on our long drive to Wales. Before we reached Porthmadog, however, and this little wooden Eventide yacht that I'd heard so much about, I had a serious hurdle to overcome. We were stopping off at Llangynog on our way to the boat, where I would meet Mike's parents, Alex and Vera, and his two sisters for the first time. The prospect terrified me. It wasn't so much the parents I was bothered about, as the sisters. For some unfathomable reason I'd conjured up pictures in my mind of two super-cool sophisticates and I was convinced I would neither compare well with them in Mike's eyes nor, even worse, would I win their approval as a suitable wife-in-waiting for their brother.

I needn't have worried. Although we barely stayed long enough for a reviving drink after our long drive from Banbury to Llangynog, it was long enough to be made welcome – and for Vera to lend me a thick, waterproof sailing coat. As for the two girls, I don't know what the panic was all about. They were cheerful and friendly and made a good job of disguising their curiosity about me, even when their brother introduced me as 'my friend Jackie'.

It was getting dark as we drove out of Llangynog and up the dramatic mountain road with its sheer drop down the slate strewn mountainsides to the valley floor hundreds of feet below. The road was unfenced and Mike was careful to keep away from the edges as he rounded blind bends in the twilight. We were soon driving over the lumpy summits of the Berwyn Mountains and I was startled to see big white boulders lumber to their feet, skitter across the road and disappear into the gloomy safety of the heather clad moors beyond. Sheep. Of course. We were in Wales, after all. Once through the hairpin bends of the descent we passed through the lakeside town of Bala. The lake, or Llyn Tegid to give it its proper name, is a popular venue for water sports enthusiasts but more importantly to conservationists, it is home to several thousand gwyniad, a herring-sized fish that is a relic of the Ice Age and is unique to the lake. It was a short hop from Bala to the bleak nuclear power station at Trawsfynydd and by now too dark to appreciate what I'd been told was spectacular scenery. That would have to wait for the daylight journey home.

According to Mike, we would be able to see some giant butterflies that inhabited the area. I was eager to see them and kept my eyes peeled, anxious not to miss them.

'We probably won't be able to see them in the dark,' I said.

'Yes we will. They're so big and bright you can't miss them,' he assured me.

'I wonder why they're so big,' I mused. 'Perhaps it's something to do with the mountain environment. Or more likely because of the power station.'

Although Mike was grinning to himself in that superior way of his, he made no reply. I don't know why but I often seemed to say things that appealed to his odd sense of humour. We motored on in silence. Then shortly before we reached Penryhndeudraeth he nudged me with his left elbow.

'Look. There they are. Over there. On the wall of that house.'

He slowed down. I looked out of the car window and there, sure enough, on the flinty walls of the cottage opposite were three, huge pale-blue butterflies...made of painted enamel and fixed to the wall as ornaments! I felt such a fool. There I was wittering on about mountain air and power stations and all the time he was having me on. These colourful butterflies turned out to be crafted by local artists and were a popular adornment on houses in the area.

We finally reached Porthmadog in bright moonlight at about ten o'clock, parked the car in front of the holiday flats on The Cob beside the harbour and walked down the strip of shingle beach to untie the waiting dinghy from its mooring ring on the wall. Once we'd loaded up Mike's single bag, my huge suitcase and our box of essential provisions I stepped gingerly on board and Mike rowed us round the corner to Cevamp. She was tied to a mooring away from the main harbour, where twice a day the ebbing of the tide left her high and dry on firm golden sands. It was close to the causeway, where the small steam trains of the famous Ffestiniog railway cross the estuary taking holiday makers and tourists to the slate-mining villages of Tanygrisiau and Blaenau Ffestiniog, high in the mountains a few miles inland.

This, then, was the first time I saw Cevamp, and even in the dim light of the streetlamps on The Cob I was enchanted.

To my inexperienced eyes, she was a real ship in miniature. Mike had already told me the story of how his father, Alex, had spent every spare minute over the previous thirteen years building the twenty six foot yacht in a barn at the back of the family's pub in

Llangynog. I'd seen the photographs of her being craned over the rooftops of the New Inn and heard how she was transported over the Berwyn Mountains to be launched at Porthmadog. Now, on that first evening, as we climbed from the wobbling dinghy up the boarding ladder and onto the deck, I was anxious to see her for myself. While Mike worked his way through the key ring, opening hatches and lockers, I eagerly soaked up every detail from the magnificent, if slightly pretentious, bowsprit sticking out at the front to the wind generator spinning merrily on the rails at the back.

Inside, through landlubber's eyes, I marvelled at the detail, at the personal touches and compactness of it all, from the clever device that held the mugs in place to the cooker which swung on gimbals to keep everything safe. There was even a plastic bag containing several bars of marine soap that was supposed to lather in sea water. Alex had thought of everything. This was my first time on a sailing boat, and everything was deliciously new. I didn't even know bow from stern, and really hadn't a clue about the technicalities of sailing, the peculiar terminology or how to raise a sail. To me, a painter was someone who decorated your house, a sheet was something you put on the bed and a tack was something handy for fixing your stair carpet. I obviously had a lot to learn.

There were two steps down to the main cabin, with shelving in an alcove on the right to hold the instruments. Inside the cabin, on the left, was a dining table fixed between two settees and another much smaller table which dropped down from the wall .This, Mike told me, was the chart table. The settee cushions lifted up to reveal lockers underneath and the sturdy wooden table top dropped down between the settees to make a good sized double bed. On the other side of the cabin was a stainless steel sink with a funny little water tap. You operated the tap by pumping with your foot on a pedal on the floor. Under the sink was a double cupboard, with loads of space for storage, and to the right of the draining board was the cooker – two burners, a grill and an oven. Mike showed me the gas tap behind the cooker and impressed upon me the importance of turning off the main supply before turning off the cooker taps, to stop any unused gas sinking to the floor and lying dangerously in the bilges.

All around the varnished wood-panelled cabin were proper electric strip-lights and little curtained windows with brass window frames and a strange system of screws for opening them. My fascination with the window fasteners evaporated later in my sailing career. They lost their attraction after they'd poked me in the eye on numerous occasions as I struggled to keep my balance, make the coffee and plot a course on a wildly bucking bronco! There was an electric fan, to keep you cool in hot weather, two or three fire extinguishers and an asbestos fire blanket. I was impressed at all the safety gear on board. Mike showed me where the flares were stored, and explained how an EPIRB works. I had never heard of these devices before, and was intrigued. If you get into difficulties at sea you activate the EPIRB – Emergency Position Indicating Radio Beacon – which then bounces signals off satellites to give your position, making it easier for rescue teams to find you.

The main cabin was separated from the front section of the boat's interior by a curtain, which we later discarded. On the left was the toilet, which I was intrigued to hear was called the heads and opposite was a roomy wardrobe with drainage holes in the floor, for wet oilskins and other sodden clothing. At the front was another double cabin and right at the very front, where the cabin narrowed to a sharp V, was a box for stowing the anchor chain.

It was on the shelf in the toilet compartment that I found Vera's contribution to Cevamp – two books: Gone With the Wind and The Book of Prayers for Sailors. I couldn't think of anything more apt!

The next day we left our mooring at high water, just before half past nine. I felt fairly useless and just sat there while Mike did everything. Watching him, I knew there was no way I would ever master all these complicated procedures or even understand what he was talking about, so I sat quietly in a corner taking it all in and ready to do as I was told.

With its protective armour of towering grey mountains, wide estuary and wonderful light, Porthmadog is a beautiful harbour but not one to be treated casually. The ever-shifting sands and constant changes to the deep water channel mean that its approaches have to be treated with respect and you ignore the buoyage system at your peril. As we chugged up the channel on that first morning Mike attempted to teach me some basic navigation.

'Starboard is the right hand side of the boat as you look at the front and port is the left. When you're going in and out of harbours the deep water channel is usually marked with buoys. You keep the red buoys to the right, or starboard, and the green ones to the portside of the boat on your way out of the harbour, and vice versa on your way back in. It's easy when you know how.'

'Yes,' I said dubiously. 'But how do I actually remember that port is left and starboard right? I've forgotten already.'

Mike also attempted to explain to me the rules of the road.

'Now this is dead simple. It's just the opposite of the rules of the road when you're in a car. The first one to remember is that you pass oncoming boats by keeping them on your port side. It's important to learn the rules if you want to avoid collisions.'

Hmmm. I could see already that I wasn't going to find this sailing business easy. We picked our way carefully along the deep water channel, following the harbour-master's hand-drawn chart of the buoyage system, got safely past 'White House Conspic', and reached the fairway buoy, which marks the end of the shallow channel, at a quarter past ten.

'Right,' said Mike. 'It's time to get the sails up and head out to sea.'

We sailed happily along the craggy coastline of Tremadog Bay, where the slate mountains come down to dip their toes into the sea, and reached Bardsey Sound about mid afternoon. Mike warned me that this was a lively stretch of water between the rocky tip of the Lleyn Peninsular and Bardsey Island and we could expect a bumpy ride. We weren't disappointed. He pulled on a few ropes to make the sails as small as possible while still giving the boat some stability. Then he switched the engine on to give him enough control to keep the boat away from the outcrop of rocks and the jagged shoreline under the menacing, spray-lashed cliffs. Or at least, that's what he told me he was doing. My ignorance meant I wasn't aware of danger and therefore I felt no fear, so I thoroughly enjoyed the experience of bouncing through the waves and by the time we moored up at Porth Dinllaen for the night I knew I'd become addicted. I loved the way you only had to move from one side of the boat to the other to make her tip over and I soon learned that once underway everything has to be firmly anchored down. You tend to get the hang of these things fairly fast, once you've had a couple of hot drinks in your lap.

Sailing, I now knew, was definitely the life for me. I became an instant expert, and in my new role as police press officer and editor of Thames View, the Thames Valley Police newspaper, I even wrote an authoritative centre page spread in about the in-house Sailing Club. That, of course, is one of the skills you have to develop as a journalist: you get to know very little about a great deal and yet manage to convince other people you know what you are talking about.

My role that first weekend set the pattern for my future sailing career. In the log Mike wrote 'Jackie Douglas crew/cook'. This suited me. I knew I could never be skipper, and I love cooking. I was very happy to be the galley slave, a phrase I thought I had cleverly invented but one I later discovered is used universally by the sailing fraternity. For all my enthusiasm, though, that first cruise did not really do justice to my onboard culinary skills and I wouldn't have been surprised if I hadn't been asked again. All the while Alex was building Cevamp, the dream that spurred him on was the enduring one of long-distance blue-water cruising, to the Mediterranean and maybe even further a-sea. So it should not have been a surprise to find, on my first weekend as crew/cook, that the cupboards were stuffed with enough tins to see him and Vera through a three week becalming. At least. There were tinned carrots, tinned peas, tinned potatoes, tinned beans, tinned tomatoes and…forty eight tins of braised steak and kidney.

Remember, this was my first ever trip to sea, with a man I had only known four months. I was desperate to impress indelibly on him the fact that I would make him the perfect wife. But, oh dear! Our first meal on board together was, to be absolutely honest, somewhat less than the unqualified success I had hoped it would be – although to be fair, it did undoubtedly impress itself on his memory.

It was just after noon on the first day that I offered to make some lunch. So far Mike had done everything and I needed to show willing. We were sailing along with what I now knew to be the main sail and the genoa out fully and making pretty good time. We'd covered about twelve miles, St Tudwal's Islands were glinting in the sun off our port bow and the sea air was sharpening our appetites. I went below to see what I could rustle up for lunch, from Alex's store cupboards.

We had tinned potatoes, tinned peas, tinned carrots and, of course, hefty, man-sized portions of the ubiquitous tinned braised steak and kidney. This was followed by a pudding of tinned peaches and tinned rice pudding. Mike, never a man not to leave a clean plate, politely forced it all down, and bravely polished off his final mouthful of rice pudding. Then, without a word he got up from his seat, slowly and carefully made his way to the back of the boat, draped himself elegantly over the transom…and neatly parted company with the entire, vile concoction. From that moment I decided that if this sailing lark was to be a permanent feature of our relationship then I had better take control of what food we took on board. It could only get better.

If Friday's lunch was the low spot of the weekend, Saturday evening provided the highlight when, sailing back towards Criccieth, we took it in turns to dive off the back of the boat and swim along behind her, hanging on to a rope and being towed through the cool emerald water at an exhilarating six knots.

The weekend seemed to end almost before it had begun and it was the beginning of a pattern which was to shape our lives. We spent long weekends each month sailing Cevamp with longer, two or three week cruises each spring and summer. My knowledge, skills and love of the sea grew and Mike's confidence increased with every trip, as we ventured further and further afield. Even in winter, Cevamp dominated our lives, with hundreds of hours spent servicing her engine, painting her top-sides, scrubbing her bottom and looking after her every need. It soon became clear that, sadly, Alex wasn't really fit enough to skipper his own boat any more, and Vera wasn't really interested. Phil was working abroad, Chris and the children liked coming out for the day occasionally but that was as far as it went and Liz, like Vera, had no real interest in sailing. So Cevamp became, to all intents and purposes, our boat. We were always more than happy to take other members of the family out sailing with us, for Alex to help us repair any damage she suffered at our hands and, of course, she was there for any of others to use if they wanted to. But they didn't. Gradually she began to feel like ours, we kitted her out to suit ourselves, replaced Alex's tins with our own stores and it wasn't long before our lives revolved around our boat, our sailing and each other.

5

Hungerford

On Wednesday August 19, 1987 Michael Ryan went crazy with a Kalashnikov rifle in the peaceful market town of Hungerford in Berkshire. He shot dead 15 people, including one of our own officers, before turning the gun on himself. It was one of those slow moving days, hot and bright with the harsh sunlight of high summer. Some time after mid-morning in the police press office we updated the media line with the announcement: 'It's another peaceful day in the Thames Valley. No news for you'.

An hour later the first terrible messages started coming in to the central control room and as the full horror of what was taking place began to strike us the phones in the office started to ring. A small team of us worked in shifts round the clock for the next thirty six hours, dealing with media enquiries from all over the world and trying to cope, ourselves, with the shock and tragedy of what had happened. We never did have time to change the message on the media line and it continued to make its ironic announcement for the rest of the day.

The professionalism of Thames Valley's officers was tested to the full that day and in the days that followed, and while they were being stretched to breaking point at the scene we were doing our damnedest to support them forty or so miles away at police headquarters in Kidlington, just outside Oxford. It was obvious at a very early stage that the enormity of what was unfolding at Hungerford was going to need massive back-up from headquarters and the major incident contingency plan swung into action. Ryan's shooting spree had started in the Savernake Forest, between Hungerford and Marlborough, continuing into Hungerford itself and leaving a trail of dead and injured people in his wake. One of these was his mother, Dorothy. He was firing indiscriminately in the streets and into people's homes, and the police could only be sure the shooting had stopped after they had recovered Ryan's own body, having first checked to make sure he hadn't booby trapped himself. People felt besieged and were panicking, afraid to leave their homes but terrified of what may have happened to their families and friends. The casualty bureau telephones rang non-stop as specially trained police officers and civilian support staff did their best to provide answers and offer reassurance to those people for whom they had no answers. And in the press office call followed call, giving us no time to put the phones down before the next press enquiry came through. Time lost its meaning as our small team carried on throughout the day and into the night, dealing with British television, newspaper and radio enquiries, as well as those from Australia, Canada, the United States and other parts of the world. Our difficulties were compounded by a lack of information from the scene, partly because of the enormous workload being put on BT's system and partly because Hungerford was in a radio 'black spot' meaning the police radios were not functioning properly. In some cases the journalists at the scene knew more than we did.

At about midnight Chief Constable Colin Smith returned from Hungerford and called in to the press office to thank us all. He looked tired and drained and we appreciated the gesture. I was sent home to grab a few hours sleep and then it was another busy day with the media, trying to ensure their reports contained more fact than conjecture and doing our best to act as an information barrier between the media and the officers on the ground.

Media interest remained high for months afterwards, which kept the press office busy, but there were more important issues to be faced. Bereaved families pleaded for privacy to mourn and those who were injured had to try to recover from their physical and mental scars. The town of Hungerford needed time as a community to recover and many members of the emergency services who were directly involved on the day of the tragedy needed help in coming to terms with the trauma. Funerals and inquests were inevitable and the media cooperated with police and family requests to limit the amount of intrusion by operating a pool system and sharing information among themselves. Members of the media were not allowed to witness Michael Ryan's funeral at Reading crematorium on the morning of September 3, 1987. This was a low key, subdued affair which I attended on their behalf and then briefed them on it afterwards. There were wider issues to be tackled too. Immediately after the shootings pressure mounted on the Government to tighten-up controls on the possession of firearms and eventually the law was changed.

It was with an overwhelming sense of sadness that I joined Mike on the Thursday evening for our second long weekend's sailing together and I was, for me, unusually subdued during the five hour drive to Porthmadog. While I was looking forward to the weekend, part of me wanted to stay behind to help and I felt guilty at leaving my colleagues at such a busy and difficult time.

Now that I'd passed the test, by not only enduring but actually enjoying my first weekend's sailing, Mike and I had spent the previous four weeks wishing our lives away as we anticipated and planned for this, our next mini-cruise. We didn't go quite so far afield this time, as our late arrival on the Thursday night meant we overslept and missed the morning tide. By the time we stirred ourselves Cevamp was high and dry on the sand...so we went back to bed.

Having lost the day's sailing we cast off from our mooring on the evening tide and motored out in the warm, damp air to the fairway buoy. Mike raised the sails and we enjoyed the sudden blissful silence as he cut the engine and Cevamp allowed herself to be powered along by the breeze instead. At dusk we dropped anchor and sat quietly on deck, enjoying the view across the estuary where the dark and brooding ruins of Harlech Castle were just visible in the fading light. Built on a cliff by Edward I, Harlech was one of the English king's 'iron ring' of Welsh castles. These massive fortresses formed a chain of coastal defences that eventually stretched from Flint to Aberystwyth and helped to keep the troublesome Welsh from rising against their English rulers. That worked for just over a century, until Owen Glyndwr led a national uprising and laid siege to the castle at Harlech. It eventually fell to his forces in 1404 and became Glyndwr's headquarters until it was retaken by the English in 1408. Construction of Harlech Castle began in

1283 and finished six years later: when work was at its peak in 1286 around 950 stonemasons, labourers and craftsmen were working on it. A fortified 200 foot stairway led from the castle to the sea below and in the days before the hungry tides ate into the cliff and left the fortress glowering over vast stretches of sand, most of its provisions were delivered by ship to be lugged up the stairs to the garrison above.

The next morning there was no wind but we woke up to the sound of heavy rain beating on the coachroof so instead of the planned early start we lingered over our breakfast of bacon, eggs, sausages and beans while the weather cleared. The smell of frying bacon wafting out of a boat's galley and mingling with the dewy fresh morning air is one of life's great pleasures and gives an added edge to already healthy appetites.

Mike mopped up the last of his egg yolk with a buttery crust of toast, pushed his plate away, stood up and stripped off his clothes.

'Coming for a swim?' he said, and without waiting for an answer he dived off the back of the boat. I was dubious.

'Is it cold?'

'No, it's lovely. Once you get used to it'.

Well I'm not the competitive type and I don't like being cold. But on the other hand, this was too good a chance to miss for showing him how compatible we were.

'Race you round the boat,' I shouted as I flung off my robe and plunged into the water. It was...exhilarating.

After a couple of laps of the boat we clambered back on board, had fun towelling each other down and finally set sail south towards Barmouth. The wind played hide and seek with us all day until, tired of messing us about, it picked up late in the afternoon and chased us all the way back into Porthmadog harbour.

6

Learning the Ropes

What with robberies and rape, muggings and murder, traffic accidents and road safety campaigns, one way and another I was kept busy with my engrossing new career. But come weekends, I couldn't wait to get away on the boat with Mike and we carried on sailing as late into the season as we could.

Gradually I learnt more about it, got to know Cevamp more intimately and even began to recognise other types of yachts. Gradually I began to understand the difference between long keel, fin keel or bilge keel boats – Cevamp's long keel was enhanced by twin skegs so that she remained upright on the sand when the tide went out. Always an avid reader, I soaked up every scrap of knowledge I could from magazines and books on sailing as well as from Reed's Nautical Almanac and the numerous sailing handbooks on board Cevamp. Mike's dad had forgotten nothing when it came to kitting Cevamp out and there were books on celestial navigation, knots, weather forecasting, international regulations for preventing collisions at sea, first aid for yachtsmen, 'going foreign', flags and signals. I was a theoretical expert after two weekends sailing but practical expertise? That's something you learn over a lifetime.

The more I read the more my confidence increased. I learned that a well-designed, well-built yacht was just about the safest craft on the sea and Cevamp certainly fitted both these criteria. Alex, Mike's dad, had left nothing to chance in Cevamp's construction and we knew the Maurice Griffiths design, with its instantly recognisable lines, had been well and truly tried and tested: there are many records of Eventides crossing oceans. I began to understand how the weight of the keel keeps a yacht from rolling over and Mike made sure I was familiar with all the safety procedures, where the flares were kept and whether to use orange smoke in daylight or red flares at night. He taught me how to use the radio and how to transmit an emergency message, just in case he was swept overboard, or knocked unconscious by the boom. I read about some of the tragedies that take place at sea, when sailors abandon their yacht in a storm and take to the life-raft. All too often they are lost, while the yacht is later found to be still afloat. And I came to understand that more lives are lost in dinghies in harbour than are ever lost off-shore, either because of overloading, under-inflation or inebriation among crew members after a night ashore.

Although I struggled, then as now, with the art of tying proper knots I developed a fascination for the timeless instruments of navigation and the private, secret language of the sailor. The navigational Douglas protractor, the brass dividers, Captain Fields' parallel ruler, and the cute little hand-bearing compass became my intriguing new toys as I slowly learned how to take a fix and work out our position on the charts. Hitherto familiar words such as deviation and variation took on new meanings as I struggled to understand what they meant and the difference between them. Mike was patient.

'Variation is the angular difference between magnetic north, where your compass points, and true, or geographical, north. The angle decreases a tiny bit each year because of the movement of the magnetic pole. Deviation is what happens when the magnetic influences on the boat, such as its electrical systems or the ferrous metals in its engine or keel, pull the compass needle away from magnetic north, either east or west.'

Yeeees. I got that okay. It was the next bit that had me struggling. Somehow you have to apply the rules of variation and deviation when you want to plan or plot your course on a chart. Mike tried to explain the rules to me, something to do with the mnemonic error west compass best, error east compass least but to this day they remain a mystery.

That other mystery, the effect of the moon on the rise and fall of the tides, and the fact that there is nothing man can do to influence it, was a constant source of wonder to me and I sat quite happily for hours on end when we were in harbour, just watching the ebb and flow of the tide. We had a little blue book that gave the times and heights of the tide at Liverpool, our nearest standard port, and the time differences that had to be applied to discover the relevant times for local harbours. Not being blessed with a head for figures, I spent ages working them all out while Mike concentrated on the more technical aspects of passage planning. We could tell from the tide tables as well as from our own observations whether we were on neap tides or springs and for once I found it easy to remember which was which: neaps mean highest lows and lowest highs while springs mean lowest lows and highest highs, something that can make the difference between getting safely in to harbour or having to spend the night bouncing around at anchor a little way off shore. What was startlingly new to me was that you get neaps and springs twice every lunar month, with the changing phases of the moon. Previously I thought neaps came with the autumn equinox and springs with the spring one. Something to do with harvest time and turneeps, I suppose!

All this book learning makes me sound very knowledgeable. I'm not now and I certainly wasn't then. I still had everything to learn about the practicalities. I hadn't a clue how to raise the sails and I became horribly disorientated when we had to tack.

'I can't see the logic of going miles out of our way to get from one place to another just because the wind's blowing from the wrong direction,' I grumbled.

An hour later we're still tacking, still making no obvious progress.

'I've got a good idea. Why don't we just switch the engine on and go straight there? It would be a lot faster that way.' And what's more, I thought to myself, I'll be in harbour in time to go and have a hot shower.

Oh dear. I still hadn't got to the point of understanding that a sailing boat was for sailing in and part of the pleasure, I was told sternly, was in sailing it.

'The idea isn't to get from A to B as fast as possible – if you want to do that find someone with a motorised gin palace. On this boat we're here to sail!'

So I sailed. It wasn't always easy for me though. As someone who was used to whizzing around by car, foot to the floor, four-or-fewer miles an hour seemed, at times, to be unbearably slow. You sit gazing at the same stretch of coastline for hours on end, go below, have a sleep, cook lunch, eat it, have a nap, bake a cake, make a cup of tea and then when you emerge again, expecting to be nearly at your chosen anchorage, there it still is – that same old bit of mountain looming over that same old bit of shore. Neither could I understand that sailing is, in any case, often faster than using the boat's engine. I didn't realise that although the log may only be showing four knots, you could be going considerably faster if the tidal stream is going your way. What's more, when the conditions were right we could often sail at speeds of more than four knots, even in a ploddy little boat like Cevamp, while the engine's top cruising speed never reached more than four or five. Gradually I began to get the hang of the slow pace and accepted that it could take four or five hours to travel the fifteen miles or so up the coast from Porthmadog to Pwllheli, a mere twenty minute hop by car. All this came later, much later, but I must admit that even now, hundreds of sailing miles and several years later, Mike's stubborn determination not to switch on the engine to get us into harbour after a long day at sea can still leave me bursting with frustration.

But there were other, more serious problems for me to grapple with, not least the concept of tiller steering, which I found incredibly difficult to grasp.

'You just point the tiller the opposite way to where you want to go,' Mike would explain, not quite through gritted teeth as, for the umpteenth time I got it wrong, spilling the wind from the sails, causing the boom to clonk over to the other side of the boat and ensuring that yet again we had gone drastically off course. Worse than that was the sheer panic that overtook me every time Mike left me alone to steer, while he clambered onto the cabin roof to do something manly with the sails. I simply could not steer into the wind and hold the boat steady at these times. I knew why I had to do it, to let the wind out of the sails to make them manageable, but I just could not do it. No sooner did I get it right, craning my neck to peer up the rigging to look at the fluttering red and green telltale ribbons that told me which way the wind was blowing, than I would lose it. Then I would frantically put the tiller right over to the other side, which meant we would oversteer, then realising what I had done I would pull it just as far the other way, meaning we would oversteer again. How Mike managed to keep his patience, not to mention his balance, I will never know.

My other problem was that I was inordinately clumsy and was for ever falling over, bumping into things or tripping up. It seemed to me that everything hard and pointed on the boat was at thigh height, and my legs were always a mass of green, yellow and purple bruises after a couple of days at sea.

I suppose my one saving grace was that I was never seasick, thanks to a cast iron constitution inherited from my father. However bad the weather and however much the boat slammed, plunged and reared into the waves, I was never ill. The only thing that induced a slight queasiness was the sickly sweet smell of the chemical that was supposed to deodorise the toilet. Sailing alone or with his father, Mike had never used it, both of them preferring to do what they had to do over the side. But having a woman on board for the first time brought his natural gallantry to the fore. Concern for my lavatorial sensitivities and the polite decorum of the early stages of our relationship decreed we would use the loo. And use it we did. But only for a short while. The wretched thing had to be emptied, which was not only an embarrassing but considerably less than fragrant task. Then there was the added frisson of danger that in heavy seas its contents would spill onto the cabin floor – not what most sailors want to have slopping around in the bilges. So sometime during our second weekend of sailing together we agreed to throw modesty to the winds and revert to the good old bucket-and-chuck-it method instead.

Day to day life on board Cevamp was usually geared towards listening to the shipping forecast, broadcast four times a day on BBC Radio Four. The unexpected poetry of those peculiar place names, which I remembered hearing as a child being chanted like a mantra on the wireless while my father waited to hear the news or the football results, now took on a real, new meaning. Lundy, Fastnet and Irish Sea actually had a relevance to my life.

By September I had learned as much as I could. I'd taken out a subscription to Yachting Monthly, invested in some new thermal underwear and bought myself a pair of sailing wellies. I was ready for my first long voyage.

7

Mike sails solo

Optimism was the better part of discretion when we sat down to decide where to go for our early autumn sailing holiday and we hit on the droll idea of a British Isles cruise, visiting harbours in England, Ireland, Scotland, Wales and the Isle of Man and having a glass of the local tipple in each country: real ale in England, whisky in Scotland and Guinness in Ireland. Wales and the Isle of Man presented a bit of a problem, as we had no idea what their national drinks were. Never mind, we thought, we'll think of something.

Mike had already booked three weeks leave but I could only get two so we decided that he would drive up to Porthmadog a week before me and sail round to Dickie's boatyard at Bangor, where he would meet me off a train a week later. Once, during his annual appraisal at work, Mike was described by his boss as having 'terrier-like qualities'. He certainly needed them over the first four days of the trip, as conditions during most of his solitary eighty miles were appalling. This is his account of his first attempt at sailing single-handed.

I faced my first hurdle even before I left Porthmadog, where so many boats were rafted up against the harbour wall that I was unable to get a hose from the tap to fill up with fresh water. It was a Sunday morning in late September and my first port of call was Pwllheli. I arrived without mishap at lunchtime and spent the afternoon at anchor in the harbour entrance, drying out the sails and waiting for high tide before going in to the harbour for the night. This was before the marina development really put Pwllheli on the map for sailors in this part of Wales and the harbour at that time consisted of a shallow estuary draining from a large circular pool that dried out at low tide.

The following morning I made myself some breakfast, stowed everything away and left on the tide in a stiff breeze just after noon. It was pouring with rain and there were heavy seas, which grew steeper with every passing hour. As I crossed the aptly named Hell's Mouth conditions worsened steadily and by the time I was off Aberdaron I could hardly make out the coastline, even though I was only a few miles off shore. Huge waves pounded the boat on all sides and I still remember the icy tingle as stinging rods of rain drove into my face. As I got closer to the treacherous tip of the Lleyn Peninsular the tiny unlit islands of Ynys Gwylan-fawr and Ynys Gwylan-bach kept appearing and disappearing off the starboard bow, straining my nerve to the limits. I made up my mind to call Jack as soon as I could get to a phone and tell her the holiday was off. The thought of going through the overfalls of Bardsey Sound single handed in such bad conditions was a bit daunting but luckily the tidal stream was in my favour. Once clear of the narrow stretch of boiling water I tucked in under the shelter of the cliffs and made good progress, reaching Porth Dinllaen in failing light at eight o'clock in the evening – thirty two tough miles in little less than eight hours.

The next morning dawned warm and sunny and I dried out all the life jackets and other waterlogged gear from the cockpit lockers before setting off for Caernarfon. As I approached the shallow water of Caernarfon Bar, at the southernmost end of the Menai

Straits, the sea became very lumpy and Cevamp really had to battle against the out-going tide. Many craft have foundered here over the centuries and I was reminded of just how dangerous it can be when I spotted a recent shipwreck of a small coaster that had gone aground. By now I'd had enough for the day and was looking forward to resting in still waters.

Caernarfon's narrow harbour is protected from the wild elements by its massive thirteenth century castle. Another of the chain of castles built in Wales by Edward I, this was the one from which England was to rule Wales. But it wasn't to give shelter to Cevamp and me on this occasion. The water was too low to get into the harbour, and we soldiered on for another four or five miles into the Menai Straits to Port Dinorwic where, according to the almanac, there were moorings for visiting yachts. But no: fate and the elements were obviously against us, and this wasn't to be either. Tide and wind were flowing and blowing too fast to pick up a mooring buoy so I decided to carry on up the Menai to Plas Newydd. There, with help from the local sea cadet crew of HMS Nelson, I moored up and was able to rest for the night. From there, it was a mere eight mile hop the next day to Dickie's at Bangor, where I enjoyed a reviving couple of days peace and quiet, before Jack arrived.

I passed the time giving Cevamp a good scrub, drying out wet clothes and sails and going to the launderette to do my washing. The night before Jack was due to arrive I visited the local swimming pool and enjoyed the luxury of a hot shower. It was great to feel the jets of hot water against my skin and then to replace my damp, dirty clothing with freshly laundered jeans and my nice clean Cevamp sweatshirt. I was pleased with my domestic skills. I may have been a single man but that didn't stop me from looking after myself properly. Jack, I thought with satisfaction, would be impressed.

It was low tide when I got back and I eyed with distaste the deep covering of black, slurping, stinking ooze that passed as sea-bed in the drained harbour. It was too early to go to bed and I've never been one to sit twiddling my thumbs. I had a couple of hours to kill so to give myself something to do I pulled on my boots to go down into the mud and inspect the log impellor. This was a small, spinning wheel that protruded out of Cevamp's hull to record speed and distance on an instrument in the cockpit of the boat. It occasionally became jammed when bits of seaweed got caught up in it and I made a habit of checking it every so often at low water. On this occasion, I wished I hadn't. As I trudged round the boat the ooze exerted a powerful and irresistible suction on my wellies and I lost my balance, falling flat on my back in the mud in my nice clean clothes.

There was no weed on the impellor.

8

Lifeboat to the rescue

The following evening, having paid another visit to the launderette, Mike met me and my excessive amounts of luggage at Bangor railway station and told me he was taking me out for dinner. Out was the operative word. As we walked along the road back to Dickie's we tucked into a meal of sausage and chips bought from an American style drive-in take-away. He certainly knows how to spoil a girl.

It was good to be together again and we spent what was left of the evening catching up on each other's news and making further plans for our holiday, before settling down for the night. The drop-down table in the cabin made a good comfortable bed but it was a real pain to make up every night and then have to put away again in the morning.

'I don't know whether I can face doing this every night for the next two weeks,' I complained as I heaved the seat cushions into position.

'Why don't we try sleeping in the forward cabin instead? Then we can leave the bed made up and not have to start messing around with sleeping bags, duvets, pillows and what-have-you after a hard day's sailing.'

No sooner said than decided. We put the thick black cushions from the settees in the saloon on top of the thinner brown ones in the forward cabin to give us a bit of extra bounce. The extra layer of mattress restricted our headroom in bed considerably but we thought it would be worth it to save the extra work. We snuggled into bed but as the night went on a horrible sour, damp smell from the brown cushions permeated through our bedding and the foul odour of wet seaweed from the anchor chain locker wafted around our faces. It was a long time before we slept in there again.

Next morning, we got up early and went over to the loos in Dickie's yard where we used the spotless facilities to have a good strip wash. We didn't know how long it would be before we would enjoy the luxury of hot running water again so we made the most of it and we were both very impressed at the cleanliness, the soap and towels and the carpet, all in a tatty little brick building with creaky doors and a corrugated roof. Over the years we became experts on the comparative merits of public toilets in towns and harbours all around the coast of the Irish Sea and the one at Dickie's always remained high on our list.

The city of Bangor dates from the sixth century when a Celtic monastery was founded there. These days it is dominated by buildings of the University of West Wales perched on a rise to the west of the town centre, while its attractive, though modest, High Street is what most of us would expect to see in a market town rather than a city. It was lined on each side by small branches of big banks, building societies and independent shops including ironmonger, greengrocer, butcher and baker. The only big high street name we noticed was Woolworth's, which wasn't surprising as there seems to be one in most Welsh towns. But it was the butcher's, greengrocer's and especially the baker's that caught our eye as we explored our surroundings. We stocked up on meat and vegetables for a stew and enough sticky buns to sink a battleship. Once we'd done our shopping and had a quick look round the town we headed back to the boat, stowed our stores snugly in the lockers, had a quick cup of coffee and by eleven o'clock we were ready to set off for Port St Mary on the Isle of Man.

Navigation as taught in the classroom is a precise science, until you get to the bit about making adjustments for wind and tides. Then it becomes an imprecise art, especially for sailing boats. When planning our longer passages Mike always spent time with the tide tables, charts and a mildewy old book of tidal streams to work out the best time to leave, the best crossing to take and the estimated time of arrival. With the Isle of Man, though, it was a lot simpler, and Mike devised his own navigational rules. He explained them to me.

'Port St Mary is about fifty miles north of here and the tide flows roughly six hours east and six hours west. So if we steer due north the effect of the tides will balance out and we can make final adjustments once we see the light on Chicken Rock off the Isle of Man. If we average four knots, it should take us about twelve hours.'

Easy. If only.

The cold, the exhaustion and the discomfort of sailing in rough seas into a head wind were bad enough. But they were nothing, compared with the utter, blind terror I experienced during the afternoon. In a display of confidence which I did not share, Mike went below to lie down, leaving me nervously wielding the tiller and trying hard to concentrate on keeping the wind in the sails while holding our course. This is something which requires great eye, hand and body co-ordination, all of which are alien to me. People who have been my passengers would probably say I find co-ordination a bit of a problem even when driving a car, but at least a car does more or less what you ask of it.

Despite my misgivings and the big waves slamming into her bows Cevamp held her own for a while, but then she began to heel over. Waves flooded over the sides and into the cockpit and all of a sudden the mast was tilting at a crazy angle, pointing to the sea rather than the sky. I knew too little about the dynamics of sailing to shift the tiller seawards, which would have spilled the wind from the sail and righted the boat. Instead I did what came instinctively. I froze. Mike must have sensed something was wrong – perhaps it was being tipped off the settee that did it – and he came out and calmly took over. I collapsed, a quivering sobbing heap on the sopping cockpit floor. The entire incident probably lasted less than a minute but to me it seemed like a lifetime and my knees didn't stop shaking for hours. I blamed the temperamental sails, of course, and convinced myself that if only we'd had the engine on it wouldn't have happened. After a while I let myself be persuaded to try again but it was no good. My confidence was shattered. Still later I was forced to take the tiller while Mike took bearings but I was still frightened of the sails and silently willed him not to take long. I dreaded him asking me to do it again.

It was an epic crossing, lasting nearly eighteen hours. So much for 'fifty miles at four miles an hour'. We averaged less than three knots and it was a very lumpy ride, with a stiff wind on the nose practically the whole way. It was impossible to cook in those conditions and we made do with easy-to-grab-hold-of snacks throughout the day rather than the warming stew that I'd planned to make en route. This taught me, the galley slave, a good lesson in preparing hot food in advance of a voyage and we never again made the mistake of waiting until we'd arrived before we cooked our meal. It was quite cold too, especially during the darkness of the night, which seemed to go on for ever. It was four forty in the morning when we finally tied onto a buoy in the middle of Port St Mary's outer harbour before falling exhausted into bed. We never did have our stew, bought with such optimism in Bangor a lifetime earlier.

We woke up late on Saturday morning and moved Cevamp over to the wall of the outer harbour, where we rafted up to a fishing boat. The relief harbourmaster appeared.

'So you're the heroes who tied up in the night,' he said. I was quite proud of that as by now I was on terra firma and could afford to be blasé, so I was happy to let him think I'd been sailing in those kinds of conditions all my life. He told us there was plenty of room further in so we untied our ropes, fired up the trusty Yanmar and set off in search of a more convenient spot to moor. The inner harbour was a pickle of buoys, lines, dinghies, yachts and fishing boats but we managed to find a space alongside the high brick wall. It was the time of the first Gulf war and the harbourmaster watched Mike pick his way carefully round all the obstacles, taking care not to catch any surface ropes in Cevamp's propeller.

'You could get a job in the Gulf – you'd be good at finding your way round the landmines,' he said, making us both smile. With the easy friendliness that we found all over the island the harbour master urged us to make use of the showers and toilets at the yacht club, and invited us along to the club for a social they were holding that evening.

We went for a walk round the town and then we went for another walk to the railway station, making our way back along the shoreline round the horseshoe shaped bay. When you're on a sailing holiday you usually only see as much of a place as you are prepared to walk and we always liked to explore as much as we could. We commented on the cleanliness and the lack of vandalism or graffiti and we were particularly struck with the way people were evidently confident about leaving expensive surfboards and dinghies lying on the beach without feeling the need to lock them up.

'Must be the cat,' Mike decided, referring to the cat o'nine tails, a form of corporal punishment which was still available as a punishment to offenders on the island. It was clearly an effective deterrent against petty theft and vandalism. Yet another walk took us up some steep lanes to have a look at the 'flying saucers' we'd noticed earlier on a hillside and which turned out to be Ronaldsway, or 'the air ministry' according to an amenable islander who stopped for a gossip. We never did find out weather he meant Ronaldsway Airport or the coastal weather station, known to most British sailors from the shipping forecast's 'reports from coastal stations.' The scenery all around Port St Mary was beautiful, very old fashioned with small fields protected by ancient hedgerows which, even that late in the season were ablaze with the colour of wild fuchsias. We wandered on the cliff path high above the sea and looked down on Calf Sound, a narrow, rocky channel that runs between the southern tip of the island and Chicken Rock, whose lighthouse had been such a welcome sight on our approach to the island.

Then we decided to visit Port Erin, about a mile and a half away, to get some diesel for the boat. We'd only gone a few hundred yards when a frail and elderly man, whom we'd noticed earlier changing the tide tables on a glass fronted notice board, stopped and offered us a lift in his eye-catching, apple green Citroen 2CV. Despite his assurances that you don't need seatbelts on the Isle of Man we nevertheless took the precaution of strapping ourselves firmly in. His driving was, to put it kindly, eccentric, and had us thinking that perhaps you don't need to pass a driving test on the Isle of Man either.

Once back on Cevamp I set the table, designed place cards and a menu and finally got round to cooking a proper dinner. Tonight's main course was, of course, Cevamp Stew. This we left bubbling gently and aromatically on the cooker while we wandered over to the yacht club to soak up the bliss of a hot shower. Then it was time for good chinwag with some of the regulars over a couple of beers. We couldn't help smiling when one of them told us in gleeful detail the story of how he'd managed to hoodwink the local bobbies late one night and shake them off his tail when he was driving home in a drunken haze. As we got up to go back to Cevamp for our dinner, the man had a question for Mike.

'What do you do for a living then?'

'I'm a police officer,' said Mike with a grin.

Despite heavy drizzle we could just see land on the distant horizon as we passed through Calf Sound shortly after noon the next day. Mike had radioed the coastguard to notify our passage plan and estimated time of arrival, and we were already tucking into bacon sandwiches with mugs of steaming tea. We were bound for Ireland and our first port of call was Ardglass. Just south of the entrance to Strangford Lough, Ardglass is about 25 miles from the centre of Belfast and we were confident we would have little trouble finding it, even in the dark. According to the chart there was a distinctive beam from the lighthouse, shining red, white or green and the angle of your approach determined which of the colours you would see.

'I want you to take the helm for this crossing,' said Mike, to my horror.

'It'll give you more sailing experience and it'll help get your confidence back. You'll never get over this fear of sailing into the wind unless you learn how to do it,' he said firmly. Who was I to argue? I was so mad about him that I would have walked on water if he'd asked me to, and of course I didn't want him despising me as a girlie wimp.

'Just give me a shout if you need anything.' And with that he deposited a salty kiss on my equally salty lips and went below to put the kettle on.

It may only have been a ruse, but it was a good one and it worked. My nerves soon disappeared and I actually began to enjoy the magic of the sails. With un-reefed main and full genoa we were averaging four knots and soon after setting sail we could actually make out the faint grey shapes of the Mountains of Mourne in the distance. We remained in sight of land all day and even as darkness fell we could still see Peel Tower, Port Erin beacon and Chicken Rock lighthouse behind us on the Isle of Man. Of the three-coloured light at Ardglass, however, there was no sign. By eight o'clock it was quite dark, the temperature had dropped and the sea was getting decidedly choppy. Mike went below to heat up bowls of left-over stew and an hour later, with genoa rolled in and the mainsail fully reefed we started the engine.

For the next three hours we sat there stoically squinting through the darkness at the horizon, which beckoned tantalisingly some twenty miles ahead.

'We wouldn't normally be sitting out in the garden in the middle of night at the end of September pouring buckets of cold water over each other's heads,' I remarked dryly to Mike, as the seas grew bigger and the icy spray cascaded down our necks.

As we sat there, stiff and cold in the cockpit, I began to realise that I had a higher endurance threshold than I'd previously given myself credit for. Always a creature of comfort, I was nevertheless coping pretty well with the long hours of tedium, the hard wooden seat, the constant straining of muscles against the bucketing of the boat and, above all, the penetrating cold. My knees and hands had lost all sensation hours earlier. But the night had its compensations. It was beautifully clear, perfectly dark and the stars were diamonds on a swathe of sooty velvet. We lost count of the shooting stars that appeared above our heads and hung briefly in the night sky before disappearing into the blackness and I was transfixed at the way the phosphorescence appeared jewel-like above, among and below the waves, providing us with a sub-aqua light show. Sometimes the strange translucent lights, palely tinted with the faintest green glow, appeared to flutter and skip above the sea's surface like ghostly seagulls swooping around the boat and I began to understand how nature could play tricks on the imagination. It was no mystery to me that ancient mariners were such superstitious old sea-dogs and I recalled John Masefield, himself a merchant seaman before becoming a poet, describing an old Danish belief that the souls of old sailors follow the sea in birds' bodies until they have purged their years of penitence.

At midnight we gave up the ghost and admitted that even if we stayed out there all night there was no way we were ever going to find Ardglass light. Even Mike's famous terrier like qualities had been overwhelmed by weariness so we decided to find shelter close to shore and drop anchor till morning, when we could see exactly where we were. We motored gently into a calm bay with the ghostly seagulls still swirling above and around the boat when suddenly we saw, very close, some big rocks looming above us out of the darkness. I knew then that the ghostly seagulls had been warning us. Mike switched on Cevamp's powerful search lamp to scan the shoreline and as soon as we were clear of the rocks we dropped anchor for the night. It was then we noticed lights flashing from the shore and vaguely wondered if someone was trying to signal to us.

'Is that Morse, do you think?' I asked Mike.

'Don't know. Might be. Can you read Morse then?'

'I did a bit of Semaphore in the Brownies and I know SOS but otherwise, no. I don't do Morse.'

'Neither do I. So even if it is there's not much we can do about it. Let's just get to bed and worry about it in the morning. I'm shattered'.

He was right. We were both very tired by now so I busied myself filling hot-water bottles and getting the bed sorted out while Mike got on the radio to Belfast.

'Belfast Coastguard, Belfast Coastguard, Belfast Coastguard, this is Yacht Cevamp, Yacht Cevamp, Yacht Cevamp. Just to let you know we've arrived safely and are now going off watch.'

'Ah yes, Cevamp. Where exactly are you?'

Oh dear. This was the question Mike was hoping he wouldn't be asked, as we didn't really know. All we did know was that we'd failed to find Ardglass, and we weren't admitting that to anybody.

'Position believed to be just south of Killard Point, near the entrance to Strangford Lough.' This last said nonchalantly.

'Can you see lights flashing on shore?

'Affirmative,' said Mike, with a growing feeling that he wasn't going to like what was to come next.

'You're at Guns Island. The lifeboat will be with you in a few minutes.'

Oh no.

It turned out that a night-time angler on shore had watched us picking our way in to the bay and, thinking we were about to run aground on the rocks, flashed his car headlamps to warn us before calling for help on our behalf. A few minutes later we were surprised to see a flashing blue light approaching out of the darkness and seconds later a big orange inflatable lifeboat whooshed to a stop beside Cevamp. The burly three-man crew, each of whom had undoubtedly been dragged away from a cosy fireside or a warm wife in a snug bed to come out to us, were amazingly good natured and dismissed our embarrassed apologies in gruff Belfast accents before zooming off into the night again. Only another sea-farer will understand how reassuring and humbling it is to know there are men and women like these who are willing to put their lives on the line for people like us. The next RNLI collecting box we came across received a hefty token of our appreciation.

After a sound night's sleep we were up and away by nine o'clock. It was calm, mild and hazy without even a zephyr of a breeze to ruffle the mirrored sea. The sails drooped in the still air so we motored the short hop north to Portavogie. On the way we spotted a dozen or so recumbent seals basking on the green, weed-strewn boulders of North Rocks Beacon. As we approached they slid into the water and watched us as we drew nearer. Just the footballs of their heads were visible above the water as their dark liquid eyes gazed at us in reproach for disturbing their solitude. We took their photograph for posterity and motored on, arriving at Portavogie just in time for lunch.

Portavogie harbour was hard at work and it was easy to tell by the smell that fishing was what kept it that way. Fish and chips for lunch, we thought. We rarely ate them at home so when we were on holiday we bought them whenever we had the chance. But our hopes were soon dashed when we discovered that although the town looked a fair size from the sea it was actually quite small, with little more than an amusement arcade and a Mace supermarket where we were able to stock up on food supplies.

Cevamp's navigation lights had blown a fuse the night before and we were looking for a spare. When we realised there was no chandlery or electrical store we thought we were out of luck but we'd reckoned without the legendary generosity of the Irish. The man in the amusement arcade gave us a fuse from one of his machines when he heard of our plight and wouldn't hear of taking any payment for it.

We eventually got our fish and chips as well, from a mobile fish and chip shop parked beside the harbour. Ironically, it didn't sell traditional battered cod or haddock, just frozen whiting or fried scampi and chips, so we plumped, not surprisingly, for the scampi. We took our food back to the boat, poured ourselves a lager shandy each and sat on deck to enjoy our feast in the sunshine. Despite the lateness of the season it was warm enough for Mike to bare his body and we sat seal-spotting for a while. Three big old seals lived in the harbour and, according to the woman in the fish and chip van, had done so for years. She told us everyone worried that one day they would be chopped up in a ship's propeller but as far as we could see they seemed pretty adept at avoiding the danger.

After we'd eaten we decided to abandon our plan to wait for the promised delivery of milk at the Mace, and set off for Donaghadee, our planned anchorage for the night. By now there was a gentle breeze, blue sky with fluffy white clouds and the sun was shining. Within half an hour we had the mainsail and genoa fully out and an hour later, after some mysterious and complicated fiddling around with sail bags, ropes and a long metal pole Mike had the cruising chute up for the first time.

Cevamp was truly dressed to kill. Her silky gown of red, white and blue billowed and rustled as she danced goose-winged across the water to the tune of the wind and the waves. Mike and I were captivated and we enjoyed a magical couple of hours sailing. For me, from that day onwards, sailing goose-winged in the sunshine with the cruising chute up will always be the ultimate sailing experience, on a par with galloping on a horse or skiing down a deserted glacier in deep virgin powder.

The harbour wall at Donaghadee was something of an enigma. It didn't go anywhere. It was just an isolated wall in the middle of the harbour. But we tied up to it anyway, and Mike entrusted me to the dubious care of two Irishmen in a rowing boat with one oar, who offered to take me ashore to get milk, while he inflated the dinghy. I was deposited safely on terra firma by my ferrymen and Mike joined me a few minutes later. We went for a walk around the town, bought a spare fuse and some postcards and visited a slightly seedy harbour-side bar for our promised glass of Guinness. In our naivety we were blissfully unaware that to walk into a bar in Protestant Northern Ireland and ask for two pints of Guinness was a potential source of conflict, but we got away with it just the same.

We'd noticed a castle which looked very pretty from the harbour so we went for a closer look. It wasn't pretty at all, close up. We were struck by the run-down appearance of the town and were conscious of an air of tension about the place. This was the only harbour we ever visited where we made a point of securing all Cevamp's doors and lockers before leaving her. It wasn't that we doubted the honesty of the local people but more because of the then very real terrorist threat and the fact of Mike's profession which we felt, perhaps unreasonably, made us a possible target. This was long before politicians' peace talks and IRA ceasefires and we were still no more than a stone's throw from Belfast. It all seems a bit ridiculous now, looking back, and perhaps we were being over-dramatic, but there is no denying the very tangible feelings of unease that we experienced at the time.

Next on the itinerary was Portpatrick on the Scottish mainland, a relatively short passage across the North Channel. We left Donaghadee under motor at half past ten on a Tuesday morning with an ETA of four in the afternoon. Forty minutes after leaving the harbour we had the mainsail and cruising chute up and the rest of the day was sheer perfection. The weather was warm and sunny, the sea was gentle and visibility was good. All in all it was one of those rare, exquisite sailing days when nothing goes wrong and you actually know why you're doing it. Mike was in seventh heaven and the sound of his fine tenor voice rang out across the water as, unable to contain himself, he gave vent to his euphoria and burst into song. A Life on the Ocean Wave seemed to be a special favourite and he alternated between its rousing chorus and Rod Stewart's pop classic, Sailing. Nothing if not appropriate.

We steered a somewhat erratic course on the approaches to Portpatrick, thanks to various distractions on board, but despite this we arrived exactly on time for once. It's an interesting harbour to get into, with orange-painted leading lights on the harbour wall and on a shop in the high street. All you have to do for a safe entrance into the harbour is make sure the two orange markers line up as you approach and then keep them lined up until you are safely in. At the entrance to the harbour an evil looking lump of rock pokes its jagged snout out of the water. It's called Half Tide Rock, for the obvious reason that the amount of rock visible at any given time is dependent on the state of the tide.

Portpatrick is small, sedate and pretty with a putting green and seats around the harbour wall providing the main attractions for its elderly visitors. More energetic souls enjoy the challenge of rugged cliff top walking above the harbour and along the coast. We forswore that pleasure for the sensuous self-indulgence of hot showers in a harbour-side hotel followed by a nip of whisky, now that we had reached Scotland. We got chatting to a couple of amiable inebriates who were propping up the bar. One of them said he was a radio operator at Portpatrick radio and commented on Cevamp's zigzag approach that afternoon. I just hoped he wasn't watching our antics too closely – we were still getting to know each other, after all.

9

I didn't drown him after all

We knew we'd been lucky with the weather so late in the sailing season and were wondering when our luck would run out. We soon got our answer. We awoke the following morning to grim skies and an alarming early morning shipping forecast. We climbed the hill above the town to get a better look at conditions outside the shelter of the harbour, to find strong winds and stormy grey seas.

I knew Mike was eager to start heading for home as we both had to get back to work by the end of the following week and we still had a long way to go. Alex always made it plain to us that as far as he was concerned our safety was paramount and if necessary we should leave the boat safely in some distant harbour rather than risk trying to get her home in bad weather. We both recognised the sense in that, but pride and stubbornness sometimes got the better of us and we always got her back to Porthmadog. That's not to say we were foolhardy. We would never put out in a storm or if the forecast was bad, and we always followed the old adage of 'it's better to be in harbour wishing you were out than to be out, wishing you were in.' We knew what we could cope with, were confident in the boat's capabilities and never considered ourselves to be fair-weather sailors. We didn't mind a bit of discomfort. On this occasion, though, we decided not to risk it and to wait another day to see if conditions improved. Instead of setting sail we enjoyed a bus ride into nearby Stranraer, once the home of Sir John Ross, the Arctic explorer who discovered the North Magnetic Pole in 1831. We planned to buy some wood for a flag-pole and to treat ourselves to a feast of food from Marks and Spencer. We got the wood but there was no M&S and the few shops we saw were enjoying half-day closing. We managed to buy some food at a small supermarket and spent the rest of the afternoon in a cafe, drinking tea, eating cakes and waiting for the school bus which was to take us back to Portpatrick. It was strange to be flying along on a bus after our sedate progress at sea and it was weird to see the scenery changing so rapidly as it flashed past the windows.

All good things, unfortunately, must come to an end. However much we liked Portpatrick, and we both liked it very much, we knew we would have to leave the next day if we were to complete our tour of England, Ireland, Scotland, Wales and the Isle of Man in time to get back to work. We still hadn't visited England and we were running out of holiday.

We motor sailed out of Portpatrick just before ten thirty on the morning of Thursday, October 1 into a choppy sea, with grey sky and a veil of mist. Another yacht, a ketch called Cigaro, left around the same time. We'd noticed her in the harbour and although we never got round to speaking to her skipper, we made up our own stories about him and decided he was a Parahandy type of character who sailed where his fancy took him, getting causal jobs as he went. We were heading south, still undecided as to our destination, while Cigaro was going west and we kept her in view until she vanished into the distance.

Once we were underway Mike unfurled the genoa, switched off the engine and got on the radio to Belfast coastguard to say we were heading either for the Isle of Man or Cumbria, but it was another four hours before we got back to them with the final decision. Because of the wind direction on the day and our lack of time we eventually decided to give England a miss and head down the west coast of the Isle of Man, returning to Port St Mary. We settled down to the prospect of a long day in hefty seas, with visibility never better than about two miles. The hours passed uneventfully. We coped with the tedium by giving ourselves regular treats in the form of food, sweets, biscuits and drinks and eventually we sighted the Calf of Man light blinking away in the distance.

We finally reached Port St Mary at one o'clock in the morning, nearly fifteen hours after setting out. It was low water and there was a very strong easterly wind so we were forced to drop anchor outside the harbour for what remained of the night. We were desperately tired but the heaving, crashing and pounding sea meant we got very little sleep. We were close to land but it gave us little protection and part of Mike's consciousness kept him alert to the possibility that we may drag our anchor and run aground. At one point during the night we'd just managed to doze off when we were snapped into wakefulness by a loud crash. Thinking the life-raft had been ripped from its stowage place on top of the cabin roof, Mike jumped to his feet, quickly pulled on some clothes and struggled out into the cold, dark and stormy night. I felt sorry for him, but not that sorry. By the time he came back to bed I was asleep.

'What was that crash last night?' I asked him when we woke up yet again shortly before dawn.

'Oh,' he said casually. 'It was that washing-up bowl full of dirty pots and pans that you left on the draining board last night. It fell onto the cabin floor in the swell.'

Oops. He said no more and I admired his restraint.

Just after six thirty it was light enough to see what we were doing and with daylight to guide us we motored into the harbour and tied up against the wall. Mike's final entry in the log that morning ended with the heartfelt words 'sleep at last in still water!'

It was late when we woke up and while I was still struggling to come to my senses Mike went off to the sailing club for a shower. The club seems to have an ever-open door to visitors and there was never any problem about using the facilities there. We decided to have a leisurely day to recover from our late night but as I dawdled off for my shower I met him coming back. 'You're going to have to get a move on,' he told me. 'The train for Douglas leaves in less than half an hour'. I grumbled a bit. I was tired, why did I have to hurry, I thought this was supposed to be a holiday, I wanted to wash my hair and put some make-up on. He listened to me droning on, before coming out with just the right words to speed me up.

'You do want to go to Marks and Spencer, don't you?'

As it happened, we didn't catch the train after all. The harbourmaster gave us a lift into Douglas, pointing out the Isle of Man airport on the way.

'Flights here are a bit unpredictable because of maintenance problems with some of the elderly aircraft,' he told us.

'Hm, I can see what you mean,' said Mike, looking across the runway at the geriatric aeroplanes lined up on the tarmac.

Douglas is the capital of the Isle of Man and home to the Tynwald, the island's parliament which was founded by the Vikings more than a thousand years ago. It is also host every June to the famous TT motor cycle races, which attract hordes of enthusiasts from around the world. Other attractions for visitors include horse drawn trams, which have operated along the promenade since 1876, the Manx electric railway which winds its way to the summit of Snaefell and, of course, Marks and Spencer which is where hungry sailors stock up on all sorts of delicious food. Which is exactly what we did. Regardless of the fact that we had no fridge on board, let alone a freezer, we filled our trolley with pies and pizzas, cheesecake and chocolate cake, thick double cream and mountains of fresh vegetables. Anyone would have thought we hadn't seen food for weeks.

We arrived back at the railway station in plenty of time to catch the return train to Port St Mary. The station was stuck in a time warp. With its steam train paraphernalia and flower boxes full of geraniums it could have been lifted straight out of a scene from The Railway Children. There was a sign saying the ticket office would be open ten minutes before the train departed, but it stayed firmly shuttered. Mike went in search of the ticket man. He was an elderly gent.

'You'll have to pay at the other end,' he said firmly.

We were disappointed when our train turned out to be diesel rather than steam, but the journey itself more than made up for it. We travelled at a leisurely pace through the prettiest, unspoilt countryside imaginable. From time to time the train rumbled through tiny stations or halts, flagged on by a man or woman at the side of the track. When we disembarked at Port St Mary we attempted to buy our tickets but the man in the ticket hut refused to take our money.

'Off you go. It's too late to buy tickets now.'

We looked at our watches. It was five o'clock in the afternoon.

It was a pleasant interlude, but we had to move on. Our next port of call was Beaumaris on Anglesey, which was even further than the fifty eight miles from Portpatrick to Port St Mary. We left on the tide just before mid-day on the Saturday and our ETA of late evening or early morning was only accurate because it was elastic. After we'd been going for a couple of hours we must have run over some weed and caught it in the impellor as the log stopped working. Mike put out the trailing log so we could keep track of speed and distance until the main log cleared itself and got going again. The trailing log fitted to a bracket in the cockpit and a lead from it trailed in the water behind the boat. When the main log clicked back into action we noticed it recorded a slightly faster speed than the trailing log and Mike reckoned that was because the part that gives the reading is dragged through the waves rather than riding up and down them and is therefore more accurate.

Even with the main fully reefed and the genoa two-thirds furled we got some good sailing in, recording an overall average of just over four knots. Conditions deteriorated steadily throughout the day and by the time we sighted Point Lynas light on the north eastern corner of Anglesey we were sailing into driving rain and heavy seas, with very poor visibility. Even the glowering bulk of Great Orme's Head was invisible in the murky night. It was low water by the time we passed Puffin Island at two thirty on Sunday morning and from the shore at Black

Point, or Trwyn Du, we could just make out the mournful sound of the bell clanging from the lighthouse. An hour later we tied to a buoy near Beaumaris Pier to snatch a few hours sleep while we waited for high water.

It was very still, dank and overcast at half past seven when we left Beaumaris to motor down the Menai Straits, and there wasn't even a whisper of wind to help us on our way. We'd missed the early morning shipping forecast but had a shouted conversation with the skipper of a passing sailing school yacht, who told us it hadn't been too promising. Casual though this may seem, especially considering the poor conditions the previous day, this shouted boat-to-boat sharing of information is all part of the camaraderie enjoyed by leisure yachtsmen and in any case we knew we would get regular weather updates throughout the day over the boat's radio. I also knew enough by now to realise that when a sailor says 'not too promising,' what he probably means is 'not enough wind to sail,' so we weren't particularly concerned by the man's remark.

I enjoyed the Menai Straits. It was the first time I'd been there and although visibility was poor I could see how pretty it would be on a fine day. We saw a heron flying low over the water from one bank to another and I admired the graceful arch of Thomas Telford's famous suspension bridge which takes traffic from mainland Wales across to Anglesey. The most exciting bit of the Menai for me was negotiating the notorious rips and races of the Swellies, an area of whirlpools, eddies and strong currents that can spin a yacht out of control unless you know what you're doing. I thought it was interesting and fun, but of course I wasn't the skipper and responsible for our yacht's safe passage. Mike took it very gently. Although it was slack water, the time close to high and low tides when the least current is running, there wasn't much of it and even though Cevamp has a fairly shallow draught Mike was tense, anxious that we would run aground. Once we were safely through the Swellies he relaxed and was soon ready for bacon sandwiches and coffee.

Late morning saw us across Caernarfon Bar without mishap and we raised the mainsail to give it a chance to dry. An hour later the wind picked up. We managed a good hour's sailing before it dropped away again and we motored the rest of the way to Porth Dinllaen, arriving just in time for our Sunday lunch. What Sunday lunch? We were getting a bit low on joints of beef and Yorkshire pudding, so we made do with bacon and egg sandwiches instead.

Then all of a sudden it was a beautiful afternoon, with blue skies, a soft haze shimmering over the hills and the sun shining warmly enough for us to take some clothes off and think about swimming. This was the magic of Porth Dinllaen and we came across it time and again. However bad the weather was 'out there', the sun always seemed to shine on us here.

'Funny,' I mused. 'How come today's bit of the journey purred like a pussycat when I did it but according to you it roared like a lion when you sailed through a couple of weeks ago? Must be the feminine influence when I'm on board.'

We stripped off but in the end we didn't take the plunge and just sat around in the sun till it was time to go to bed. All right, I know six o'clock was a bit on the early side, but we were exhausted and had a lot of sleep to catch up on.

The final day of our cruise dawned and there was a

slight drizzle as we slipped our mooring after breakfast to head back to Porthmadog. We made steady progress in the fresh breeze and to start with we averaged about five knots under sail.

'This is promising,' I said.

'It won't last,' predicted Mr Gloomy. He was right. It didn't. We were ripe for a drama. Conditions began to deteriorate but we were happy enough and I was pondering on progress.

'Do you realise we've logged over six hundred miles in two weeks?'

'Mmmm,' said Mike. 'Impressive.

'And we've managed to live together at close quarters without coming to blows. And we've had a good time doing it. Best holiday I've ever had,' I added.

'Mmmm, me too'. A man of few words, that's Mike.

Sighing happily, I huddled myself deeper into my usual place in the cockpit in the rain, privately congratulating myself on this major achievement and feeling pretty pleased with myself

'I'm not a bad crew,' I boasted. 'I'm never seasick, I keep us well fed and watered, I don't mind being beaten at Scrabble and I do as I'm told.'

Complacency was obviously the order of the day.

'I can steer a course on the compass, I never argue with the skipper and I don't get frightened.'

I was clearly getting a bit big-headed and was due for my come-uppance. They say pride comes before a fall...The words had no sooner left my mouth than something happened which made me very frightened and nearly caused me to lose Mike over the side into the bargain.

We were getting close to the overfalls off Bardsey Island at the time and the sea was getting lumpy. Mike dug around in a locker for life jackets, safety harness and lifelines.

'Better put these on before it gets any worse.'

'I don't think I'll bother with mine,' I said. 'It's such a performance taking them off when I need the loo.'

Mike was in no mood to argue. 'Just put them on.'

Then we ran into foul weather. The wind started gusting and the waves grew bigger and more powerful with every heave. The wind was deafening.

Mike gave me the tiller and told me to steer into the wind. My old bête noir. Even after many hours at sea and countless hoistings and lowerings of the main sail, I was still unable to co-ordinate this simplest of sailing tasks. This was my worst effort. The time when I was paralysed with fear, thinking the boat would capsize or, worse, that I would cause Mike to fall overboard and drown. And almost as bad, to leave me on my own in a boat that I still didn't have a clue how to sail. As his feet began to slide from under him he made one last attempt to get through to me.

'Tiller away from you!' he bellowed, in desperation, as his feet slid from under him and he began to lose his grasp on the mast. 'Steer into the wind. Let go of the tiller!'

Light dawned. I released my vice-like grip on the tiller. Cevamp responded instantly, righted herself and pointed her nose obediently into the wind. She didn't even need me to do it for her. The violent slamming ceased, the clamour abated and Mike found his feet.

My heart was hammering against my ribcage. I'd done it again.

Instead of letting the wind out of the sail I'd been steering so that the wind was hitting us broadside on, filling the sails and forcing the poor boat further and further over onto her side, subjecting her to immense stress. By the time Mike had finished reefing the sail and tucked all the ends neatly away I was a quivering wreck, trembling with the aftermath of fear and with my hood pulled well down over my face so that he wouldn't see the tears mingling with the rain streaming down my face. Nothing had changed. I was just as useless as I had been a fortnight before. Despite Mike's patient, painstaking and oft repeated attempts to explain it to me it was a long, long time before I could put the theory of steering into the wind into practice when I needed to. Even now I have my moments of incompetence. Much as I love sailing I am obviously doomed to be a bit on the slow side when it comes to grasping even the most basic techniques.

We'd no sooner recovered from this little episode than we were faced with drama number two. We were motor sailing with the main fully reefed but still straining in the wind, and girding up our loins in readiness for the difficult passage through Bardsey Sound. The swell was increasingly heavy on the approaches to the rips and it was an effort to keep on course, so when the shackle-pin on the main sheet worked loose and flew out it was a diversion we could have done without. Luckily we had a spare pin and Mike managed to get it into place before we really started to bucket around in the bad tempered waters. We battled our way through the sound, with big waves constantly breaking over the back of the boat, determined to knock us off course and onto the rocks. But once again, thanks to Mike's strength and his ability to 'read' the waves, we got through. Wet but safe and heading for Hell's Mouth.

The wide sweeping bay was every bit as bad as it had been when Mike sailed through solo two weeks earlier.

We endured a couple of hours of heavy rain, lumpy seas and poor visibility as we crossed the wide bay and then suddenly there was a loud bang, apparently from the engine compartment, and we lost propulsion. It was time for another drama. The engine seemed to be working but Cevamp had stopped moving forward. Mike looked serious.

'I don't know what's happened but I think we've lost the prop. We'd better switch the engine off and keep going under sail, until we can find out what's going on.'

Even with both sails up and a fair following breeze we still wallowed and floundered and made unbearably slow progress. Then an hour later, when we were just south of Pwllheli, we discovered the cause of the problem. We'd struck one of the myriad marker buoys that litter the coast all around Cardigan Bay, and the line that secured it to the heavily weighted lobster pot on the sea-bed was wound tightly around Cevamp's starboard bilge keel. The iron flag-pole on top of the buoy was jammed tight around the keel and we were obviously dragging the pot. Mike hung precariously over the side, prodding and poking at the flag pole with the boat-hook, but even when he managed to control the long wooden pole in the bouncing boat, his efforts were fruitless. Then, as suddenly as it had struck, the pot-buoy freed itself and we catapulted clear of our manacle. That was the signal for the rain to stop and we sailed on a broad reach the rest of the way to the fairway buoy at the entrance to Porthmadog's deep water channel, making the most of the opportunity to dry the sails in the wind.

As we entered Porthmadog harbour we felt as though we were bold explorers, returning from a long voyage to unknown places. But there were no cheering crowds lining the route, no bunting on the buildings and no welcoming blasts from ship's hooters. In fact, no-one at all watched us return and I don't suppose anyone even noticed our absence either. So we tied Cevamp up to the harbour wall and went to get some fish and chips. We still didn't know what the national drink of Wales was so we settled for cans of cola. By now we were famished and that meal, which we ate in the dark, seated on the damp wooden seats beside the bus stops in rainy Porthmadog High Street, was just about as good as they come.

Next day we arranged for Robin Kuffyn, the owner of Porthmadog boatyard, to crane Cevamp out of the water for the winter. 'Four tons is too much for my old crane,' he muttered, as he did every time he lifted her out. It was certainly nerve-wracking to see her being swung out of her element and over the wall, but the crane coped without mishap. As it did every time. Once Cevamp was safely on her blocks of tree trunks we inspected her for damage from her run-in with the pot-buoy. To our relief we found the prop was unscathed but the starboard skeg had suffered some minor damage.

'Dad'll enjoy repairing this for us,' Mike predicted confidently as he poked at the hull and keels with a screwdriver. And it was true. Alex never balked at giving us a hand to repair the damage we'd caused to his precious yacht. I think he was only too glad that we were getting such pleasure from sailing her.

We agreed we'd had a great holiday. Although I had my inadequacies as a sailor – see above – I felt I was making progress. By the end of the two weeks I could steer a course, pump out the bilges and was even, apart from the odd hiccup, learning to love the sails. Having said that, I still didn't have a clue about how to raise them or how to set them and my knots were a mystery even unto themselves. But I could learn!

We arrived home on Tuesday, October 6 1987. Just over a week later we had reason to be thankful we were not still afloat. During the night of Thursday, 15 October a great storm struck parts of the British Isles. One hundred mile an hour winds tore across the country, leaving the worst scenes of devastation on land and around the coast in living memory. Buildings were damaged and destroyed, millions of trees were ripped up, a cross Channel ferry and countless small boats were flung ashore like bits of driftwood. That night, two people lost their lives at sea.

10

'It's safe to take the ground'

Mike's priorities, I decided, were his boat, his squash, his horse-riding, his job and me, in that order. These days I know I am higher in his charts but in that first delicate year I was happy to be placed at all. I may be wrong but I think the low rating may have had something to do with the way I drove him mad with the camera. Every time he looked up I had the lens pointed skywards, landwards, seawards or at him.

'Put that damned camera away and hold on,' became a familiar, irritable, instruction. Having worked for years with press photographers, who are never happy with just one shot of a subject, I adopted their technique of taking a series of shots of every picture. Sails up, sails down, sails goose-winged. Top-sides, hull, keel. Cevamp sailing, Cevamp on a mooring, Cevamp high-and-dry, Cevamp being lifted out of the water. I was still too close to my life as a local newspaper reporter not to see everything that happened to us as a 'good story'. And, of course, every story had to have a picture.

'You're more interested in taking photographs of the yacht than you are in learning to sail her,' he grumbled.

In a way he was right, but what he didn't know was that this was photography with a purpose. I was working on his Christmas present. During the summer I'd been agonising over what to give him. I wanted it to be something special, something classy and something that would demonstrate to him my impeccable taste. Then I hit on the perfect gift. A painting of Cevamp, copied from photographs. But Mike was – is – such a fuss-pot, such a perfectionist, that I knew it couldn't be just any old painting, hence the photographic binge. I couldn't afford to leave any detail un-snapped.

My sister Trish and brother-in-law Mick recommended an artist from Tisbury in Wiltshire. Gilly McLaren is well known locally for her wonderful drawings of people's homes, which was how Trish and Mick came to hear of her. The previous year Gilly produced a beautiful set of pictures of their centuries-old Dorset long-house but she'd never done a yacht before. She blanched a bit when I told her that as the picture was for a perfectionist it had to be technically perfect, as well as aesthetically pleasing. Nonetheless, Gilly bravely accepted the commission, and said she would enlist the help of her husband, a keen sailor, if she needed a technical opinion. I handed over my precious stock of photographs for her to work from, together with a ridiculous deadline: I wanted to collect the picture early in December. It was now the end of October. Gilly gulped, but she didn't let me down and delivered the painting on time to Trish. A week or two before Christmas Trish, my mother and I arranged a secret rendezvous on a rainy night in Swindon, the half-way point between Trish and Mick's home in Bourton and mine in Banbury, and I took delivery of my precious painting. A framed water-colour – what else? – of Cevamp riding the waves at Porth Dinllaen, cruising chute flying spectacularly and the misty grey mountains of Snowdonia in the background. I was absolutely delighted with it. I could hardly contain myself till

Christmas but the suspense and skulduggery were worth it. On Christmas morning Mike unwrapped his not very cunningly disguised present – it's difficult to make a painting look like anything else – and was speechless. Yes. He loved it and it has taken pride of place on our sitting room wall ever since.

With Christmas and New Year out of the way we joined thousands of other nautical Walter Mittys for the annual pilgrimage to the Earls Court Boat Show, where we drooled over dreamboats such as Victorias, Vancouvers, Halbergs, Najads and big Moodys, with their sumptuous interiors and smooth teak decks. We cast a disdainful glance or two at the luxurious motor yachts and made smug remarks about real boats having sails and real sailors not being seen dead on one of those floating gin palaces. We sat on the littered floor of the main exhibition hall to tuck into our picnic of ham sandwiches, apples and Mars bars and spent the rest of the day filling our now empty Sainsbury carrier bags with scores of glossy brochures, leaflets and price lists. Then it was back to reality. We binned our brochures almost as soon as we got them home. They were lovely to look at but we knew they were out of our league, unless we struck lucky on the Premium Bonds.

As the January days lengthened and winter relaxed its grip we knew we had to lock our dreams away for another year and face reality. It was time to head back to the boatyard and scrub Cevamp's bottom.

During snatched weekends in Porthmadog over the winter we were full of good intentions but the west Wales coast can be very cold, wet and windy. This meant that we spent most of our time in the boatyard huddled under Cevamp's hull, eating cakes and waiting for a break in the rain so we could get on with a bit of vital maintenance to the engine and woodwork. Sea water is cruelly uncaring of varnish, paint and polished brass and there was a lot to do. The worst task of all was cleaning and rubbing down the hull ready for a new coat of anti-foul paint.

'I hate doing this,' I complained, frequently and fervently, from my cramped position under the bilges. If the cold muddy water wasn't seeping through the knees of my jeans because the only way I could work was by kneeling in a puddle, it would be pouring up the inside of my sleeves as I stretched above my head to scrub off last year's paint, slime and barnacles.

'Well don't do it then,' was Mike's muttered response, as he tackled some equally unappealing task. With Cevamp on blocks she cleared the ground by no more than ten or twelve inches, which made for extremely cramped and uncomfortable working conditions, and our patience with each other, as well as the job in hand, was a bit thin. Still, it gave me the opportunity for a spot of martyrdom.

'I get the pleasure of sailing in her. I'll do my share of looking after her, too,' I said piously, when all I really wanted was to wash the paint out of my hair and nails before sitting down in front of a blazing fire with a cup of tea and a plate of hot, buttery crumpets.

By the time we arrived in Porthmadog for our spring cruise in mid April there was still an awful lot to do before we could put to sea again. We spent the first four days of our holiday in unremitting hard labour, scrubbing, cleaning, rubbing down, painting and renewing (the boat, that is, not ourselves). For once the weather was on our side and we revelled in the warm sunshine. The azure skies melted into a soft violet haze over the mountains and, most importantly, there was a promising breeze. Our efforts were largely directed towards giving Cevamp a new colour scheme. We painted her white on top and grey underneath, with a bright red stripe round the waterline and a matching new red name, computer-designed for us by a sign writer who worked from a small industrial unit just outside the town. We protected the rubbing strakes and locker lids with two or three coats of deep-teak wood-paint from Woolworth's in the High Street and we emptied out the lockers, jettisoning all Alex's odds and sods which he'd stuffed into Cevamp's nooks and crannies 'in case they come in useful'. Mike directed operations.

'The only things we'll put back on board will be the things we really need,' he decided, restricting his selection to spare parts, tool kits and safety equipment. Among the things to go was an ancient navy blue, roll-neck fisherman's sweater, more holes than sweater, which Alex had been photographed wearing on fishing trips at least twenty years previously. We found it in the bottom of a locker, smelling sourly of wet wool and incubating a nice crop of fungus in its musty folds. Next we dug out mountains of soggy polystyrene sheets and granules. Especially granules. When he built Cevamp Alex stuffed every possible nook, crack and cranny with the horrible stuff in a bid to increase Cevamp's buoyancy. It undoubtedly succeeded to start with but as time went by more and more water came over the sides and insinuated itself through small fissures in the hull. The polystyrene got wet, bits broke off and stuck to everything they touched, more determined to stay put than teasels in a spaniel's ears. We were fed up to the back teeth with the stuff floating around in the bilges and appearing as if by magic in our tea, our sandwiches, our pockets and our bed.

We completed Cevamp's refit by threading fresh cord through the spray dodgers and Mike adjusted the rigging while I added final touches. I was very proud of my bright new red and green ribbons, which fluttered from the stays. Not only did they look very pretty, they had two serious navigational functions. One was to help me distinguish between port (red) and starboard (green) and the other was to indicate the direction the wind was coming from, a useful bit of information for novices who can't steer into the wind.

At last we were finished and Cevamp was craned back into the water on the Saturday morning. We planned to set sail for Ireland the next day, but fate took a hand in the form of neap tides and we were delayed at an inelegant angle on the mud for another couple of days. We made the most of it by pottering around the boat (me) and tidying up the mooring lines (Mike). There's always something to do when you have a boat, especially a wooden one, and my fantasy of basking on deck in the sun, sipping something cool and alcoholic had long since evaporated: apart from the problem of unreliable weather in the Irish Sea, there simply isn't the time.

The tide tables promised deeper water with Tuesday morning's high tide. We prepared for an early start, filled our fresh water tanks, set the alarm to wake us in time for the early shipping forecast and were in bed before sundown. At half past three the following morning, Mike nudged me awake.

'We're afloat. Let's go.'

Half an hour later we were on our way.

Damp grey skies, smoky haze and penetrating cold do not for pleasant cruising make, and the next few hours were not pleasant. We were bone-achingly weary and our eyes ached from the strain of peering into the in the greyness of the day. For the past three nights our sleep had been disturbed, either by the maddening noise of enraged halyards flapping against masts or because of Cevamp's crazy angle on the mud and by the time we slipped, gently for once, through Bardsey Sound shortly after ten o'clock we were also beginning to feel the effects of having got up so early. The promising breeze of the previous few days had dropped away to nothing and we motored through silky smooth waters, knowing that the merest puffs of wind would have raised our spirits as rapidly as it would have filled the sails. We steered a steady 285 degree course and took it in turns to sleep the day away, perking up only for our lunch of hot soup and toasted cheese sandwiches.

Finally, just before eight o'clock and after a couple of hours of 'yes it is' and 'no, it isn't', we knew that the shadowy shapes looming in the mist weren't figments of our imagination or tired eyes playing tricks. It definitely was land. From our calculations we reckoned it to be Mizzen Head and we changed course to head north up the coast to Wicklow, where we finally tied up to the wall of the outer harbour just after ten o'clock. Hunger overcame fatigue and we tucked into a huge plate of stew, cleverly prepared by the galley slave the previous day, before falling into the deep dreamless sleep familiar to exhausted mariners.

'Anyone on board?' The distinctive Dublin tones cut through our slumber and we struggled onto deck, stretching and yawning. It was morning and the harbourmaster had come to collect his £3 mooring fee.

'English money okay?' asked Mike.

'Oi'll take anything,' came the co-operative reply. 'But you'd be better off in the inner harbour. There's plenty of room and it's calmer in there.'

It was a bad move. The water in the inner harbour was filthy, with what looked like raw sewage outlets spewing out their contents all along the harbour wall. The unappetising morsels bounced and bobbed around Cevamp's water line, nudging and nibbling at our lovely new paintwork.

'I hope people don't think that's ours,' I muttered to Mike, as I unpegged the towels from the guard rails where they were airing. I was anxious to get them in before they fell into the fetid water.

After breakfast we set off to explore the town. Dark alleyways and narrow streets led up from the harbour to the town centre, where we treated ourselves to coffee and cakes in a coffee house on the lower side of the split level high street. Among Wicklow's more famous sons was Captain Robert Halpin, under whose command the ironclad steamship Great Eastern laid the first transatlantic cable in the mid-nineteenth century, but we didn't linger long enough for sightseeing. The capricious wind was now beckoning seductively from the north east and it was time to set sail for Dun Laoghaire.

The next six hours gave us the only decent day's sailing of the entire holiday and even then it wasn't perfect. Because we were sailing north we had to steer a zigzag course of tacks to keep the wind in our sails. To me this seemed pointless and incomprehensible.

'Why do we have to keep changing direction?'

I was worn out from hauling on ropes and trying to get from one side to the other of the cockpit without tripping over, whacking my head on the boom or getting caught up in a flailing line.

'Because if we didn't tack we wouldn't be able to sail in the direction we want to go,' said Mike, not for the first time. 'You can't sail into the wind. We have to tack to keep the wind in the sail and to keep us going where we want to go.'

It still didn't make sense to me.

'But why do we have to sail? Why can't we put the engine on?' I persisted.

'Because we're here to sail,' was the uncompromising reply. End of debate. We sailed. And it was fun. The sun played hide and seek with us, one minute beaming brazenly over the cockpit, the next vanishing coyly behind Cevamp's sailcloth skirts until we again changed course.

'It's strange,' Mike mused as we skimmed along the coast, 'but I never get bored when I'm sailing. Even though the scenery hardly seems to change there's always something new to look at, even if it's only the clouds changing shape.'

It was true. He could spend a lifetime huddled into his corner of the cockpit with the tiller tucked under his arm, squinting at the horizon or lining up transits on land as a way of judging our gentle progress. As if to reinforce Mike's remark a huge block of flats appeared from nowhere, shimmering in the sunlight as it floated across the sea's surface towards Dublin. We gazed at this outsized mirage in disbelief and then reached for the binoculars to get a better view. It was the ferry, Saint Patrick II – or maybe III – steaming purposefully towards Dublin where it would disgorge its impatient cargo of cars and lorries before turning round and heading back to Holyhead with another load.

'It's a miracle that with so much above the water it doesn't fall over,' I said. 'But I suppose the weight of trucks and cars helps keep it stable, like the keel on a yacht. Don't you think?'

But Mike didn't answer. He had lost interest in the

ferry and had already found something else fascinating to look at, this time on land. The coastal railway winds its way along a rocky ledge above the shoreline between Wicklow and Dublin, where the thinly grassed lower slopes of Sugar Loaf and Little Sugar Loaf mountains are washed by the waves; we watched vivid green trains disappearing into the rock and re-appearing from the mouths of tunnels, munching their way along the track like hungry caterpillars through an emerald forest. Then as we drew nearer to Dun Laoghaire we came in closer to land and in between navigating our way inside a chain of dark, rocky outcrops with their icing of cormorant guano, we were able to admire the smart houses with their private slipways and Lilliputian harbours at the end of their gardens.

Light was fading as we entered Dublin Bay and Mike's final log entry of the day spoke for us both.

'Moored up in Dun Laoghaire inner harbour. Time 21.30 hours. Distance travelled: 29 miles. Time taken: six hours twenty minutes. Ready for dinner.'

We savoured the warmth and flavour of our re-heated left-over stew and having satisfied our inner needs we clambered ashore to use the facilities of Dun Laoghaire Motor Yacht Club to deal with our external ones. You have to have experienced the difficulties and indignities of strip-washing in a cramped cabin, where it's impossible to stand upright and every jugful of water has to be pumped through a quarter-inch pipe then boiled in a kettle, to understand the bliss of a hot shower on a sailing holiday. Our last was on the previous Thursday and it was now Wednesday night. Our delight in standing under the comforting streams of hot water was in direct proportion to our days of deprivation. Cleansed, refreshed and considerably sweeter smelling, we adjourned to the bar for a convivial glass of Guinness and to chat to some of the local sailors.

From where we stood we could see Cevamp snuggled up against the Old Trade harbour wall, but were content to enjoy our drink without worrying about her. We knew from studying Reed's Nautical Almanac that this was a sound mooring with a sandy bottom and Mike had left enough line to allow for the rise and fall of the tide – not so much that she would drift far out from the wall when the tide came in, and not so little that she would be hanging from the wall when it went out. We got talking to one of the chaps at the bar and pointing to Cevamp Mike asked him whether we were on a sound mooring, on the basis that a little local knowledge is a valuable thing. 'What sort of keel does she have?' the man asked.

'Twin. Is it safe to take the ground where we are?'

'Sure, you're safe enough there. That mooring doesn't dry out.' Reassured by his answer we finished our drinks, said our goodbyes and went back to the boat.

We were jolted from our slumbers a few hours later. Crash! Bang! Crash! Bang! Cevamp was rocking violently from bow to stern and the crazy motion was accompanied by a horrible cacophony of crunching, banging and grinding noises. We leapt out of bed and rushed out into the darkness. The helpful chap in the yacht club was right. The harbour didn't dry. About six inches of scummy grey water remained. And although Cevamp didn't need much depth to stay afloat she needed a damned sight more than six inches. With the movement of the ebbing tide our centre keel was striking the ground. And the ground consisted of jagged rocks and boulders. From what we could make out in the darkness we had landed on one of them and it was acting as a pivot. Every time a wave rolled in it lifted Cevamp's nose so that the stern crashed down and hit the bottom. Then every time it rolled out again it lifted the stern and the nose crashed back down.

For the next two hours there was nothing we could do except wait for the tide to turn and put Cevamp out of her misery. Every thud was a physical blow to us. We felt Cevamp's pain, and while we longed for daybreak we dreaded seeing the full extent of the damage it would reveal. We lurched back inside and sat on the bed, silent in our misery, waiting for the water level to rise. Suddenly there was a loud bang. Mike leapt up just in time to see the tiller sliding away through the pushpit. He lunged towards it, thwacking his ribs painfully on the gunnels as he did so and just managed to grab the heavy tiller seconds before it dropped off the back of the boat during another violent lurch. The rudder had banged down onto one of the rocks with such force it had lifted from its mountings and we were lucky not to have lost it altogether. The next half hour lasted forever. With both of us struggling to keep our balance, I shone a torch so we could see what we were doing while Mike hung over Cevamp's stern and, muscles straining, eventually managed to re-position the tiller on its pinion.

So much for local knowledge.

11

Cevamp takes the ground again

In the morning Cevamp seemed none the worse from her pounding but the early forecast was a bit off putting and we decided to spend the day in Dun Laoghaire rather than heading for home. As sometimes happens, the shipping forecast bore no resemblance to weather on land and it turned into a glorious day. We mooched around the 150 year old harbour looking at yachts and spent the afternoon pottering on the boat, sunbathing, washing our smalls and eating.

Dun Laoghaire's ancient origins were largely lost on us but we enjoyed looking in the shops. We were shocked at the high prices for basic food and amused to see butchers selling 'round mince', not to mention an 'Irish Italian' restaurant that was closed for lunch. There was an abundance of semi-tropical trees and plants and I've never before seen so many dogs wandering around, occasionally stopping to cock a leg casually up a shop door or a greengrocer's fruit and veg stall on the pavement.

Mellow and relaxed from our day in the warm sunshine, we were in bed by eight o'clock and were just dropping off to sleep an hour or so later when we were startled by a thud against the side of the boat and heavy footsteps on the roof. Mike hurriedly pulled on a pair of old tracksuit bottoms and went to investigate. He found a couple of sailors rafting their yacht alongside us.

'We're planning to leave at about seven thirty tomorrow morning,' said Mike. 'You'd be better off tying up inside us, unless you don't mind being woken up when we go.'

'Oh don't worry,' said the skipper. 'We're not staying on board. We're going home. We're just down from Dublin but we only live twenty minutes away. We've been to collect our new boat and bring her home.'

We helped them tie up their boat and declined the left-over cheese and pickle sandwiches that they generously offered to us by way of thanks. They trundled none too steadily off into the sunset, leaving us to keep an eye on their yacht.

'I can't believe it,' I gasped once they were out of earshot. 'That's a brand new yacht and they don't know us from Adam. How do they know that we can be trusted to tie her up properly in the morning? I can't ever see us being that blasé where our boat's concerned.'

We were incredulous but not surprised next morning when neither of them had put in an appearance by the time we were ready to go. We carefully manoeuvred the gleaming new yacht round to Cevamp's nearside and tied her tidily alongside the harbour wall before motoring east out of Dun Laoghaire and straight into a force five. We knew at once that this was going to be a bit of a slog and we weren't disappointed. Once clear of the harbour we put the sails up and spent a frustrating couple of hours tacking. But we were only making two knots and had about 60 miles to go so in the end Mike bowed to the inevitable and switched the engine on.

Five hours later we had still only covered 15 miles or so. The engine seemed to be lacking power, making the boat sluggish, and the sea was lumpy, which slowed us down even more. The fan belt was squealing, too, and in the end Mike decided to change it. After half an hour with his head in a hot engine compartment on a heavily rocking boat he was sick and felt ill and nauseous for the rest of the crossing.

It was an unpleasant passage, into a headwind all the way. Visibility was down to about three or four miles and it was very cold. Even with several layers of clothes underneath storm proof suits we both felt very chilled and for some reason I really felt it in my knees.

Time passed unbearably slowly and the only nice thing about it was a little green bird that landed on the guard rails and stayed with us for a while before being lifted into the wind and disappearing. We couldn't identify it, and other than making a silly remark about it being an Irish wren because it was green, the closest we could get was that it was a warbler of some sort, taking a break during its spring migration.

As the day limped interminably on we took it in turns to take naps. It makes you very drowsy when visibility is poor, you're out of sight of land and you don't have any sails to worry about. Before leaving Dun Laoghaire I'd put soup in a flask and made a supply of sandwiches but Mike still couldn't really face food and ate his with less than his usual gusto. All that really kept us going was cup after cup of hot orange squash, with the obvious effect.

'What on earth are you doing down there. It can't take that long just to have a wee.'

'Huh. It's all right for you. You're a man. All you have to do is unzip yourself and take aim over the side. It's not so easy for me. I have to balance on a bucket in a bouncing boat when the sea's this choppy. And I have to struggle out of my safety harness, life jacket, storm jacket, fleece jacket, storm trousers with Velcro flap and stubborn zip, jeans, long johns and knickers. No wonder I've lost all sense of modesty.'

Living accommodation on a twenty-six foot yacht is snug, to say the least, and however private a person you are you soon accept that modesty comes a poor second to intimacy when two people are sharing a space no bigger than the average family car. In less than a year I'd thrown most of my inhibitions to the wind, along with the contents of the bucket, and now felt perfectly at ease sitting on my pail and chatting to Mike, a few feet away, as I answered a call of nature.

By seven in the evening, visibility was down to about one or two miles and apart from the lights of a few big ships crossing the shipping lanes out of Holyhead we felt we were alone on the ocean. There was none of the magic in the stars we enjoyed on previous night passages and nothing at all enjoyable about the experience. Tired, cold and grumpy we knew we just had to stick it out.

Two hours later we saw the first beam from a lighthouse, which meant land was getting close, and our spirits lifted. It's fun at night, picking out the different lights and matching them against their descriptions on the charts. And, of course, it's always satisfying to end up roughly where you intended to. Mike's navigational skills are pretty good in any case so we shouldn't have been too surprised, nearly three hours later, to find we were just north of Bardsey Island on the tip of the Lleyn Peninsular. This was just a little south of our intended anchorage at Porth Dinllaen, the setting for Cevamp's portrait.

'What's the time?' I yawned.

'Nearly midnight,' Mike yawned back.

'God, that's eighteen hours since we left Dun Laoghaire. No wonder I'm exhausted.'

'I know, and I'm whacked too. But I think we should push on a bit further and try and pick up a mooring at Abersoch.'

By the time we got round the Llyn Peninsula we were both shattered and it was two in the morning before we got to Abersoch. Mike felt even worse than I did as at least I'd managed to sleep during the day and for the two hours from midnight. He, poor soul, had survived on little more than cat naps. We motored into the bay with me poised up front with the boat hook, ready to pick up a mooring buoy. It was very dark, the moon was blanketed in cloud and it was a matter of going very slowly and shining Cevamp's searchlight around until we spotted a line.

Then we ran aground. We'd gone too far in at low tide and because the night was so dark and we were so tired we hadn't noticed how shallow the water was getting.

'Hold tight,' shouted Mike. 'I'm going to see if I can reverse us out of here.'

There was a metallic clunk as the gear dropped into reverse, a squeal from the protesting fan belt, a roar from the engine and a lot of churning of water. But Cevamp just dug herself more firmly in. We were stuck broadside on to some pretty hefty waves and for the second time in less than forty eight hours the poor yacht took a real pounding.

We dropped a couple of anchors and then there was nothing more we could do but, once again, sit and wait for the tide to come in. Although the water wasn't very deep the power of the waves was immense. Cevamp is a heavy boat but with every breaker we were lifted up and dumped with a shuddering crunch onto the hard-packed sand below Cevamp's keel. We sat there, powerless, always waiting for the next crash to split the boat in two and realising, not for the first time, how the force of nature is totally beyond the control of humankind. But yet again Cevamp excelled, and with every shudder she simply shook herself down and prepared herself for the next onslaught.

Just as we thought things couldn't get any worse, they did. The rudder was again jolted off its mountings and once again Mike just managed to grab it before it slid off the stern to be lost in the waves. This time it wasn't so easy to re-position it and it took two fraught and uncomfortable hours hanging over the back of the boat before we succeeded. I shone the torch – I was getting good at this by now – onto the bottom bolt as Mike struggled against the violent rocking to guide the hundredweight rudder into place, just below the waterline. Things were made more difficult by the darkness and cramped working space. The rudder's mountings were only inches from the boarding ladder and the emergency outboard, which was mounted on the top rail of the pushpit.

And still things got worse.

The top mounting bolt for the rudder sheered off.

Mike cursed. He had a brief rest to get his breath back and restore the feeling in his hand, crushed as the rudder fell against the top edge of the transom.

'Right,' he said. 'Ready to start again? This time I'll lash the torch to the pushpit and move the outboard out of the way. You go and switch on the deck lights. They should throw a little more light on the situation and we might be able to see what we're doing a bit better.'

I scuttled below and prayed I'd remember which switches operated the deck lights. Back on deck Mike told me he'd come to a decision.

'We'll give it another fifteen minutes and if we still

haven't done it by then I'm getting on the radio and asking for a tow,' said Mike. 'I can't think of anything else we can do if this doesn't work.'

He didn't have to. With his strength and infinite patience, my extra pair of hands and an old screwdriver serving as a temporary bolt, we finally got the rudder back in place.

What a relief. But there was to be no respite. I looked round to see water lapping over the floor boards in the cabin. This was annoying rather than a problem. It is common for wooden boats to take on water and by now I was a dab hand at pumping out the bilges. After fifteen minutes or so order was finally restored and although we were exhausted we were even managing to crack the odd – very odd – joke.

By this time the tide had started to come in. Slowly, very slowly, Cevamp swung round and almost as if by instinct, pointed her nose into the wind. She was ready to go. And so were we. Mike had decided that with all our problems the best course of action was to head straight back to Porthmadog and by half past four we were again under way, with the engine on and frozen hands wrapped around warming mugs of hot orange squash.

Poor Mike was almost asleep at the tiller. I could see his eyelids drooping and his head nodding but he was worried about the screwdriver and wouldn't take a break from helming. We were also aware, by this time, that we were still making very slow progress and were taking on much more water than usual, taking it in turns to pump out whenever the level rose above the bilges.

'Look,' I said forcefully. 'This isn't doing you any good. I'm quite capable of managing on my own. Now go down below and catch some sleep.'

'But what if ...'

'I said I can manage. If anything goes wrong I promise to call you.'

'Oh all right then. As long as you're sure you're okay. But give me a shout...'

'...if anything goes wrong,' I finished for him. 'Okay, I will.'

Minutes later I peeped into the cabin and had to smile. He was lying on his back, sound asleep, snoring loudly, with his welly-clad feet poking out of the end of the duvet. Talk about being prepared.

He slept for an hour, by which time we had only just got to the big dipper at Butlins holiday camp near Pwllheli and I was very chilled. So he came up on deck and I went down to get warm, intending to relieve him after an hour. To my shame and embarrassment I was still asleep when we reached Porthmadog at half past ten.

We arranged with Robin Kuffyn, the owner of Porthmadog boatyard, to have Cevamp craned out the following morning and we finally collapsed into bed together just before mid-day.

It was normal for Robin to grumble about Cevamp being too heavy for his crane and on this occasion he probably had something to grumble about. We had already ladled out five buckets of water from the cabin floor but as Cevamp rose from her mooring and over the harbour wall she looked more like a giant colander than an ocean going yacht. Gallons of seawater poured out of her hull, adding a good half ton or more to her weight and explaining her sluggishness on the journey home.

Once she was resting on blocks we were able to examine her for damage, most of which she suffered on the rocks at Dun Laoghaire. The glass fibre skin around the port keel had cracked and the iron centre keel was damaged at the point where it joined the hollow wooden keel extension, which was also full of water. Bolts from the keel to the hull under the cabin had been damaged, splitting the seal and allowing yet more water into the bilges. Water continued to trickle out of the hull for a long time and Mike removed plugs to help channel it all out.

'Enjoy your holiday?' asked Alex when we stopped off at The New Inn on our way home.

'Well actually, Dad, there's something we need to tell you,' said Mike. 'We've broken the boat again.'

12

Nautical deafness

I've got good ears. Not in the sense, I hasten to add, that they're dainty, fragile shells lying flat and prettily against the sides of my head. What I mean is, they hear very well.

As a novice, eager and terrified young mum, I was guaranteed to hear the faintest snuffle or the tiniest whimper made by my new born infant from three rooms and two flights of stairs away. When I went off babies I lavished my affections on cats instead (less mess, less work and don't turn into teenagers). I would awaken instantly from the depths of my slumbers at the slightest piteous meow from the garden or the merest scratch of determined feline claw on bedroom door as one of the other of my pride begged to be allowed in to the warm comfort of my twelve tog duvet.

By the time the last cat went off to his happy hunting ground I was besotted by beagles and it's the same story. They've got me so well trained that every little woof in the night has me flying downstairs to see what's disturbed them – no matter that Mike and I are also disturbed in the process.

And even in my everyday life, mundane though it may often be, my ears have an unerring capacity to hear and transmit to my brain everything that is intended for them, as well as a few things that aren't.

But put me on a yacht and I go deaf.

Whether we're out at sea, battling in a heavy swell with the motor running and the ever present howl of the wind, or sitting quietly in harbour sipping a glass of wine, it's still the same. When I'm on a boat I never hear a word that's said to me.

Even when it's just the two of us sailing pleasantly along with little noise other than the occasional flap of the main and the whoosh of water under the stern, I seem totally incapable of discerning human speech.

I suppose at times it's understandable. It's so easy at sea to lose yourself in thought, in deep contemplation about such intellectually demanding matters as whether it's just a bit too soon after the last Mars bar to suggest having another, or whether the next harbour will have hot showers, clean loos and a launderette that's open all hours.

Or perhaps the most dominant questions concern fashion: will it ever be warm enough for shorts and the Italian sun top that cost nearly £50 and has only been off its hanger once, or am I just going to have to get used to wearing five layers of inelegant, damp and gently steaming clothes for the duration of this trip?

At other times I may even be searching for the answers to some of life's more complex problems, such as how many days in August in Britain is it possible to go without the sun shining? Whatever it may be, as I sit there pondering the meaning of life and trying to see how far I can follow the progress of a wave without blinking, it has the same strange negative effect on my personal auditory equipment.

Suddenly, through my reverie, I realise Mike is speaking to me.

'What was that?' I say.

And he has to repeat it. Not just occasionally, but almost every time he speaks to me. It must drive him crazy, but at least it isn't life threatening. And anyway, although he'd never admit it, he's almost as bad.

Another problem is that I have the greatest difficulty understanding anything that's said on the ship's radio, especially when the operators have Welsh or Irish accents, which partly explains my reluctance to use the hateful thing. This is quite apart from the fact that I feel foolish in the extreme, having to repeat everything three times. I was glad Cevamp had a nice simple name. Imagine having to say, as some people have to, 'This is yacht Globulin' or 'This is yacht Ben Druidh of Assynt', three times every time you call the coastguard, or even worse, 'This is yacht Fionn MacCumaill', even when I discovered you actually pronounced that one Finn McCool. Even though I had gone to evening classes to get my radio operator's licence, I always managed to find something else important to do when it was time to make a radio transmission to the harbour master or coastguard station from the yacht.

At 26 feet long, excluding the bowsprit, Cevamp isn't a particularly big boat but the three yards between cockpit and foredeck can have a very peculiar effect on how one human voice can be distorted by another human's ear, as I had already found out on more than one occasion when Mike was trying to tell me to steer into the wind, and yes, I accept that on those occasions perhaps my nautical deafness may have been life threatening.

And of course there was the day when it nearly caused me to crash the yacht. It happened at a time when Mike and I had been sailing together for about eighteen months and my confidence had grown. I had mastered, or nearly mastered, the knack of steering into the wind and reckoned I could now handle the boat pretty well on my own.

We were on our way back from a longish holiday and I was pretty pleased with myself. By now I was reasonably competent with the genoa's self-furling gear and could go about with panache. I even knew what it meant! I had a working knowledge of the use of the two-way marine radio, even if I was reluctant to use it, and had learnt how to set up and interpret the blips on the echo sounder. The electrics and engine were no longer a total mystery and I'd even raised the mainsail single-handed, under Mike's ever-watchful eye, of course.

'If anything happened to you, such as if you were knocked unconscious or broke your arms and legs,' I said cheerfully to Mike, 'I reckon I'd be able to get us back to Porthmadog by myself now.'

'You're probably right,' he agreed mildly, privately deciding to put me to the test. We were tied to a buoy in Abersoch at the time, having arrived gloriously goose winged the previous evening. We are not poseurs, not really, but we felt quite proud as we sailed into the sweeping bay, with the silky fabric of the cruising chute boomed out to one side of the boat and the mainsail boomed out on the other. The brilliant red, white and blue of the chute shone in the soft light and although there wasn't much wind there was just enough to fill both sails and keep them where we wanted them. Abersoch is a big sailing base and we were immodestly certain that everyone was watching and admiring us from the clubhouse overlooking the wide sandy beach.

It was one of those times when I was torn between the exhilaration of sailing and the desire to watch from the cliffs, so that I could get a photograph of our own boat under full sail, something that is actually quite difficult to achieve.

After a while the wind dropped to a whisper, the chute drooped and fluttered and we brought it in. Then Mike decided that, in view of our probable audience, rather than switch the engine on we – or rather I – would sail right up to a spare mooring buoy. The tough option but an unmissable opportunity to show off our boat handling and mooring skills.

Had Mike been at the helm I think we'd have succeeded. He is far more sensitive to the feel of the boat than I am and is far more experienced into the bargain. As it was, he offered me quiet advice, most of which I didn't hear, and I bungled things as usual although to be fair to myself there really wasn't much wind to help me along.

'Get some wind in the sail to get some speed and then turn towards the buoy,' he said more than once. But to no avail. The buoy would come tantalisingly close, just inches from the boat hook, then we would swing right round and have to start again. Stubbornly I kept trying, a bit like I do when I reverse the car into the garage, but eventually conceded defeat and we motored the last few yards. The effect of our glorious arrival was somewhat diminished but we felt we could live with that.

But I wasn't to be let off the hook that easily. The following morning there was a steady, gentle breeze and Mike asked me to raise the main and get ready to sail out while he attended to something – or nothing – in the cabin. Feeling rather smug and childishly hoping people were watching this experienced yachtie expertly handling the rigging, I was up on the coach roof with the ropes even before Mike had finished running through what I had to do. I don't know who was more surprised, him or me, when I realised I'd actually done it and done it right.

Then it was time to cast off and head for home. Another smoothly executed manoeuvre, but wind and tide were in my favour and conditions were not at all difficult.

I was still feeling pleased with myself but had to admit that what I'd done was nothing really. I suspect those other formidable women sailors, Clare Francis, Naomi James and Ellen MacArthur were probably doing that kind of thing while they were still in nappies but it made me feel good nonetheless and gave me cause to think for the second time in my sailing career that perhaps I wasn't such a bad crew after all.

As usual, my euphoric bubble was soon to burst. My big-headed boast 'I can manage this boat on my own' was going to look very silly, very soon.

We got back to Porthmadog that afternoon hoping we could sail right up the channel but by the time we reached the Fairway Buoy the wind, never strong and gradually lessening all day, had died completely. We were almost at a standstill so decided it would be more prudent to switch the engine on and motor in against the fast ebbing tide.

When we arrived, Porthmadog was at its best. The sun poured from a cloudless indigo sky, the distant mountain tops peeped through a veil of blue haze and the clear turquoise water was the proverbial millpond. The only sounds to disturb the silence came from the raucous gulls, screaming at each other over the schools of mullet that we could see idling on the sandy sea bed below.

There wasn't enough water to go straight onto our own mooring, which dries out at low tide, so we tied up to a spare buoy in the deep water channel with yachts at our bow and stern, to port and starboard. There was another small yacht nearby, no more than a twenty-two footer, with at least five large young men crammed on board, reading newspapers and basking in the sunshine. They were clearly strangers to the area as they could scarcely believe we had just come up the channel at such a low state of tide. I could understand their incredulity. The sandbar along the length of the channel is constantly shifting and despite the efficient buoyage system and the local chart, regularly updated by the then harbourmaster Mike Bicks, we knew from experience it was possible to run aground even at high water.

We pottered around on Cevamp, cleaning and tidying while we waited for the tide to come in and eventually it was time to move her over to her own mooring, near the causeway.

Suddenly, I went deaf again.

The engine was ticking over and Mike went up front to release the lines, having previously briefed me on my role at the tiller and the throttle.

'Once I cast off, get us away as soon as I give the word.' That was clear enough.

He untied the lines fore and aft and from his position at the front of the boat gave me the word. Cevamp's bows are really not very far from the cockpit, where I was standing, and I swear he told me to pull the throttle back to engage gear. So I did, following this smartly by thrusting the throttle forward to drive out.

Oops! What he actually said was pull the throttle back and reverse out...I realised my mistake a split second before Cevamp's long and potentially lethal bowsprit harpooned the very expensive looking yacht ahead of us.

In a bound, Mike was in the cockpit, grabbed the gear

lever at the same moment I did, and steered us smoothly out of trouble.

'Oh well, a miss is as good as a mile,' I said nonchalantly, trying to make light of my blunder.

Mike gave me an exasperated look.

'Wash your ears out,' was all he said.

13

In the doldrums

Homemade lamb goulash with apple pie and cream to follow. A fine and filling meal to celebrate the start of our late August holiday, a three week circumnavigation of the Isle of Man. Or it would have been, if I'd remembered to take it out of the freezer and bring it with me. Instead we joined the queue at Porthmadog's excellent chippy and sat under a canopy of stars on Cevamp's deck enjoying our supper and revelling in the sensuous warmth of the summer evening. It was another of those rare occasions when we actually knew what we were doing there and as we let ourselves be soothed by the barely discernible movement of the boat and the gentle lapping of the water we were hard pushed to remember how cold, wet and scary sailing could sometimes be.

It was mid August and our first opportunity to do any real sailing since we'd damaged the boat in Ireland. Alex had joined us in Porthmadog for a week in June to mastermind and help with the repair operation but we hadn't yet taken Cevamp for a proper test run. The repairs consisted mainly of a major modification to the keel and the bottom of the boat and the removal of about a quarter of a ton of wood, water, ballast and, of course, several carrier bags worth of water logged polystyrene. It was obvious by now that a lot of water had been coming in through bolt holes in the hog of the boat next to the bilge pump and these had to be made watertight too. Once Alex was satisfied that everything that needed to be done had been done, Cevamp – or Revamp as I now thought of her – was craned back over the harbour wall and into the sea. Less than an hour later we noticed water creeping over the floorboards again. When the tide receded, leaving us high and dry on the sand, and water had stopped dripping out of the bottom of the hull we carried out another inspection and found the source of the leak was at the leading edge of the keel. Mike and Alex raised the floorboards in the front section of the boat and discovered about a dozen iron bars, presumably put there as ballast when Cevamp was built but apparently forgotten about over time by Alex. They jettisoned these, along with still more soggy polystyrene and plugged the leak with silicon filler.

Once that was done Mike's mother, Vera, declared it was time she came for a short trip on Cevamp. We didn't quite pipe her aboard but Mike and I were pleased for Alex's sake that she was at last taking some interest in the boat and we took her out for a couple of hours to the fairway buoy and back. She seemed quite at home and the cabin filled with the gaseous whiff of hard-boiled eggs as she bustled around making sandwiches for lunch.

'Not feeling sea-sick then?' I asked.

I felt my sarcasm was justified. It was the one and only time she ever set foot on the yacht and my heart ached for Alex during the afternoon when he confided sadly, 'If I'd known how Vera really felt about sailing I would never have built the boat.'

But that was weeks ago and now we were looking forward to doing some serious sailing. If sitting on deck on the first night of our holiday was lovely, the first morning wasn't and we awoke to the sound of torrential rain just as dawn was breaking. The early morning shipping forecast promised southerly force five winds and by nine o'clock it was still windy, cold and overcast. I'd laden the boat with food, wine, sweets, cakes, biscuits and other stores and once we'd filled the tanks with fresh water from the yacht club tap we were eager to be off. Undeterred by the fact that the yachts Eurhythmy and Hunky were now returning to the sanctuary of their moorings after a short run out, we decided to go and see for ourselves what it was like away from the shelter of the harbour. I poured hot tomato soup in a flask to have with pasties for lunch and we left our mooring at just after midday. Anglesey here we come.

Half an hour later we turned round and came back. By the time we'd drawn level with Harlech Spit heavy seas were pounding over the sandbar, there was a strong headwind and we knew we were unlikely to get safely over the bar.

We spent the afternoon in bed and in the evening we had a cheese and wine party for two before settling down for another early night.

Next morning conditions were a bit better and we left Porthmadog shortly after breakfast. It was low water slack and we were barely half way up the channel when we ran aground. The incoming tide eventually lifted us clear and we finally made it to open water. It was hard going, with a strong north-westerly on the nose and a forecast for a gale eight later, so tired of the relentless buffeting we found some shelter under the cliffs of Aberdaron Bay. What with the slapping waves, howling wind and the clanging of the halyards against the mast we got little sleep and by dawn we were wide awake again.

The early morning forecast was for more of the same so rather than repeat the previous day's performance we stayed where we were and even managed to doze back off to sleep. Our snooze was short lived. Mike's uncanny sixth sense alerted him to something wrong.

'Come on; get some clothes on as quick as you can. We've dragged our anchors and we're drifting out. I need you on deck to steer.'

I groaned as I reluctantly joined him on deck to haul the anchors back in so we could tuck Cevamp back into the lee of the cliffs. Tea and toast, then back to bed for another couple of hours, until Mike summoned up the energy to face the day, don his wet suit and, using his sailboard as a canoe, paddle ashore to explore Aberdaron.

It is an old whitewashed fishing village on the sea shore at the mouth of the river Daron and in days gone by it was the final settlement on the mainland for the saints on their pilgrimage to Bardsey. Quiet out of season, busy in the summer and popular with holiday makers, walkers and water sports enthusiasts, it is home to the famous beach known as Whistling Sands, so named because the smooth white sand whistles underfoot. It didn't take Mike long to have a look round and he was soon back on board.

'Well what do you think?' he said. 'Shall we just go out to see what it's like and try to get round to Porth Dinllaen? We can always come back if it gets too bad.'

It wasn't a question and I trusted his judgement but privately wasn't too keen on the idea and muttered mutinously while I got ready to face the elements.

While he was waiting for me to finish getting my wet weather gear on, Mike set about tightening the alternator belt, which he thought was slipping a bit. Bad idea. What's that old saying? If it ain't broke, don't fix it! Suddenly there was a spark from Cevamp's nether regions, Mike yelped and jumped back, followed by billowing clouds of acrid smoke from the engine compartment. Thank goodness for all Cevamp's fire extinguishers. When the air had cleared we could see the main cable sleeves had all melted away and the isolator switch for the electrics was destroyed. Not only did we have no engine, but no electrics either. The solenoid on the starter motor had shorted, and because of the speed it happened, Mike hadn't been able to prevent a fire by turning off the electricity supply.

'I'm sorry love,' he said, 'but this looks like the end of our holiday'. He looked so downcast and I gave him a hug. Trying to be tactful, I didn't ask why he hadn't switched off the electrics before poking around in the engine compartment with spanners and wrenches.

'Doesn't matter. It's not your fault. The main thing is that you're all right.'

'Hmm. Well we can't stay here. We'll just have to sail back to Pwllheli. There's a guy there called Roland Marine who does electrics for boats. We'll ask him if he can come out and fix it for us.'

With that he stomped off to raise the main, haul up the anchor and prepare to retrace our route of the previous day.

Then, as if in apology for its earlier ill humour, the weather took a turn for the better. The sun came out and now that we were heading back to Pwllheli the wind direction was just right. With the mainsail fully reefed and most of the genoa unfurled we enjoyed a wonderful few hours sailing, at one point touching 7.4 knots, a record for Cevamp that she only exceeded once, later in the same holiday.

But as usual, it didn't last. We went through St Tudwal's Roads, delighted to spot deer on the smaller of the two islands, but by then our speed had dropped dramatically and we were having to tack to make any headway at all.

We soldiered on.

By eight thirty in the evening we'd been under way for six hours. The wind had dropped to a whisper, we were making one knot if we were lucky and Gimlet Rock off Pwllheli was just visible, still about a mile away. But there were compensations. A half moon was rising through the low cloud on the horizon, giving a soft glow to the grey and orange sunset, and the blue of the daytime sky had darkened to indigo high above. We finally entered Pwllheli Harbour on an ebb tide just before 10pm and dropped anchor close to the fairway buoy just inside the harbour entrance.

We awoke to a fine, mild and still Monday morning in a somewhat less than sweet smelling spot a couple of hundred yards from the first line of moorings. What had looked, in the dark, like the fairway buoy turned out to be a hazard beacon marking the end of a sewage outlet pipe. Almost as bad was the realisation that we had completely missed the litter of red and green buoys marking the deep water channel into the harbour. We were lucky not to have run aground again and as we sat on deck with our breakfast we watched the local fishing boats entering and leaving the harbour, sticking very closely to the route marked by the buoys.

Mike untied his windsurfer from the coachroof and again using it as a canoe he paddled ashore to find Roland Marine, the electrical engineers, who were based in the middle of a housing estate in Pwllheli. They assured him they would be over to us shortly.

By mid-afternoon there was no sign of Roland, Mike was getting more despondent and withdrawn by the minute and I realised I hadn't been off the boat since Friday.

'I think I'll row ashore for some fresh bread and milk,' I said to Mike. 'I'll pop in and find out what's happened to Roland while I'm there.'

Pwllheli, the unofficial capital of the Lleyn Peninsular and an ideal base for touring this beautiful part of Wales is also a popular holiday town and that day it was like a miniature Blackpool, basking in the high season sunlight. Crowds of holiday makers pushed and shoved for space on the busy pavements, squeezing past steaming fish cafés smelling tantalisingly of chips and vinegar. Various shops full of beach paraphernalia and tacky souvenirs lined the streets and buffers on the tracks at the railway station marked the end of the line.

When I got back, having first extracted a promise from Roland that he would be over first thing in the morning and a request for us to ferry him over to Cevamp, Mike was windsurfing in the bay and had cheered up a bit. But it was beautiful sailing weather and we were both frustrated by the delay. Gloomily we sat and watched as the harbour emptied itself of yachts that were full of happy people going out sailing. Then as the tide turned we watched them all come back again.

We thought about trying to sail further in to the harbour to get us away from the gut-churning stench from the outflow pipe but as we only had limited manoeuvrability without an engine we thought better of it and Mike went off to arrange a tow. Shortly after he got back the tow boat arrived.

'It'll cost you £10,' said the skipper.

'That's too much just to be pulled a few hundred

yards,' protested Mike.

The skipper shrugged. 'Take it or leave it.'

'I'll leave it then, thanks,' said Mike. He gave the man £4 for his trouble and the boat chuntered off again.

As far as I was concerned it would have been worth the extra £6 to get us away from the smell, which by now had insinuated itself permanently into our taste buds and added a certain je ne sais quoi to the flavour of the chilli con carne that we ate on deck for supper.

It was another two long drawn out and tedious days before Cevamp was finally fixed and seaworthy again but we'd now lost so much time that we abandoned the plan to sail round the Isle of Man and substituted Anglesey instead. We breathed our last lungful of sewage-scented air and motored gratefully out of the harbour on the afternoon tide. St Tudwal's Islands beckoned in the distance and our spirits rose with every nautical mile we put between us and Pwllheli. If that had been the low point of our holiday we were confident that from now on things could only get better.

14

Storm warnings

We knew bad weather was on its way, despite the brightness of the day and the warm sunshine on our backs. The first clue came from Holyhead coastguard station in a securité radio transmission: falling barometric pressure and north westerly gale force eight, imminent. The second came twenty minutes later on the Radio Four shipping forecast: winds north westerly six to gale force eight, showers.

What's more, we could see from the way the waves were building and the frequency of white caps on their crests that there was already a good force five powering us along so I went below to make sure we had plenty of soup in a flask and to check the beef and dumpling stew that I'd prepared earlier in the day. I didn't want to be caught out by a prolonged spell of bad weather with no hot food to sustain us.

As the late afternoon gave way to early evening the sea was getting pretty heavy and the sky increasingly threatening. The wind was picking up too, so while I made doubly sure that everything was secure on deck and stowed away in the cabin Mike furled in the genoa, put a couple of reefs in the mainsail and started the engine.

'What do you think?' he said. 'Shall we keep going round the headland for a bit longer to see whether we can get across Hell's Mouth to Aberdaron, or should we just cut our losses and go back to Abersoch?' He always asked me for my opinion, knowing full well that I invariably relied on him to make the decision.

I wanted to take the easy option and go back to Abersoch but I knew Mike wanted to press on and heard myself saying, 'We'll cross Hell's Mouth. Why go back when it seems reasonable enough to go on?'

An hour later we were approaching the western end of Hell's Mouth. The waves were bigger than ever and the earlier sunshine had given way to a sullen orange glow that was partially obscured by silver-edged black clouds flying overhead.

Then suddenly it hit us. Spray everywhere, howling wind, huge waves and stinging shafts of rain. Mike decided to get the main down to relieve the stress on the yacht but as he handed the tiller over to me Cevamp heeled right over. For once I kept my head. Mike's repeated instructions in the past had, at last, sunk in and I instinctively tugged the main sheet out of its cleat in the split second before he shouted at me to do it. With the wind out of the sail Cevamp straightened up and Mike clambered onto the coach roof to lower the canvas. It was still a pretty perilous operation as the sea was still heaving and pounding but nonetheless he managed to get my attention and point to the double rainbow arched against the pewter sky behind us.

'Aim for the gap between the headland and the islands,' he called.

Aim for the gap? The waves were so big that I couldn't even see the islands. By now my feet were soaking and I laughed to myself at the irony of us both having trudged around Pwllheli all morning in wellies then, in a force eight with water coming over the sides in bath-tub-loads, finding ourselves in trainers.

'Are you okay?' Mike called out from his perch on the coachroof.

I called back casually, 'It's only a squall.' How times had changed!

Still, it was fun and neither of us was frightened. In fact, it was probably just what we both needed to get the adrenalin going after our enforced few days of inactivity. Afterwards it seemed to me the whole episode had only lasted a few minutes but Mike reckoned it took about an hour for the storm to blow over.

Shortly afterwards we dropped anchor among the lobster pot marker buoys at the entrance to the fishermen's cove in Aberdaron Bay. Mike called Holyhead coastguard to say we'd arrived safely. They thanked him for his call but didn't comment on our skills as sailors or even say they were pleased we'd made it. I suppose if they thought anything at all it was just that we were mad to be out there in the first place.

The next morning saw us en route for Bardsey Sound, the treacherous tide race between Bardsey Island and the tip of the Lleyn Peninsular. Known to the Welsh as Ynys Enlli, Bardsey is said to be the burial place of 20,000 saints and some people believe it to be the legendary Avalon, where King Arthur died and Merlin the Magician was buried.

Over a beans-on-toast breakfast we discussed our options. Should we try to get through the sound straight away, when the tide was just starting to run against us, or should we leave it until the afternoon when it would be with us? Or should we just stay put until the weather improved? The early morning shipping forecast was again warning of gales in Irish Sea but, as usual we decided to put our nose out to see what it was like. It looked quite rough from what we could see of it. Perhaps we should have heeded the gale warning and stayed put. We were both tired; I had a headache and although the day was reasonably mild and dry it was overcast and very windy.

Of course, once we got going we kept going. Bardsey was its usual inhospitable self and almost before we knew it we were in rip tides in mountainous seas and a good force six or seven to boot. We could hear the wind above the crashing and banging of the boat as she reared up one side of the great rollers only to hurtle down the other. I found it exhilarating and it soon blew away my headache. The waves were huge, powerful, magnificent and breathtakingly beautiful. Because I wasn't driving and didn't have responsibility for the boat it was easy for me just to sit there, enjoy the ride and thrill to the splendour of it all. Above the confused sea and the screaming wind the grey clouds had broken up to reveal an intense blue sky. The sun glinted off the exquisite translucent jade of the waves and spindrift swept across the surface of the water as the yacht's bows forced their way through the surf.

We had just cleared the island and were still battling to get through the last of the overfalls when Cevamp was hit by a big wave that caught us broadside on the port beam. I was flung across the lockers and Mike was swept up and across the cockpit, fighting to retain his hold on the tiller. The wave crashed over the spray dodgers and right over us before tearing along the length of the boat and ripping one of the starboard stanchion posts almost from its mounting. Mike was still struggling for control of the boat. I was busy photographing the drama for posterity.

'Put that bloody camera away, grab the loo bucket and bail,' he shouted, furious with me and my obvious lack of concern. I sheepishly shoved the camera into the pocket of my oilies before dropping onto all fours in the cockpit, bucket and chucking as fast as I could. My efforts had made little difference to the gallons of water sloshing around in the cockpit when we caught another monster, from the starboard side this time. I continued bailing for what seemed like ages until the depth of water had diminished to a level that the pump could cope with.

We carried on, slowly easing our way round the tip of the peninsular and away from Bardsey Island, which seemed to be looming behind us for ever. Finally, though we got through the sound and as the seas were beginning to ease slightly I took over the tiller to give Mike a bit of a break. That was when we hit another area of rip tides and from my seat in the cockpit I saw my bag of clothes and Reeds' Nautical Almanac fly across the cabin to end up floating in the knee-deep water that had forced its way inside.

This time the waves weren't only high but wide too. They loomed vertically ahead of the boat and as usual Cevamp rode decisively up them, balanced for a breathless, motionless moment on the crest then rolled heavily down the other side. Sometimes I thought she'd never make it to the top and would have to go, like Alice, through the glassy green wall, while at other times the waves just broke right over our heads instead. But still my over-riding impression was one of indescribable beauty.

Even while all this was going on we could see through the spray to where people were strolling along the cliff path on top of the headland and we wondered if they could see how rough it was for us. But it's almost impossible to judge the height and ferocity of waves when you look down on them and although some of the ramblers waved cheerily to us most of them probably never even gave us a second glance.

When we finally reached Porth Dinllaen we anchored close to shore, exhausted, cold, wet-booted and soaked to the skin. Our faces and lips were encrusted with dried-on salt, which sparkled in the sun and gave us a slightly frosted appearance. Families were scattered on the beach, eating ice creams and making the most of the glorious weather. They couldn't have known, and wouldn't have cared, about the drama that had been going on just a few miles from where they were enjoying their picnics, playing with their dogs and children, splashing around at the water's edge or simply soaking up the sun. We still couldn't relax though. There was damage to repair and lots of sorting out to do. And most importantly, we needed a cup of tea. We spent the rest of the afternoon mopping up and drying things out and soon the boat resembled a Chinese laundry with trousers flapping from the halyards at the top of the mast and a variety of waterproofs, wellies and my spare clothes hanging from the rails and anywhere else I could find some space.

That evening, lingering over our dinner of beef stew, we talked about our experience.

'Well I don't mind admitting I was frightened,' said Mike, especially when those two big waves came over and lifted me up and swamped the cockpit.'

I thought about this for a minute. I wanted to try and be honest with myself. Had I really been as unafraid as I was making out, or was I just trying to make myself out to be cooler than I really was? I've always had this notion that as an Englishwoman I am at my best in times of adversity but was I just kidding myself? Was that coolness just a front, protecting the frightened little girl that I really was? Or had the trials and tribulations of sailing brought out nobler qualities, previously unseen? I was pleased with my decision.

'I may have been a bit anxious,' I told Mike, 'but I really wasn't that scared. Probably because I trust you and know you know what you're doing, and I truly believed Cevamp would cope. But if I'd been on my own or in charge of the boat for some other reason, say if you'd been knocked unconscious by the boom, I think I would have been terrified.'

I chewed thoughtfully on a gravy-enriched dumpling.

'Mind you,' I added, 'I'm not saying that I'd particularly choose to do it again!'

In the end we agreed we had been foolhardy to put to sea in the first place that day, especially having heard the gale warnings. Cevamp had taken a real pounding and we made a decision that in future, out of respect for the boat if nothing else, we would always stay in harbour if the forecast predicted anything above a force six. We paid close attention to the early evening shipping forecast.

I couldn't help a wry chuckle.

'We moan when we forget it, make a point of listening to it whenever we can – then what do we do? We ignore it!'

In high good spirits we took ourselves off to bed at half past seven, with a bottle of wine, a two-day-old Daily Telegraph crossword and the last of our massage oil.

15

Full circle

Early morning, not quite light, and a pair of cold hands, two damp, freezing feet and an icy cold body insinuate themselves under the duvet and attempt to use me as a body-warmer. I wake up. It is Mike. He's been out on the windsurfer to secure our mooring lines and lay an anchor from the stern, leaving the main anchor in its usual position just below the bowsprit. I shuffle an inch or two from my cosy nest into the cold half of the bed so he can have the warm bit and it is mid-morning before we finally emerge into the glare of dazzling sunshine, diamond-tipped sea and a deep blue sky. Porth Dinllaen at its best.

The day drifts lazily along, punctuated by a walk ashore, a few jobs around the boat and a lesson on the windsurfer for me. It is fun, but I am slow to get the hang of it and keep making my same old mistake of pulling the sail towards me. I spend more time flopping backwards into the sea than I do on the board and despite the sunshine I am chilled to the bone by the time the lesson is over.

Sometime during the early evening, as the warmth of the late August sun begins to fade, the sky clouds over and the brilliance of the day gives way to shrouds of grey Snowdonian mist that obscure the distant peaks and cloak the headlands on either side of the bay. We dine on an unsophisticated meal of stew and Lambrusco and, with little else to do, decide to have an early night. Mike washes the dishes while I go out to the cockpit to deal with the effects of half a litre of wine.

'Phew, there's a dreadful smell out here,' I call from the loo bucket.

'Probably my wet-suit boots.'

'Ugh. They're really awful.'

As I stand up to empty the bucket over the side a blue fishing boat, Big John, barges alongside. So that's where the smell's coming from. With such poor visibility we haven't noticed we've dragged our stern anchor and the main anchor, still hanging a few inches below its cleat on the bowsprit, is now well and truly caught up in Big John's mooring line. It is also bucketing down with rain. We throw on our waterproofs and wellies and dash out on deck. From a precarious perch on the bowsprit, and taking it in turns to take the strain from the ropes, we finally manage to prise Cevamp away from Big John. We are so busy concentrating on this that we fail to spot Cevamp's bows slotting, like the missing piece of a jigsaw, into a perfect v-shaped space formed by a motor launch and another fishing boat as they rub noses in greeting just ahead of us. They say problems come in threes. This is no exception. We hear the splosh of oars and look around to see a small and very angry man in oilskins and a sailing cap. By now Mike is aboard the fishing boat, fixing lines in a bid to pull us clear with the least possible damage to all three vessels. And it is on this man's fishing boat that Mike is now trespassing. The furious little figure shouts at us in a foreign language – Welsh? – and as he spits out odd phrases in English all I can understand is: 'Is my shaft free?'

'Whatever does he mean by that?' I whisper hoarsely to Mike.

Eventually we manage to motor Cevamp clear and drop anchor well away from all the other boats. It is now dark and still pouring with rain but Mike has yet more things to do. Again using the surfboard as a kayak he paddles out with the second anchor, drops it into the water with a splash and a rattle of chain, gives the rope a tug to make sure it has bedded in properly and then sculls off to retrieve the original line. The angry man in the rowing boat has disappeared, muttering, into the gloom and I go inside to the comforting warmth of the saloon. A consoling bar of Cadbury's makes me feel human again and I put the kettle on for a mug of hot chocolate ready for Mike. So much for an early night. This little pantomime lasted nearly three hours and Mike ends the day the way he started it, using the warmth of my body to defrost his chilled one. Cold hands, warm thighs. Mike cuddles up close. No problems here.

16

Balmy daze

Last night I dreamt I went to
Porth Dinllaen again.
A horseshoe bay of sand and sun,
a place that sees no rain;
where Snowdon's mists roll out to sea,
where dolphins call and leap;
a place of refuge in a storm
where weary sailors sleep.
For Porth Dinllaen gives shelter
from seas that foam and roar:
a place of quiet refuge
beside a Celtic shore.

Ten days into our holiday and we were beginning to shake off the pressures of work, to relax and enjoy ourselves. Mike was quite good at turning his back and closing his mind to the job as soon as he walked out of the police station at the end of his shift but I have always been someone who brings work home, both in my briefcase and in my head, and it always took me a week or so to unwind and adapt to the slower pace of sailing.

Porth Dinllaen was a favourite spot where the sun always seemed to shine for us and we decided to treat ourselves to a leisurely weekend and make the most of it. Anglesey had been around for a long time, we reasoned.

It could wait another couple of days. In any case we were still badly in need of a rest from the rigorous physical demands of our stormy passage from Aberdaron.

It was Saturday morning and we'd slept badly, thanks to the nightlong noise of the wind, the flapping of the tarpaulin that we'd tented over the boom to keep the cockpit dry and the relentless thudding of Cevamp's keel on the ground with the incoming tide. Worse, water had seeped through the floorboards during the night and our duvet, which was far too big in any case, had trailed over the side of the bed and was sopping wet. By the time we'd had our tea and toast and were ready to face the day the sky was clearing and the sun was beginning to shine. Mike thought he'd go for a sail on the windsurfer and I decided to brave the chill morning air and go for a swim. The early morning forecast had still been warning of gales in Irish Sea and eventually Mike concluded it was too windy to take the board out. He'd swim with me, instead. Damn. I'd already changed my mind, about the same time that I'd changed into my swimming gear, but pride wouldn't let me admit it to him. It was jolly cold, standing there shivering in my swimming costume, and I dreaded to think what it would be like in the water. But if I wasn't to lose face, I'd have to stick to my word. So in I went. Head first. The only way to go. And I was right. It was cold. Very beautiful translucent jade green water. But so, so cold. I was sure my gasps of shock could be heard on the beach.

Mike: 'What's it like?'

Me, through chattering teeth and salty lips: 'It's lovely'. What a lie, it was freezing.

'Once round the boat and I'm coming out,' I spluttered, knowing full well it would spur him to go twice round the boat – and get twice as cold as I was.

By the time my lady-like head-above-water-at-all-times breast stroke had taken me once round Cevamp's hull and I was ready to clamber back on board, Mike was halfway down the ladder. Sure enough, he did two circuits of the yacht before emerging, while I sat huddled in a bathrobe and watched his noisy display of macho butterfly stroke. It wasn't long before he'd had enough as well and he appeared at the top of Cevamp's ladder, blue lipped, salt encrusted and sparkling in the sunlight as he shook the water from his hair. We collapsed, cold wet and laughing onto the floor of the cockpit where we towelled each other down. There are worse ways of getting warm again. Once dressed, we made coffee and after consulting our walkers' map of the Lleyn Peninsular decided to row ashore in the dinghy and go for a walk round the bottom of the cliffs, up the coast path to the golf course on the headland then head back down the field-side track into the village.

It really was a glorious day with the blue sky creating a vivid contrast against the green of the headland, while as far as the eye could see white-capped rollers surged shoreward, gathering their strength only to spend it on the beaches along miles of deserted coast. The air was fresh and clean and you could almost smell it doing you good. This must have been how it was hundreds of years ago, when pilgrims used to break their journey and rest in the village en route to Bardsey Island. A lone skylark soared above us, a barely discernable speck against the clouds and filling the sky with song while from our viewpoint high on the cliffs we could see divers exploring the chartreuse waters of the bay below. Further offshore a catamaran flew into our field of vision, with two people trapezed out on one side and almost skimming the sea's surface as they sped along, while a visiting yacht made a more sedate approach to the harbour. We could see Anglesey clearly on the horizon where the previous night only the distant twinkling of street lights through the darkness gave any hint of the island's existence. We were tempted to get under way again and sail a bit further up the coast to Trefor but it was a temptation that was easy to resist and we decided to stay put. We were enjoying our relaxing day in the sun.

Back on Cevamp we chomped our way through a pile of ham and mustard sandwiches and then while Mike went out to play on the windsurfer I sat on deck, absorbing the scenery, soaking up the sun and the remains of the previous night's Lambrusco. Our previous visits to Porth Dinllaen and its neighbours, Nefyn and Morfa Nefyn, were out of season so it came as a surprise to see just how busy it was at the peak of the August summer holidays, with yachts, windsurfers, speedboats, motor boats, fishing boats and sailing dinghies coming and going all the time. A cluster of white-washed houses was tucked into the shelter of the cliffs and Ty Coch Inn, the beachside pub, was doing a roaring trade, making the most of the recently introduced all-day drinking laws.

The beach itself was crowded with boats, boat trailers, fishing paraphernalia, Land-Rovers, people and …spaniels.

'I've never seen so many spaniels' I said to Mike when he got back.

'Well it's not that surprising,' he said. 'Welsh Springer spaniels come from Wales.' Infuriatingly logical, as ever.

The horseshoe shaped bay was clearly a thriving and popular centre for holiday makers and water sports enthusiasts. For me, sitting there on Cevamp in the sun, it was hard to imagine it as it used to be. Not only was it once the most important place on the Lleyn Peninsula but at one time, before Holyhead was developed as a commercial port, there were even plans to turn it into the main west coast shipping terminal for Ireland.

That evening we dined in style on pork cutlets, peas, potatoes, carrots, home-made gooseberry pie and German Kabinett wine and were in bed in time to watch the lowering sun set the surface of the sea ablaze. Our lazy idyll was over. We were bound for Holyhead in the morning.

17

Picnic on Holyhead Mountain

If it's Holyhead it must be Sunday. And if it's Sunday it must be roast dinner. This had quickly established itself as a tradition for Mike and me and was part of what made Sunday special as far as we were concerned. Whatever else we are doing and wherever else we are, our Sunday dinner is sacrosanct. Roast beef, roast lamb, roast pork or, occasionally, roast chicken. Always with Yorkshire pudding and invariably accompanied by, according to Mike, 'twenty seven vegetables'. Not normally prone to exaggeration, it's his way of telling me I'm overloading the veg. Left to his own devices it would be meat, potatoes, carrots, and peas.

But I like vegetables and, never one to do things by halves, had been a strict vegetarian for a couple of years before I met Mike, even to the point of wearing plastic shoes, refusing to buy anything made from silk and declining to sit on leather armchairs. Strict, that is, until an impossible-to-ignore craving for Gibson's pork sausages enticed me back into the ways of the flesh. This craving saw me making a sixty mile round trip from my semi in Leighton Buzzard to Watford, where there was a butcher whose sausages had formed a memorable part of Sunday breakfast for the best part of my life. Their allure, after two meat-free years, was no longer resistible.

But man – or woman – can't live on sausages alone,

however succulent they may be, and my passion for veg remains. Faced with a decision over which to choose I usually opt for the adage about variety being the spice of life and get some of everything. So it's not unusual for us to have roast potatoes, roast parsnips, carrots, broccoli, cauliflower, Brussels sprouts, runner beans and anything else that catches my eye, piled up and spilling over the edges of our plates. And that's before space has to be found for meat, gravy and, of course, the ubiquitous Yorkshire pud.

'No-one has Yorkshire pudding with lamb or pork ,' Mike used to say, until my firm, unequivocal and oft repeated response 'Well I do,' made him realise he was wasting his breath.

He also gave up, long ago, trying to convince me that any more than two veg with his meat was too much and soon realised it made more sense to eat up his greens than to argue with me.

And being in a sailing boat with a tiny oven and a two-burner stove-top is not, in my opinion, a good enough reason not to cook a Sunday roast. With a decent home-made pudding to follow.

So here we were, tied to a mooring buoy in the still water of Holyhead Harbour and, fresh from scalding hot showers at the yacht club, tucking into a full roast beef dinner followed by gooseberry pie and cream. All washed down with Lambrusco for me, shandy for Mike and a quick game of Scrabble before bed.

We'd made good time on our passage from Porth Dinllaen, taking just under seven hours to cover the 33 miles and Cevamp actually topped what was for her a breathtaking 9.2 knots for an exhilarating few seconds. It was grey and windy most of the time but there was a lovely south westerly breeze and apart from a spiteful little squall off Abraham's Bosom the trip was relatively uneventful. We hauled in the sails to negotiate a nasty riptide area around South Stack Rocks, admired the gleaming white lighthouse on its jagged island and argued companionably about how many times and how often it flashed.

'Once every eight seconds.' I was adamant.

'No, once every ten seconds.'

'I know I'm often wrong but this time I'm right. It's definitely every eight. Look, there it goes again. One, two, three…'

'Okay, if you say so.'

There are times when Mike's self-conviction and refusal to argue can be so infuriating. This was one of them. I'd show him.

'Right then, I'll check on the chart.'

I clambered face first through the doorway just as Cevamp hit a particularly rough patch of overfalls and found myself pitched heavily onto my knees on the cabin floor. I lurched to my feet, hitting the top of my head hard on the corner of the chart table as I did so. I raised my hand to rub the fast growing egg on my head, dislodging the kettle, which was full of water, with my elbow, knocking it off the cooker and onto the floor. A little water goes a long way and I grabbed at the nearest towel to mop up the mess. But of course I yanked it a little too hard and snapped the plastic hook it was hanging from.

I eventually managed to tackle the task I'd gone down there to do in the first place: prove I was right about the number of flashes emitted by Stack Rocks lighthouse. I was wrong. Defeated, I hauled myself back up the companionway and out into the cockpit. Mike was looking smug.

'Everything all right down there?'

'Yes, fine. Nothing I can't handle.'

'What did the chart say about the lighthouse?'

By now I'd lost interest in the wretched lighthouse and in any case there was no way I was going to give him the satisfaction of, yet again, being proved right. More to save face than anything else, I changed the subject.

'Shall we have a cup of tea and a Mars bar then? I'll put the kettle on.'

That night, safe in the quiet waters of Holyhead Harbour, Mike was less anxious about the boat and despite the howling wind on the other side of the breakwater, we both slept well. After a late breakfast of egg, bacon and fried left-over potatoes we gathered up our dirty washing and hailed the taxi-launch that plied its trade among the yachts and motor launches in the harbour. Once ashore we set off on the long walk into town but although we were able to replenish our dwindling food supplies we ended up lugging our overstuffed laundry bags back to the boat. The launderette was closed till Wednesday. Whatever happened to washday Monday?

Later, out walking, we came across what looked like an old castle. With its turrets and towers and overgrown grounds it could have come straight out of a fairy story and Sleeping Beauty sprang to mind. It turned out to be the former Soldier's Point House, clearly grand in its day but now in a sad state of disrepair. Built in 1856, it is a replica of Hampton Court Palace and was originally the private residence of Mr J. C. Rigby, the master engineer in charge of the massive task of building Holyhead's breakwater. Eventually it was converted into a hotel but we were pleased to discover, many years after our visit, that it had reverted once again to a private house.

We'd commented on the length of the breakwater wall on our arrival in Holyhead and it took us a good hour in bright sunshine and a bracing wind to walk the length of it and back again. At 1.86 miles – or three kilometres – it is the longest in Britain and took twenty eight years to build. It was opened in 1875 by the then Prince of Wales, more than a quarter of a century before he succeeded Queen Victoria to become King Edward VII. The harbour itself was completed in 1877 and is a 'harbour of refuge'. Largely free of tidal influences it is accessible at all states of tide, in all weathers and all sea conditions. It's only when gales are blowing from the north east that sheltering yachtsmen have to hold on more tightly to their gin and tonics. We were lucky that week. The wind was a wet but warm south westerly and the only movement from the boats moored in the harbour was the almost imperceptible swing of their bows back and forth through 180 degrees every six and a bit hours with the ebb and flow of the tide.

The only vessel in the harbour impervious to the relentless tidal influences was the Morecambe Flame, a huge gas rig that had come in from its usual offshore site in Morecambe Bay for what we supposed was a routine maintenance check.

It was the first time Mike and I had been this close to one of these towering structures and we were fascinated by it. Our natural curiosity was sharpened by the knowledge that just a month previously, on 5 July 1988, one hundred and sixty seven men died when a gas leak caused an explosion on Occidental Petroleum's Alpha offshore platform on the Piper oilfield in the North Sea. It was difficult to imagine that many people living and working for weeks at a time on such a structure and I thought the Morecambe Flame bore a close resemblance to an oversized Meccano model. The red painted solid base, or hull I suppose you would call it, sat atop three massive legs, a bit like an angular, fretwork milking stool. The legs continued through the base and skywards, and perched between them was a small block of flats that I guessed was the living accommodation. The rest of the deck area was chocker-block with mainly unidentifiable equipment, a tower crane, a communications mast and, incongruously, a small encapsulated lifeboat suspended from a gantry. Most unlikely of all was the helicopter pad, a spaceship-like structure that jutted out high above the water and was attached to a shorter Meccano tower of its own. To my inexpert eye it seemed impossibly small and I marveled at the skill of the pilots who had to take off from and land on it so close to the rig's vertical girders. The slightest margin of error would, I knew, spell disaster for the pilot, passengers, helicopter and, quite probably, the rig itself although I was later told by an RAF rescue helicopter pilot that landing on rigs was easier than landing on the deck of a ship.

'Rigs don't roll,' he shrugged modestly, by way of explanation.

It was another peaceful night and we were woken shortly after five thirty by the alarm clock, followed by the sounds of Men of Harlech and Greensleeves from our transistor radio. Just as we were thinking of telling BBC Radio Four exactly what to do with a drunken sailor the station's early morning signature tune morphed into the shipping forecast and suddenly we were alert. Gale warnings in Irish Sea. Another day in Holyhead for us. After breakfast we hiked into town for stores, came back for scones and coffee then rowed ashore again. Mike had one oar and I had the other. Wind, water and swell meant it was a hard row and my ineffectual paddling with the heavy wooden oar meant that most of the time we went round in circles. Much laughter later we made it to the beach, tied the dinghy securely to a mooring ring and by noon, armed with cameras and our picnic in a paper carrier bag we were all set to do battle with a force eight gale as we trudged up the lanes to South Stack and the lighthouse.

Although the gale was in our faces we were soon high above the harbour, enjoying the views and admiring pretty, unspoilt hedgerows and small fields. We were less admiring of the dark and lowering cloud base racing over the sea towards us and we braced ourselves for a soaking.

'Let's stop here and have our picnic,' Mike suggested as we neared the top of the lane that led to South Stack car park.

'What, here? There's nowhere to sit and anyway, it's starting to rain. Why don't we wait till we find somewhere a bit more scenic? We'll get run over if we sit down in the road.'

'If we wait to find somewhere more scenic we could be waiting all day in these conditions. Anyway, I'm famished.'

While we were discussing the pros and cons of a roadside picnic spot the clouds opened. We were soaked in seconds. Not ideal conditions for eating al fresco. But the carrier bag full of food was already beginning to disintegrate and if we didn't eat there and then the food would be sodden too. Then there'd be no picnic at all.

So to the astonishment of people sitting warm, dry and snug as they passed us in their cars on their way to and from the lighthouse, we scrambled up the bank, wedged ourselves under the prickly hawthorn hedge to get what shelter we could from the torrential rain and the onslaught of wind and got stuck in to our lunch. The rain came down harder, the wind blew ever more strongly and water dripped out of our hair into our eyes and off the ends of our noses into our mouths and pasties. By this time we were past caring and had even started waving jauntily at the startled faces peering at us from passing cars. It satisfied our shared sense of the ridiculous, I suppose.

'What's that about mad dogs and Englishmen?' asked Mike.

'Yes, but this is hardly the mid-day sun,' I answered. This, for some reason, struck us as hilariously funny and by the time we'd polished off the last of our lunch we were laughing and spluttering so much it was a wonder we didn't choke on it.

Using soggy tissues to wipe the last flakes of pasty from the corners of our mouths we continued clambering up the north ridge of Holyhead Mountain to its summit which, at two hundred and twenty metres, is the highest point on Anglesey. The wind here was fiercer than ever but it didn't stop Mike from singing the same song he always sang when we walked in the hills, Robert Knight's Sixties hit 'Love on a Mountain Top'. With its lyrics about making love on a mountain it gave Mike lustful ideas and it was obvious what was going on in his mind. But it was the wrong sort of weather and I told him so. In no uncertain terms.

'Before you say another word, the answer's no. It's too wet, too windy and too cold'.

He took it good naturedly. I don't think he was really serious anyway, and we plodded on to the top of the mountain.

'What on earth are you up to?' he asked me a few minutes later, clearly perplexed to see me repeatedly running a few steps then jumping into the air.

'Trying to see if the wind is strong enough to lift me up. It would be like flying. You have a go.'

'I don't know what to make of you sometimes. Come here and give me a kiss.'

'Someone might see us.'

'What, up here, in this weather? You must be joking!'

So we shared a tender moment on the mountain top after all, with the rain beating down and the wind raging around us.

Even so, we were glad to head down to the four hundred steps leading to Stack Rock and its dramatically located lighthouse, which was joined to the mainland by a wispy little white painted aluminium bridge one hundred feet above the waves. Here at the foot of the steps the strength of the wind was incredible, blowing us around and almost taking our legs from under us. We were secretly glad that public access to the flimsy looking bridge was barred. Below us the sea was huge and pounding and beautiful to watch as it crashed in white capped splendour against the sheer granite cliffs that rose from its turbulent depths. In the old days stores for the lighthouse keepers would be carried down the steps by donkey and then carted across the bridge in a sliding basket drawn by a hempen cable. Nearly a decade after our visit the bridge was replaced by the Welsh Development Agency at a cost of £182,000 and opened to members of the public, who are now able to visit the lighthouse in groups of a dozen or so people at a time.

The first hint that South Stacks was hazardous to shipping came in 1665 when a petition was presented to Charles II but it was nearly another century and a half before the first light shone its warning beam to sailors, on 9 February 1809. The lighthouse, which is twenty eight metres high, was manned until 12 September 1984 when it was automated. These days Trinity House controls and monitors the fog signal and the 1,000 Watt/ 1,370,000 Candela light remotely, from its operations centre in Essex.

After being blown around like spume in the wind we were glad to scramble back up the steps and enjoy ten minutes respite in the steamed up café at the top, where we sipped gratefully from mugs of hot, strong tea before heading back, this time downhill with the wind on our backs. Easy.

As we made our way back to Cevamp we passed what we'd previously assumed was a monastery on a hill, to discover it was a now derelict convent in huge, overgrown grounds. Built between 1907 and 1910, Le Bon Sauveur was a girls' boarding and day school that, at the height of its success, catered for up to 150 pupils. Its church was finished in January 1937. Many years after Mike and I first noticed the building, local historian John Cave told me the school had closed in 1983 after struggling with falling numbers of boarders and facing a massive expenditure of around £50,000 for essential repairs and rebuilding work.

By December 1987 the local council had granted planning permission for 70 homes on the site and seven months later the land had been purchased by Anglesey County Council. Demolition work started a month after our visit and the following year the sisters took possession of their new house, Bryn Hyfryd – or Pleasant Hill – in Mount Pleasant, Holyhead. The church and house were retained and are in use today, the church as part of an arts centre and Nuns' House as flats for single parent families.

Exhilarated by our walk in the wind Mike and I got back to Cevamp feeling relaxed, cheerful and optimistic about the next day's weather. All our good intentions about not going out if the forecast was anything above a force six forgotten, we determined that come hell or high water we would leave for Cemaes the next day.

'What are you doing?' I asked Mike.

'I'm making up the bed, what do you think I'm doing?'

'But it's not even four o'clock in the afternoon.'

'Yes, I thought we'd have a little snooze.'

But first, I switched on the VHF radio. I'd heard the distinctive boom of maroons calling the retained lifeboat crews to action. I wanted to know why they'd been set off.

18

The Lori Lea

Captain's Log, Yacht Cevamp

Tuesday August 30
15.38   On deck in Holyhead harbour with a cup of tea,
        listening to the gulls. The double boom of
        lifeboat maroons disturbs their squabbling and
        the startled birds flap away. We switch our ship's
        radio to Channel 16, the listening channel: the
        nosey parker journalist in me can't bear not
        knowing what's going on.
15.40   The first member of the lifeboat's crew arrives by
        bike and we hear a radio transmission from
        Holyhead coastguard asking the occupants of the
        yacht Lori Lea if they are okay.
15.41   Lifeboat cancelled, we wonder why, and the lone
        crew member cycles off again. Coastguard asks
        the people on board Lori Lea why they put out a
        Mayday call but we are unable to hear the
        response. What we do know is that Mayday is the
        internationally recognised distress signal which
        indicates a vessel is threatened by grave and
        imminent danger and requires immediate
        assistance. It's not something that's done lightly.
        We guess something unexpected had happened
        to put the frighteners on the yacht's crew but

after their initial panic faded they were able to cope.

17.50 Warnings of gales in Irish Sea. Mike tackles the Daily Telegraph crossword while I prepare dinner. I don't bother to wash the organic broccoli I'd bought earlier, on the principal that cooking it in boiling water will do the job just as well.

17.55 Two more maroons go off and this time we watch the full lifeboat crew turn out in response to a second Mayday from Lori Lea. We listen in on the radio to the three-way conversation between the lifeboat, the coastguard and the yacht. Their original call for help had been triggered by a big wave that had swamped her and they'd panicked. Then they thought they could cope but conditions had worsened and now they were worried and frightened again.

The heavy throb of the lifeboat's engines vibrates through the water. I wipe the steam from Cevamp's windows and peer through the mist just in time to see the sturdy orange and blue vessel disappear round the end of the breakwater as she puts out to sea. I feel an irrational surge of fear for the crew of the stricken yacht and a pulse of anxiety for the lifeboatmen as they head out to help. If the seas are dangerous for yachts they will be dangerous for lifeboats too.

The smell of beef stew wafts around the cabin and we tuck into our dinner. Succulent chunks of beef, perfect waxy potatoes, dumplings to die for, thick gravy and a mixture of vegetables. The organic broccoli is less of a success. I really should have washed it. I gaze at my plate in horror. Floating in the gravy are scores of plump green caterpillar bodies. My dinner goes in the bin. Mike, stoic as ever, doesn't turn a hair. 'It's all extra protein,' he says, his mouth full of dinner, 'don't worry about it' and we continue to listen to the ongoing drama on Channel 16. The lifeboat gives Lori Lea an estimated time of arrival of thirty to thirty five minutes. By now it's pouring with rain and visibility is poor. It's a spine tingling, real life crisis. To listen to the incident unfold, knowing there is a yacht out there in danger while we are safe in harbour, makes me feel excited and fearful at the same time. It could have been us. There is nothing we can do to help.

18.20   Radio crackles back into life. Lori Lea's skipper gives their position as 'Carreg'. Coastguard tells them the lifeboat is 'just round Stack Rocks'.

18.23   Lifeboat to Lori Lea: We've just rounded Stacks and will be with you in 30 minutes.

18.45   Lori Lea to lifeboat: Please hurry.
Lifeboat to Lori Lea: We're having to slow down quite a bit because of weather and sea conditions.

Mike and I clear the table and open the forehatch to get rid of the lingering aroma of broccoli and braised caterpillars.

18.55   Lifeboat on scene. It radios Lori Lea's crew to stand by and look out for them for now. Lifeboat to coastguard: Seas pretty confused and high out here. Don't propose towing at the moment.

We make coffee and unwrap a large bar of fruit and nut. Mike makes a tin foil aeroplane from the wrappings and aims it into the sink. It misses.

19.00   Conversation between lifeboat and Lori Lea's
         skipper, who now sounds more relaxed: We're all
         right but we've been apprehensive – there's me,
         my son, daughter and son-in-law. We've taken a
         lot of sea on board and it's nice to see a lifeboat.
         Lifeboat to Lori Lea: it's just about slack water
         now. You're making three knots and seem to be
         going quite nicely. We'll stay with you all the
         way.
19.08   Coastguard asks lifeboat for present weather
         conditions: Swell 15–20 feet, visibility 4 miles,
         wind SW7.

'Doesn't sound very nice out there,' I say to Mike, and
pour us a second mug of coffee with a whisky chaser for
him and a brandy for me.

19.20   Lori Lea to lifeboat: Is it safe to go towards South
         Stack and could you give us directions for the
         course and by the way, it's lovely to be able to ask
         someone what we should do.
         Lifeboat to Lori Lea: You should be all right to
         head for South Stack on a course of zero-six-zero
         degrees.

We breathe a sigh of relief that they are all heading safely
for home, and get the Scrabble board out. Playing
Scrabble with Mike is something of a self-fulfilling
prophecy for me. I know I'll never beat him, but I enjoy
the challenge just the same.

19.45   Lifeboat to Lori Lea: Can you put up a bit more
         headsail? You're making too much leeway, not
         enough headway. 'How can they not be making

any headway in this,' I say to Mike, incredulous. 'They've got a gale blowing right behind them.'

'Yes, but if they haven't got enough sail up and there's a bit of tide running as well, then they'll be going sideways rather than forward,' he explains.

19.50   Lifeboat to Lori Lea: Good, you're making better way now. Stay on zero-six-zero for an hour, still heading for Stacks.

It's getting cold in Cevamp's cabin. I bow to the inevitable, accept I will never match Mike's ability to place seven letter words on a triple word score, and clear the Scrabble away. I put the kettle on to make hot water bottles, drop the table top into its runners and start to make up the bed.

20.10   Lori Lea to Lifeboat: the drinks are on us when we get back – wherever you say!

'They're obviously feeling more relaxed and cracking jokes now,' I say.

Lifeboat to Lori Lea: Nearly there now. We'll escort you all the way – and we'll let you know about the drinks!

20.20   Dusk is falling and we get our first glimpse of Lori Lea and the lifeboat as they come into the sanctuary of the harbour. Their steaming and navigation lights are bright against the greyness of the evening sky and the lifeboat's engine thrums gently and reassuringly in the still air. We feel ridiculously emotional to see them safely back, the fragile little yacht and the big strong lifeboat with its brave crew of volunteers, and I can't speak because of the tears constricting my throat. For the second time in my short sailing career I feel humble to know these men will risk their lives to help people like us wherever we are, however stupid we may have been and whatever the conditions.

20.35   Final radio transmission of the day from Lori Lea: Safely moored in Holyhead harbour.

We switch off our radio, give Cevamp a final pump-out for the night, turn out the cabin lights and go to bed. Perhaps tonight we'll get a decent night's sleep.

19

The disappearing jetty

We weren't disappointed. It was one of those rare nights, still and clear; the sky was sequinned with stars, and once the wind dropped we both slept like logs. Mike listened, I half heard, the dawn forecast and we finally awoke to a sparkling, sunny, slightly chilly morning. After breakfast we rowed ashore for showers at the yacht club, returned to collect our laundry and set off once more to do the washing. Two machines, two driers and lots of twenty pence pieces later we got back to Cevamp just before mid-day and were delighted to see Lori Lea moving around the bay, draped with wet clothing.

The prospect of being back under sail made our spirits soar. Together we stowed our stores and put away the laundry then Mike carried out the engine checks while I prepared enough food and drinks to keep an entire armada afloat. At last, we thought. Cemaes Bay here we come.

Cevamp was also glad to be underway again and once we were clear of the boats in the harbour we raised the mainsail, unfurled the genoa and sailed in stately fashion past the harbour wall. As usual when leaving a harbour there was plenty to look at, including two helicopters and an RAF launch practising rescue drills. I felt the same surge of gratitude towards the helicopter crews that I always experience when I see a lifeboat, and was childishly excited when they actually leaned out of their aircraft doors to wave back to me.

It turned into a fine day and by the time we were ready to change course to go around the Skerries we'd stripped down to shorts and tee shirts. The name Skerry comes from an Old Norse word, sker, meaning rocky reef or island, while the Welsh name Ynysoedd y Moelrhoniaid, means the islands of the bald-headed seals. We didn't actually see any seals, grey, bald-headed or other-wise that day, so you'll have to trust me on that one!

A group of rocky islets, the Skerries lie a couple of miles offshore from Carmel Head on Anglesey's north west coast and they are transformed every spring into a breeding colony for sea birds. Scores of puffin, kittiwake, herring gull, lesser black-backed gull and the rare, but fiercely aggressive, Arctic tern return here year after year to breed and they are occasionally joined by another rare visitor, the Roseate tern.

The Skerries are also popular with scuba divers, who enjoy exploring the wrecks of vessels that have foundered on the rocks. These are dangerous waters for shipping and despite being marked by a lighthouse, a sturdy white tower with a broad red horizontal stripe, the Skerries have seen their share of disasters over the years. Several tides collide in this area, resulting in a potential hazard that is made worse by the hilly nature of the sea bed. The resultant overfalls between the Skerries and Carmel Head can, and often do, make for tricky sailing conditions.

'What do you think it'll be like round there today?' I was sitting comfortably on a pile of cushions, tiller under one arm and, with my mouth full of Nuttall's Mintoes, bearing a strong facial resemblance to an over-fed hamster.

Mike didn't answer for a minute. He was busy with the tidal streams booklet and working out the time of slack water, the safest time to pass through the overfalls.

'What if we've missed slack water? What if we've missed slack water and the wind picks up? What if we've missed slack water and the wind picks up and the engine breaks down? What do you think would happen to us?'

Mike didn't appear to have heard my manic burblings and I was just about to repeat them when he closed the book and put it back in the chart table drawer. Confident as ever, he didn't seem too worried by what his deductions told him and we were soon safely round the Skerries, admiring the sight and sound of waves thundering onto the island of West Mouse ahead of us. His reply, when it eventually came, was matter of fact.

'It's about an hour after high water slack and the tides are running against us. We'll just have to keep going towards Carmel Head and see how we get on. We can always put the engine on if we need extra power.'

No sooner had he finished speaking than we entered the short, steep seas that are so typical of rip tides. After an hour of going nowhere in an unpleasant heavy swell, Mike made a decision.

'I don't think it's worth persevering with this. We're making hardly any headway and we're being swept in towards the headland. The longer we leave it the harder it's going to get and I think we'll be better off further out. You switch the engine on and I'll get the genoa in.'

Once clear of the rips we switched the engine off again and enjoyed another hour's sailing. Then Ramsey coastguard broadcast a warning that force eight gales were expected 'soon'.

'What does "soon" mean?' I asked. 'I know "imminent" means pretty well straight away but do you think I ought to go and batten down the hatches? At the rate we're going the gale will hit us before we get into harbour.'

'Don't be such a drama queen,' said Mike. 'When they say imminent they mean within six hours, when they say soon it's six to twelve hours and when they say later it'll be more than twelve hours. We'll be in harbour long before then. But you're right. We should put the engine back on to give us some extra stability and we'll leave the sails up as well to give us a bit of extra speed.'

I needn't have worried. The weather stayed fair for the rest of the afternoon and we dropped anchor in the crescent-shaped bay at Cemaes at six o'clock. The tide was in the dying stages of its ebb and Cevamp grounded on the sandy bottom soon after we arrived.

After beaching, Mike untied the windsurfer from the guardrails and paddled ashore to check out the harbour. As the last of the tide drained away I walked across the firm wet sand to join him. It was here that we had our first experience of the kindness and generosity of people in Cemaes, the most northerly village in Wales. We got chatting to a man who had been watching our arrival as he walked his dog on the beach. He was really interested in Cevamp and wanted to know everything about her, from the length of time it had taken Mike's dad to build her to the height of the mast. No sooner had we asked him the way to the public toilets than he insisted on taking us home to use his loo, introduced us to his wife and offered us drinks. I think he would have invited us to dinner too, if we'd let him. I wouldn't have minded a night off cooking and would have accepted but I knew

Mike wanted to get back to the boat. I reluctantly left the warmth, comfort and stability of their bungalow and the two of us set off over the cliff paths. We hoped we'd get a better view of the harbour from up there, to find ourselves a safe mooring.

'Hang on, wait for me,' I puffed as I struggled to keep up with Mike. My heels were blistering painfully where my sailing wellies were slipping up and down and he was walking, as usual, at top speed – anything less and he wouldn't think he'd had any exercise!

'I feel like an Indian wife, trailing along behind at a respectful distance.'

'Well you should walk faster then.'

I could never get through to him that from my permanent position six paces behind him I could see that my legs and feet were moving just as fast as his, but his strides were longer, meaning he always outpaced me.

'No, you should slow down a bit. Then we could walk together.'

'You know me,' he said, taking my cold hand in his warm one and pulling me alongside him. 'I don't hang about.'

'No, I know. I think I'll have that written on your gravestone: "Here lies Michael Williamson. He didn't hang about." Then every time I come to put flowers on your grave it'll make me smile.'

The views from the cliffs were spectacular. From where we stood we could see towering cliffs, sandy beaches and the harbour with its picturesque cluster of houses. The sun was still glinting on the sea, tracing a wobbly golden path to the horizon and sea birds wheeled overhead, their familiar call loud in the afternoon silence.

'You can see why this is an area of outstanding natural beauty,' I said. 'Did you know they composed that old song "Red Sails in the Sunset" at Cemaes?'

I didn't either, but it was on a leaflet I picked up in the village so it had to be true.

The next cove along looked perfect to my eyes but Mike was uncertain about the quality of the seabed and, on second thoughts, I didn't fancy the long walk back to the shops from there. But we were both taken with a small jetty a short distance in from the corner of the bay and not far from where Cevamp was currently squatting on the sandy foreshore. There were no other boats and it looked ideal, quiet and sheltered.

'That's a nice spot. What do you think?' I asked Mike. 'We'll have the place to ourselves by the look of it. '

'Should do nicely,' he said. 'The jetty looks nice, except it's a bit slimy and the mooring rings are all covered with weed too. It doesn't look as though it gets much use at all. I wonder why no-one else is tied up to it.'

He stopped briefly and waited for me to catch up with him again. Then he spotted something else.

'I wonder why those dinghies over there are tied to the railings. It would make more sense to tie them to the jetty so you don't have to drag them over to the water every time you want to use them.'

'Oh, you know what some people are like,' I replied. 'Lazy. They probably just don't want to walk the extra few yards to the wall.'

A boy of about twelve or thirteen was standing on the wall watching us.

'No-one ever uses that jetty for their boats,' he said.

'Oh, why's that?' Mike asked.

The boy shrugged. 'Dunno. They just don't.'He

wandered off, hands in pockets, kicking stones over the side of the wall.

We thought nothing of his remarks and made plans to move Cevamp as soon as there was enough water. Mike reckoned that it would probably be about midnight before she was properly afloat again and we both thought it would be nice to have the jetty to ourselves.

That evening we went to the Stag for a drink and to use the loos. We thought it would do us good to mix with normal people for a few hours and in any case we had time to kill before the tide came back in. But after living in the open air for two weeks Mike and I, both non-smokers, found the pub unbearably smoky and stuffy. Our eyes met and we both knew instinctively what the other was thinking. Without saying a word we placed our half-full glasses of lager on the bar and left the pub. By now it was way past our usual early bedtime so we were surprised how dark it was outside. But it was a good job we left when we did. The tide was already coming in fast and if we'd stayed in the pub any longer we'd have had a long swim back to the boat. We made up the bed, changed into our tracksuits and then struggled to stay awake until there was enough water to move Cevamp.

Half an hour later we were afloat, it was raining hard and as thunderclaps rumbled overhead we put waterproofs on over our nightwear, started Cevamp's engine and shunted her carefully into position alongside the jetty. I was just washing the smelly green slime from my hands when Mike had a thought that was identical to something I'd mentioned to him earlier in the day.

'With these high tides, what if the sea comes over the wall? We'd better move back into the bay'. Perhaps he just hadn't heard me, but at the time I thought was ignoring it as being one of my stupider remarks. Funny how my drama queen suggestions became sensible ideas when Mike thought of them. I wasn't best pleased.

Muttering murderously under my breath I dragged myself back outside, helped untie the knots, stow the ropes, push us off from the wall, motor back out into the bay and lower the anchor. Then it was back into the humid warmth of Cevamp's cabin with its lingering aroma of cabbage, wash the smelly green slime from my hands again, wellies off, oilskins off and into bed.

We turned out the last of the cabin lights above the bed and I was soon in that delicious relaxed state of near sleep. A breath away from drifting off altogether.

'Hey Jack.' Mike's voice jolted me awake. 'I've just thought of a way of tying her up so we could stay tied to the wall after all. D'you fancy giving me a hand to move back to the jetty?'

I snored loudly, to let him know I was asleep. There was no way I was moving again.

It was an appalling night, with whistling wind and heavy side to side rocking. Neither of us got much sleep and we weren't surprised to hear the early morning shipping forecast warning of winds south easterly six to gale force eight, increasing to cyclonic gale force nine and more rain. We pinched and punched each other in recognition of the start of a new month, September, and at six-fifteen we dragged ourselves out of bed, got dressed and moved Cevamp back to the slimy jetty. Still water. Still raining. Heavily. The boom continued to groan. What, I thought, happened to the dream – secluded cove, drop anchor, swim, sunbathe?

'Fancy a lesson in ropework before we go ashore?' Mike had to shout to be heard above the rattle of chain. The tide had turned and he was out on the bowsprit, lowering the anchor to stop the front end of the boat swinging out as the sea flowed in.

'What sort of lesson?'

I was suspicious. I found ropes and knots a challenge. Mike, on the other hand, was a wizard with both. He could even do a bowline, the most complicated knot of all as far as I was concerned, and one which I never really mastered. My knot-tangling – sorry, tying – skills started and ended with the simplest one of all, the reef knot, so I was easy to impress. Anything more advanced, such as a round-turn-and-two-half-hitches – a really useful knot for tying your boat up to a mooring ring – was doomed, when tied by me, either to become a messy cats-cradle or to fuse permanently into a tight clump that had to be cut away because it was impossible to untie. Mike made them all look so easy it gave me an inferiority complex.

'We need to set a spring to stop the boat moving too much against the wall. You do it and I'll help you.'

'What's a spring?'

'It's two extra mooring lines that stop the boat surging backwards and forwards against the wall.'

I was still confused.

'But we've already tied ropes from the front and back to the harbour wall,' I protested.

'Yes but we need two more to stop the boat surging. It means she'll be more secure and I can go ashore without worrying about her.'

So I helped set the springs. It was a complicated arrangement involving two ropes. The first one went from the front of the boat to a mooring ring on the quay near the back of the boat. The second one led from the back of the boat and across the first one, to be tied to a mooring ring on the wall near the front of the boat.

Finally the last knot was tied to Mike's satisfaction and he felt able to come ashore with me with an easy mind. We left enough slack in the ropes – I mean mooring warps – to allow for the rise and fall of the tide and he was confident that Cevamp would be safe in our absence.

It was a cool day and looked like rain so we wore oilskin jackets over t-shirts, long trousers and trainers. We did our shopping and headed back to Cevamp to have lunch.

A shock awaited us when we got back to the steps leading down to the jetty.

'Bugger,' said Mike.

The jetty had disappeared. The sea had risen over the top of it and Cevamp was floating serenely on the water where the jetty used to be. The tide was rising fast. We had to act quickly.

'Give me the shopping, get your trousers off and get back on board,' Mike ordered.

'No way am I wading through that. It's freezing.'

'Don't be so bloody stupid. How else are we going to get back on board? Just do it. You go first and I'll follow.'

Mike had never spoken to me like that before. It made me realize how serious the situation was and without arguing I went down the steps, took off my trousers, clenched my teeth to stop myself from squealing as the cold water lapped around my thighs and waded carefully over the slippery jetty to the safety of Cevamp's ladder.

The first thing I saw once I got back on board was my camera. This was too good a picture opportunity to miss. Mike was just climbing back on board, trousers rolled above his knees...and an exasperated expression on his face at the sight of me pointing the lens in his direction. 'For goodness sake put that camera away. We've got more important things to worry about than taking happy snaps. If we don't soon get this boat moved the tide will go out and she'll be left straddling the jetty. God knows what damage that will do in this wind.'

The water continued to rise and the wind continued to blow. Mike took stock of the situation and weighed up the possibilities.

'I don't suppose it's helped by us setting those springs,' I ventured helpfully. 'It means we'll have more ropes to untie now.'

'I think the best thing we can do is release everything, raise the anchor if we can and drift over the wall. Then we just have to motor back into the bay.'

'What if we can't get the anchor up? What if it's caught round the ladder or hooked itself into a crack in the wall?'

'Well if that happens, we'll cut it free. I don't want to have to do that but it'll be a damn site cheaper than it would be if the boat smashes her bilges on the jetty.'

'Hey, Cevamp.' A young local yachtie shouted to us from the bridge nearby. 'Have you heard the forecast? This weather's going to get worse. There's room in the harbour. I'll help you in if you like.'

'Thanks for that,' Mike shouted back. 'We'll see you round there.'

That was it then. Decision made. It was time to act. With the engine running in neutral, Mike let out the ropes at the back. I sat up front and pulled on the anchor chain so we floated slowly over the jetty.

'Watch the ladder handles on the top of the wall,' Mike yelled. We missed them by a hairsbreadth, Mike released the bow ropes and we were safe. He slipped the engine into gear and we motored round into the harbour where the young yachtie and two other lads helped us to tie Cevamp between a small trawler and a boat called Miranda, whose wheelhouse bore the proud sign announcing she was available for 'trips in season'.

'Thanks lads. You've been great.' Mike, happier now that we were in calm water, relaxed a bit. I looked around to get my bearings. Miranda on the outside was tied to Cevamp, Cevamp was tied to the trawler Sheilamay, and the trawler, complete with rows of hooks hanging all along the safety wires, was tied to the harbour wall. That meant that as long as we stayed there we didn't need to worry about adjusting our mooring lines as the tides rose and fell. As long as the fishing boat was moored properly, and we could only assume her skipper and crew valued their livelihood sufficiently to ensure that she was, we would simply rise and fall with her. And we didn't even have to row ashore. All we had to do was step out of Cevamp onto the fishing boat, pick our way across the tangle of tackle on her decks to the rusting iron ladder set into the harbour wall, climb to the top of the ladder and then walk ashore from there. Even the pervasive smell of fish wafting towards us from Sheilamay was welcome.

Once again, our arrival attracted attention and several people gathered on the wall to ask us about Cevamp and to share their knowledge of wind, tides, moorings and the like.

'By God,' said one man. 'You'll be safer here than where you were before. Lots of people have been worrying about you, you know.'

With all the excitement we'd missed the lunchtime forecast but Arthur had heard it. Captain Arthur V. Orchard was Sheilamay's skipper, a friendly, wind polished man with deep lines etched into his face, a wide smile and skin the colour of ripening conkers, who usually long-lined off Ayr and Portpatrick for spurfish and skate .

'I'm not putting out tomorrow,' he told us firmly, blue eyes bright against his tan. 'And if you've got any sense, you won't be going anywhere either.'

20

'Sail south till the butter melts'

By mid-afternoon we'd recovered our equilibrium, enjoyed a late lunch of cheese and pickle rolls with apples for pudding and were all set for a cliff top walk to Llanbadrig Church. Whenever we were stuck in harbour because of bad weather we always tried to have a walk over the cliffs, to help us work out our best route for when we were able to leave. It was overcast and blowy to start with but the sun broke through and we enjoyed spectacular views as we trudged up and down the well-trodden path, remarking on the fact that everything in the area was named after St Patrick.

According to local legend, St Patrick – or Badrig – was on his way to Ireland to convert the Irish to Christianity in the fifth century when his vessel foundered on the rocks now known as Ynys Badrig or Mouse Island. He managed to get ashore and sheltered in a cave and later, to show his gratitude for being saved, he built a wooden church on the cliff top. The cave was subsequently named Ogof Badrig in his honour and the nearby spring, which kept the saint supplied with fresh water, is called Ffynnon Badrig – St Patrick's Well.

The present church is a simple place of worship, dating from the fourteenth century, and is probably the only one in Wales that is dedicated to the patron saint of Ireland.

We had a look round the tranquil little building and admired its simplicity.

'I wouldn't mind being buried here,' I said to Mike. 'It's so tranquil.'

'Yes, but it would be difficult digging a hole for your grave. It's solid rock.' That's Mike. Always practical.

'Well it wouldn't be my problem. I'd be dead.'

We carried on past the Church until we were looking out at Middle Mouse. The rocky uninhabited island is about half a mile or so from shore and is notable mainly as the northernmost point of Wales. It is also the place where the steamer SS Liverpool sank with its cargo of Cornish tin ingots in 1863 following a collision with the barque Laplata, a three masted sailing vessel on its way to the Peruvian capital, Lima.

'Just look at those rip tides down there.'

I didn't much like the look of the frantic waves below us.

'If big ships can come to grief here there's not much hope for us in our little one. Perhaps our best course will be to go further out and right round the island rather than risk trying to go between the rocks and the coast.'

'No, I don't think we'll need to do that.' Mike was reassuring. 'I think we'll be able to get round the headland okay. If we hug the coastline we should avoid the tide races no problem.'

We turned and retraced our steps. Back on Cevamp we were about to indulge in afternoon tea when Arthur appeared. He couldn't go out fishing so he had all the time in the world to chat.

We listened to the shipping forecast together. It wasn't good. A warning of gales in all sea areas except Trafalgar and south east Iceland was followed by the local area forecast, which heralded winds southerly five, veering south westerly six to gale force eight in Irish Sea. We must have looked as crestfallen as we felt and Arthur took pity on us.

'Forget the weather for now. There's nothing you can do about it. Come on up to my house for a cup of tea and a bath.'

As a fisherman and sailor he knew what is was like to go for days, weeks even, without a bath. He also knew how good it was to have one. I jumped at the chance of a long, relaxing soak in hot water.

'That's an offer we can't refuse,' I said and popped down into the saloon to get towels and toiletries before Mike changed his mind.

Arthur drove us out through the village in his car and up a steep hill to his house.

'Oh, what gorgeous views.'

'Yes,' said Arthur. 'That's why we've got an upside down house. We've got the living rooms upstairs and the bedrooms downstairs so we can look out of the windows and enjoy the scenery.'

He opened the front door and we stepped out of the bright sunlight into the shadows of his hall. Arthur pointed to a door in front of us.

'The bathroom's there. Take as long as you like then come upstairs for a chat. See you later.'

The bath was amazing. It was a huge affair, taking up the entire corner of the room. I turned the taps on and while Mike enjoyed his first shave in hot water for two weeks I poured in enough shower gel to make the water foam as it gushed into the bath. I swished it around with my hand, checking the temperature, and when I was happy with it we climbed into the bath together. I eased myself into the fragrant silky water and slid through the cool, lightly crackling bubbles until I was submerged, with just my nose poking hippo-like through the froth.

'Make way, make way, let me in.'

My ears were full of water and I could barely hear Mike's muffled voice, but I knew what he was saying by the way he shoved my legs to one side with his foot. I surfaced with a great heave and a theatrical sigh and he sat down. From our positions at opposite corners of the tub we could just about make each other out through the sandalwood scented steam. I lay back and closed my eyes. Bliss.

'I wonder what this button does,' said Mike. He pressed it and we jumped as a motor whirred into life and the water started splashing and vibrating around us. Arthur hadn't thought to tell us it was a Jacuzzi.

'Turn it off, turn it off,' I hissed anxiously, as the churning bathwater created great mountains of froth that threatened to spill over the sides.

As the sound died away I became aware of another. It was coming from the direction of the door. It was the rattle and squeak of the door knob being turned and the thud of someone's shoulder against wood.

'Someone's trying to come in,' I hissed again. Mike stood up, showering me with water and foam, and quickly wrapped a towel around his waist. With all those bubbles he could just as easily have preserved his modesty by staying in the water.

The rattling and thudding stopped. We heard footsteps receding down the hall.

'Muuuum.'

A girl's voice echoed loudly through the hall and up the stairs.

'Mum,' she shouted again. 'There's some people in our bath.'

There was the faint sound of a woman's voice from a

room above us. We couldn't make out her reply but it sounded cross. Very cross.

'We'd better get dressed and go and show our faces,' said Mike, in a hoarse whisper. 'I don't think we're going to be very popular.'

I didn't need a second bidding. I felt embarrassed and as guilty as if we'd broken into the house and were using the bath without the owners' knowledge. I got dressed in record time and quickly stuffed our wet towels back into their plastic carrier bag before going upstairs with Mike to face the music.

Upstairs, Arthur's wife Brenda was watching Emmerdale and wasn't too pleased to see us.

'Don't mind me,' she said grumpily. 'I'm in a bad mood. Arthur's always doing this sort of thing and I'm fed up with bloody boats. It's all he ever talks about.'

As she went out to the kitchen to put the kettle on she told us there were people in Cemaes who, apparently, didn't want Arthur's boat in the harbour and the previous night, she said, they interfered with all his ropes.

Arthur paid no attention to his wife's grumbling. He'd heard it all before.

'Don't worry about her,' he said. 'She doesn't mean it. She just gets fed up with my boat stuff cluttering up the house. She bungs it all in the attic.' With this he clambered into his loft to lend us his copy of Coastal Sailing Around Anglesey, a local pilot book written by Dr Robert Kemp.

He told us the Sheliamay was a deep sea trawler and the only one to boast an automatic baiting machine, which Arthur was trialing for the White Fish Authority. He sold his catch to middlemen John the Con and Mark the Shark from Anglesey, and they sold it on to the big dealers more than two hundred miles away in Grimsby. As well as the trawler, Arthur owned a small sailing yacht, a Cobra, which he kept round on the mainland, at Bangor. But he was clearly smitten with Cevamp.

'Tell you what,' he said. 'I'll swap my Cobra for Cevamp. Minus equipment, of course.'

Mike smiled and explained that even if Arthur was serious Cevamp wasn't actually our boat to swap.

'Dad built her but it took so long that by the time she was finished he wasn't really fit enough to sail her. Mum isn't interested, my brother works abroad and my sisters aren't really interested either. So although Jack and I have more or less exclusive use of her, she isn't really ours.'

But Arthur wasn't really serious. His dreams were of sailing to the Caribbean.

'One of these days I'm going to sell the Cobra and buy a big catamaran. When I've done that I'll sail south till the butter melts, then turn right.'

There was a longing, faraway look in his eyes. He knew life wasn't that simple.

'But first I've got to persuade Brenda.'

21

A meal to remember

Less than a week later our holiday was over and Mike and I were back in the fast lane. Fields and hedges flashed past the periphery of our vision and the low autumn sun ambushed us with dazzling strobes of light through the car's side windows as we sped home. In another two days we would be back at work and the holiday would be another chapter in our shared history.

We'd enjoyed the intimacies of a small yacht for three weeks and I was dreading the moment when Mike would kiss me goodbye at my house in Banbury and head back to his, fifty miles away in High Wycombe.

Reluctant to exchange our domestic compatibility for the single life again before I absolutely had to, I reminded him of the lamb casserole and fruit pie that was waiting for us at my house in Banbury, prepared by me more than three weeks ago and left behind in the freezer.

'I'm looking forward to that. We'll have a bottle of wine with it and I'll go back to Wycombe in the morning,' he said.

Was he reluctant to return to bachelordom too, I wondered.

As we clocked up the miles, through Shrewsbury, Telford, Kidderminster and Evesham we looked back on the holiday and talked about our love hate relationship with Cevamp. Throughout the trip she managed to present us with problems on almost a daily basis. Either the engine refused to engage gear, the hull leaked or, more annoyingly, the pump refused to pump, leaving us to take it in turns to bail out the waterlogged bilges by hand. But as is often the way, it's the things that go wrong that leave you with the best memories and during the drive home we had fun re-living the worst bits.

We'd left Porthmadog in scorching sun that morning, the first really hot day of the entire holiday, and decided to visit Snowdonia. Neither of us had been there before and although we didn't have time to walk up the mountain we stopped to admire its reflection in the mirrored waters of Lake Gwynant before driving on to the famous Swallow Falls at Betws-y-Coed where we stopped for lunch.

All in all, though, the final week of our cruise had been relatively uneventful compared with the first two. The morning after our bath at Arthur's we were woken in the early hours of the morning by the unearthly howling, whooshing and shrieking of the wind. At this point we gave up all hope of leaving that day, accepted that Arthur had been right about the weather and resigned ourselves to another day in harbour.

But the next day, a Saturday, dawned warm and sunny. At twenty past six I gradually became aware of Mike moving around and dragged myself, reluctant but unprotesting, from a dream of shopping for beautiful clothes in Paris.

'Wakey-wakey, rise and shine,' he called cheerfully. 'Ready to get up and move? It's a lovely day. We'll motor out into the bay so we're in deeper water and soon as the tide turns in our favour we can get away.'

Dreams of Paris forgotten, I pulled on my old faithful tracksuit. It was unsmart, unlovely, unsexy and definitely not Parisian chic, but it was also warm, loose and comfortable.

We moved Cevamp into the bay, had tea and muesli and went back to bed for an hour, enjoying the rocking of the boat and luxuriating in the warmth of the sunshine pouring into the cabin.

We eventually waved farewell to Cemaes Bay and within half an hour the engine was off, the mainsail up and fully reefed and the genoa three-quarters out. With the wind behind us we were running goose-winged – just – and Mike was smiling again.

'A life on the ocean wave,' he bellowed exuberantly. 'This is the life for me.'

Four hours later we were tied against the wall at Dickie's of Bangor and Mike sat down to write up the log.

'Do you know what day it is today?'

'Saturday?' I suggested helpfully.

'I joined the police fifteen years ago today. I'm halfway there.'

'Halfway where?'

'Halfway to retirement and my pension.'

Two months off his thirty sixth birthday and he couldn't wait to retire!

Dinner that night consisted of large pork chops, cauliflower, carrots, potatoes, gravy, apple-and-blackberry crumble, very thick double cream and Lambrusco. Afterwards we changed into our tracksuits, made up the bed and got in it. The weather had changed again and we sat companionably side by side with our mugs of cocoa and studied the yachts-for-sale details we picked up in Dickie's earlier.

'I love this,' I told Mike. 'Being here with you, snug

and dry in our little boat and listening to the rain drumming down on the roof.'

He looked up from the sheets of paper spread over his knees on the duvet and looked at me. His face was serious but his eyes sparkled.

'Listen to the pouring rain listen to it pour, and with every drop of rain you know I love you more,' he sang softly.

'Soppy old romantic,' I told him, snuggling up closer. He was no Jose Feliciano but he was my idol and I was his number one fan.

Next day was Sunday and I made the most of the warm weather to dry out our supply of damp salt and transfer some of it out of the plastic tub where we usually kept it, into a salt pot. As usual we enjoyed a gargantuan Sunday lunch, sitting on deck in the sun. Roast rib of Welsh beef, Yorkshire pudding, carrots, cauliflower, broccoli, roast potatoes, gravy, apple and blackberry crumble and cream. Rather than fiddle around carving the joint we just cut it in half, even though there was easily enough for four.

'How's this for gracious living?' I said, waving the now full salt pot over my food with a theatrical sweep of my arm. The top fell off.

Oh no,' I grumbled, frantically using my knife to scoop the soggy salt out of my gravy.

'I thought you liked salt.'

'I do like salt but an entire pot full on one potato is a bit too much, even for me.'

After dinner we inspected a couple of the yachts in Dickie's yard. They'd caught our fancy when we were looking through the brokerage list and we'd arranged to go and have a look at them. It wasn't that we were even considering buying one but it was always nice to dream and we often wandered around boatyards to see what was on offer. We were particularly interested in a Westerly Centaur that was on the hard-standing outside the office. Westerlys are popular in the Cardigan Bay area because most of the smaller models come with the option of twin keels. Deep water marinas in Wales were few and far between and twin keels meant you could moor your boat in relative safety in harbours that drained at low tide. They just settled themselves gently on the sand or mud as the tide went out and, if you were lucky, they remained on the level until the tide came back in.

The salesman propped a rickety wooden ladder against the Centaur's stern and we clambered aboard, eager to see how the inside compared with the yacht's sturdy, workmanlike exterior. We were disappointed. The main cabin was tatty and unloved, the sink was stained and the cushions were mildewed from being left on board. The whole boat smelt damp. There was no instrument panel and none of the unique, finishing touches that made Cevamp so special.

The other boat, a brand new Colvic Countess, couldn't have been a greater contrast. She was so beautiful inside that it brought a lump to my throat. We could still smell the resin and sawdust. Breathtaking, smooth, solid wood, expertly crafted drawers and cupboards, wooden mouldings and even adjustable bookshelves. The galley was perfect and in the heads I drooled over a sea toilet, a burgundy fold-up wash basin and, luxury of luxuries, a shower.

'It's just like the Marie Celeste,' I whispered. 'I know she's not finished in here but you can see just how much love and skill and attention to detail has gone into fitting her out. It's as though the owner's just downed tools and gone for a tea break. I wonder why they're selling her?'

Back at Dickie's office I asked the salesman what the story was behind the sale of the yacht.

'It's tragic, really,' he said. 'The man who owned her was fitting her out himself and he died suddenly, quite recently. Understandably, his widow wants, or maybe needs, to sell the yacht.'

'What a tragedy,' I said, 'to build something that beautiful and not live to see it completed. At least Alex finished Cevamp and can still sail on her with us whenever he wants to.'

Mike and I were both enchanted by the yacht. The asking price was not unreasonable, although at £16,000 it was still more than we could afford, and she still needed all electrics and the interior to be finished. But what a boat to be proud of when done.

We sailed out of Dickie's that afternoon, motored through the Menai Straits, past Caernarfon Castle and over the sand bar into a lumpy sea to the small harbour of Trefor on the Lleyn Peninsular. Here we endured a terrible night, thanks to a heavy broadside swell, and only slept for two or three hours. We were so tired that we didn't clear up as thoroughly as usual and left a few things on the work-top when we went to bed. Two cups, tea caddy, tea pot, coffee jar, half full milk bottle, water jug and, just to add to our misery they all went crashing onto the cabin floor in the middle of the night.

We stuck it out until half past four then moved the boat fifty or so yards further back and dropped anchor. Things improved considerably and we slept, first until the shipping forecast and then again until half past seven, when Mike brought me a mug of tea and a bowl of muesli.

'You know we were planning on a lie in and a leisurely breakfast before we head off to Nefyn to wait for high water?' he said.

I knew what was coming next. I was right.

'I think we should set off straight away. We could be at Bardsey by early afternoon and get through the sound at low water slack.'

I wasn't very enthusiastic so leaving me in bed he put warm clothes on under his oilskins and left me to dream on. I heard the rattle of chain as he raised the anchor, the clomping of his wellies on the coachroof over my head as he hoisted the sail and half an hour later I felt Cevamp bobbing out to sea. We were under way again.

I felt guilty lying there while he did all the work but nevertheless I found it quite easy to justify my idleness.

'He doesn't really need me here at all,' I told myself. 'In any case, he always does all the technical stuff himself. I expect it's nice for him to be out there on his own. I'll get up soon, put the bed away and make us a drink.'

When we arrived at Porth Dinllaen it was bathed in sunshine as usual, and we enjoyed bacon and eggs on deck before leaving at noon, a little more than an hour later.

Mike was not at all happy with Cevamp.

'This bloody pump's broken again.'

'I told you it would.'

'Well I'm peed off with this boat. If it's not the engine it's the pump. There's always something going wrong. We've still got to get through Bardsey and if we take on water we're going to have to pump out by hand.'

'We'll manage,' I said philosophically. 'We've managed in the past.'

'We shouldn't have to manage. The bloody thing should be working properly. It's so infuriating. It's typical of Dad. When the electric pump went wrong he took it out but he never did get round to having it repaired. And it was under warranty at the time. Get me the Araldite and I'll see if I can fix the damned thing.'

He spent the next fifteen minutes sticking the broken bits of pump back together, and we waited for the glue to set. I went down below to make a cup of tea.

'Bugger.'

'What's up?'

'I don't believe it. The glue's set but now the handle's stuck too.'

I kept quiet. I'd already heard him swear more times in that one day than all the times put together since I'd known him and didn't want to say the wrong thing and put him in a worse mood than he already was. For some reason I felt it was all my fault, but I didn't know why it should be. It wasn't me that had broken the stupid pump, or got the handle all glued up.

By the time we left Porth Dinllaen I was feeling awful. I was very tired and miserable, with sore eyes from the wind and lack of sleep but I perked up when we reached Bardsey. I took the helm to motor through the sound between the island and the mainland and was surprised at how easy it was. Although I was quite pleased with myself it was almost too easy and I missed the sense of achievement there would have been had it been rougher. It wasn't as much fun, either, as it was when we went through at the start of our holiday.

We spent the night at Abersoch and sailed for Porthmadog the following morning. It was a pleasant day, overcast but mild with the sun trying to shine.

'Our last day's sailing is the first without having to wear coats,' I said. Then it rained.

By the time we got back to Porthmadog it had stopped raining, the water was like a millpond, the air was still and the barometer was way up to about 1035. It couldn't go much higher if it tried. It was obvious the weather had changed for the better. I knew tomorrow would be lovely. The day we had to go home.

We went ashore for a celebratory slap-up dinner, our first restaurant meal of the trip, and then sat on deck the way we had on the first evening. It was a beautiful still, clear and starlit night with phosphorescence sparkling in the water around us as we relived the highs and lows of our circumnavigation of Anglesey.

We were satisfied we'd set out to do what we'd intended, which was to sail round an island with frequent stops to go exploring but we were disappointed that engine problems and bad weather meant it wasn't the island we'd been planning on, the Isle of Man.

We talked too about the places we'd seen, the people we'd met – especially the eccentric Arthur and his Jacuzzi – and, of course, the weather. Particularly the weather, which had been consistently and unremittingly terrible, with torrential rain, horrendous and persistent gales, rough seas and numbing cold.

By ten o'clock, full of good food and deeply content in each other's company, we were ready to fall into bed. But first, of course, we had to bail out the bilges.

It was a calm night and we awoke refreshed at quarter to six the following morning, the first time in nearly three weeks that Mike had slept right through the night. 'Like a baby,' he said.

He made some tea and we sat up in bed marvelling at

the beauty of the pre-dawn sky through the open door of the companionway.

'Look Jack,' said Mike, pointing. 'Can you see the moon? And there's the Plough up there too.'

I pondered the inky black heavens for a few moments.

'Have you noticed how dark it's getting in the mornings now?' I remarked.

'Well what do you expect? Summer's over and we're well into autumn now. We'll be putting the clocks back in another few weeks.'

'Yes I know, but it seems to have happened overnight. I'm sure it wasn't this dark yesterday.'

'You weren't awake at this time yesterday.'

He was right. I wasn't. Not at four-thirty-five in the morning, which a quick glance at the clock confirmed it now was.

'Oh no,' said Mike. 'When I looked at my watch when I woke up I looked at the time the alarm's set for instead of the actual time. And we don't even need to hear the shipping forecast today.'

It was early evening when we got back to my cottage in Banbury.

'I'm looking forward to this dinner you've been telling me about,' said Mike. 'I like lamb goulash. I like apple pie. Especially when you make it.'

'Well it won't take long, once we get the oven warmed up.' I gave him what I hoped was a seductive look through lowered lashes. 'While dinner's heating through we can have a soak in the bath and a glass of wine.'

We unpacked the car and carried everything round to the back door. I turned the key in the lock, opened the door and we stepped into the kitchen.

'Ugh,' said Mike. 'What's that dreadful smell?'

I buried my nose and mouth into the neck of my jumper to stop myself from gagging at the stench.

'I don't know,' I said, my face still buried in my clothes. 'I think it's coming from the freezer.'

Mike opened the freezer door and we both recoiled in horror. There on the shelf, slithering towards us like something from a horror movie, were the translucent, putrefied, semi-liquid remains of our lovely casserole and apple pie, not to mention all the other food that I'd stocked up on before the holiday.

'Someone's turned the freezer off,' said Mike, checking the switches.

'No they haven't.' I was mortified. 'I defrosted it before we went away and forgot to turn it back on again!'

Launch day: Cevamp sets off for Porthmadog

Cevamp and Alex: first sea trials

No hands sailing: en route from Bardsey to Arklow

Sailing back to Pwllheli at sunset, following the fire in the engine

The disappearing jetty at Cemaes Bay on Anglesey

Jackie at the helm as we round the Fastnet Rock

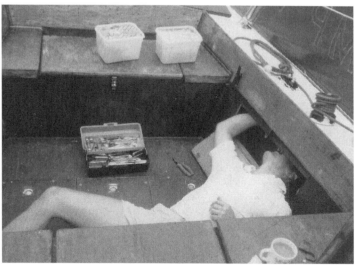

What is it this time? Gearbox? Alternator? Both? Engine repairs at New Quay

Alex takes the helm as he joins us
for a day's sailing. Photo: courtesy
of Vera Williamson

Cevamp tied to Sheilamay in
Cemaes Harbour

Cevamp – now Gipsy Maiden – as she is today, sailing off Findochty,
Morayshire. Photo: courtesy of Ron Billing

22

What's on the menu?

In my opinion the art of cooking at sea hinges on the three Ps: planning, preparation and...packets! And what's more, also in my opinion, you can't be a good cook without making a mess.

Making a mess? How can you make a mess when there's barely enough space for a chopping board in the galley of a small yacht?

And why go to all the trouble of cooking when you're supposed to be on holiday?

So already, we have some contradictions creeping in – cooking at sea? Is it even possible? There are those, I know, who think I'm mad and produce nothing more interesting out of their galleys than cheese and pickle sandwiches, relying on yacht clubs and harbour-side pubs for more sustaining or exotic fare. But I like cooking and enjoy meeting the challenge of producing good meals on board. What's more, making the most of your own galley helps keep costs down, an important consideration with such an expensive toy to keep afloat.

'Owning a yacht is just like standing on a harbour wall and tossing torn-up £10 notes in the water' Mike would grumble every time we had to fork out for yet another exorbitantly priced bit of kit, vital to ensure Cevamp remained safe and seaworthy. Non sailors would be staggered to learn the prices of replacement winches and cleats, carabiner clips and shackle pins, all of which have to be in expensive stainless steel or bronze to counteract the effects of continual immersion in corrosive salt water, not to mention the routine costs of mooring, maintenance and insurance.

If I can help by providing all our meals on board I am happy to do so and, apart from the disastrous dinner I prepared on our first weekend sailing together, Mike is more than happy with the food I cook for him.

Having said that, however, nothing can prepare you for the practical difficulties and that's just something you have to get used to. Bumps and bruises, slops and spills become all part of the fun of cooking in a rocking kitchen with few of the mod cons we have at home. Even something as simple as making a cup of tea can be fraught.

First you have to rouse yourself from the cold-induced lethargy into which you have undoubtedly sunk as a result of someone's bright idea to spend the day sailing. Then, having overcome the arm-achingly difficult task of descending a short but vertical staircase into the galley, only to find the floor is not only at an angle of forty-five degrees but also coming up to meet you, you have to fill the kettle.

Banging your shins on the bulkhead, you heave the five litre bottle of drinking water from its locker and hold it with one hand as you stand a one-litre plastic jug in the sink. Next you unscrew the lid of the water bottle, struggling to keep your balance because you only have two hands and at this point you can't use either of them for holding on to a grab rail, and put the lid in your pocket so it doesn't roll off the worktop into some hitherto unknown crevice on the floor. Then you pour, or attempt to pour, enough water for two mugs of tea into the jug. Quite a lot of it pours down the sink, quite a bit more pours down you and some goes into the jug. You replace the lid of the water bottle and again bang your shins on the bulkhead as you wedge it back into the locker – a ridiculously tight fit but necessarily so if the bottle of water isn't to fall out the next time the yacht heels over.

'How's that tea coming along,' calls the skipper from the cockpit.

'Okay. Won't be long,' you say. You don't let on the water isn't even in the kettle yet, and it's taken you a good five minutes to get that far.

You raise the hinged whistling cap on the kettle spout and attempt to transfer the water from the jug into the kettle via a one-inch diameter spout. Some goes in the kettle. The rest goes over the cooker, meaning you have to dry the gas outlets on the burners before the gas will even light. You get the gas to light on the second or maybe third attempt and as you finally put the kettle on the flames you singe your sleeve on the guttering stove. Once the kettle boils life becomes even trickier. You are now dealing with boiling water and are lucky to escape with only a minor scald to the hand that's holding the cups. Success. You've made the tea, got milk into the mugs and struggle back to the cockpit.

'Tea up,' you cry in triumph, handing a steaming mug to the skipper. The boat lurches. You are thrown off balance. The mug flies upwards and hits the deck.

'No problem,' you say, womanfully. 'I'll go and make some more.'

There are many cookery books available for sailors but with a few exceptions I think their authors sometimes forget that not all yachts have fridges, microwaves and ovens and very few have enough storage space to transport a larder full of stores and the range of utensils that most of us enjoy at home. On a yacht you can actually get by with very few basics for cooking: kettle, pressure cooker (or similar sized saucepan with a lockable lid), frying pan, vacuum flask, sharp knife, bread knife, tin opener, large plastic mixing bowl, plastic measuring jug and wooden spoon are my absolute minimum. It might sound Spartan but, with the help of a few pre-packed sauces (Schwartz and Colmans casserole mixes for example) they will just about do the job. Every cook is different, of course, and it's up to individuals to fit out their galley in the way that suits them best. If you need a cookery book get one of those one-pot recipe books to make life, and washing up, easier. Remember that when you're sailing you need food that is hot, nourishing, filling and easy to eat from a bowl, preferably with a spoon. Chilli con carne with rice, sausage casserole, chicken curry and beef stew all fit into this category.

At the start of a trip I always take on board a pressure cooker full of stew or other hearty casserole that I've prepared at home, a big apple pie and a substantial home made fruit cake, which takes care of the first two days dinners, pudding and treats.

Then, because we always try and get into a harbour at night, I shop for fresh meat, bread, milk and greengrocery on a daily basis. There are times, of course, when you get caught out, either arriving after the shops have shut or leaving before they open and it is always useful to have emergency stores to fall back on. Tinned soup, baked beans, tinned corned beef and tuna can all be turned into quick and easy meals with very little trouble.

Mike and I are lucky that we rarely suffer from sea sicknesses, other than a slight touch of nausea when the boat wallows heavily from side to side. Most of the time the only difference to our appetite when we're sailing compared with when we're at home is that it's bigger. Our staple diet tends to be simple and substantial. Cereal for breakfast then once we're under way we have bacon sandwiches. Elevenses may be cakes, scones or biscuits and lunch might consist of tinned soup, cheese sandwiches and some fresh fruit, usually an apple. On calm days I prepare lunch as we go along but if it looks as though it may be rough I make up the sandwiches and put the soup in a flask before we set off. I usually prepare our evening meal, invariably some kind of casserole, once we arrive in harbour, and always make enough for two nights.

Then there are the treats. When we're sailing Mike and I are like naughty children, gleefully eating all the things we know we shouldn't – too much wine, real cheese, fried bacon, white bread instead of our customary granary, real butter and lashings of thick double cream. Not to mention the mountains of chocolate bars, chocolate biscuits, sweets and cakes that disappear almost as fast as we buy them.

Drinks are easier to plan for, if not to prepare (see tea-making scenario above). Tea, coffee and instant drinking chocolate are the obvious staples but there are times when you can't really face any of these and the best thing of all to have then is hot Ribena. It goes down a treat. Hot and sweet and comforting.

Wine bottles can be a nuisance clinking around on a boat and we usually take three-litre wine boxes on board. Of course, once the sun goes over the yard arm we enjoy the occasional gin and tonic and from time to time, after dinner, we'll have a whisky or brandy with our coffee.

Cheers!

23

Good news, bad news

'It's time to crane the boat out, Autumn's here again
The tide is high, the crane is booked, I hope it doesn't rain.
Let's motor up on Sunday, put her beside the wall,
then Monday morning we'll be there, before the tide can fall.'
We climbed aboard on Sunday, the ropes they were all set.
The tide was high, the wind it blew, we knew that we'd get wet.
'Go and switch the batteries on,' said Mike to me on deck.
I turned the key, he pressed the switch. No engine. What the
    heck?
'Oh bugger,' said my captain, oh hell, oh shit, oh fuck.
'We should have guessed about this. It's just our bloody luck.'
We took the battery home again and put it on to charge;
then took it back down to the boat – by now more like a barge.
We got it all connected, I stood by skipper's side.
It started up no problem, but whoops, oh dear, no tide!

As the hired seven and a half ton lorry trundled down
the motorway I gradually became aware of something
warm and wet spreading over my lap, trickling between
my thighs and soaking into the upholstery of the
passenger seat. Min had wet himself.

Fourteen years old and half Siamese, with unblinking
green eyes and a silken black coat, Min was my cat and
we were moving house. He gazed up at me indignantly
and shifted himself over to a drier place on my lap, still

186

purring his special loud vibrato and totally unabashed at his breach of manners.

The move was the climax to an action packed year, and we were still only three days into February. Things got off to a good start early in January when Mike and I enjoyed our usual New Year jaunt to the London Boat Show, where we window-shopped, day-dreamed about buying an expensive yacht and ate our picnic lunch, brought from home to save money.

The following evening we went to the High Wycombe police inspectors' dinner with the superintendent. It was a good night and we all enjoyed the rare opportunity meet up and get to know each other's wives and partners. Normally, because of the shift system, the inspectors managed little more than a few words with each other as they handed over at the end of each shift and most of the partners rarely met each other, or the other inspectors, not to mention the superintendent.

Next day we slept late, making the most of a midweek morning off work. Mike woke up, rolled lazily towards me and wrapped his arms around me.

'This is nice. I love having you here. What would you think about us moving in together?'

My stomach lurched. I wondered if I'd misheard.

'Where? Here? What about my kids? What about my cats? What about my house? Yes. Okay.'

Decision made. The children were old enough by now for me to be able to make this kind of decision. At 21 and 19 years of age Sarah and Claire were already living independent lives and 13-year-old Alex was at boarding school, sharing his occasional weekends home and holidays between me and his father. He and Mike had already met and spent time together so I didn't foresee any real problems. In any case, I had no time to worry about the finer points of what it would all entail. I had an interview to prepare. A day later, almost before I'd had time to catch my breath, I was being invited over the flag-stoned threshold of 10 Downing Street, led up a staircase lined with paintings of previous incumbents and into the presence of the prime minister. Margaret Thatcher was charming and elegant and I was terrified! But she poured coffee, put me at my ease, asked me questions about myself as though she was really interested in my answers and I was soon enjoying myself. The interview was for Thames View, the Thames Valley Police newspaper, which I edited. Because the police service is apolitical I felt obliged to steer clear of political issues so really, from a police perspective, the interview was a wasted opportunity. I also felt intellectually intimidated – which was everything to do with my lack of confidence and nothing at all to do with the prime minister – and was afraid to get involved in a debate over, say, police salaries or manning levels in case I made a fool of myself or let the side down. So I simply accepted what she said without probing deeper and concentrated on personal issues instead.

The resulting article would have been ideal for a woman's magazine but I think most of the roughie-toughie male police officers in Thames Valley were fairly disgusted with my timidity as they read about the prime minister's skin care routine, the secret of her strong marriage, her love of mountains and her dislike of snakes and lizards. The female officers were probably also pretty unimpressed with it, too. Nevertheless, I was still on a high from Mike asking me to move in with him and I was on cloud nine as I travelled home on the train. I felt both honoured and privileged to have not only met the prime minister but also to have walked through the same doors and up the same staircase that so many powerful, influential and historic figures had trodden before me. I thought, not for the first time, that journalism gives you experiences that you would never otherwise have a chance to enjoy, and was grateful for them.

I'd no sooner got my feet back on the ground than they went, literally, from under me, as Mike and I joined a group of police officers and their other halves for a week's skiing in France. It was our first time on skis and we loved it. We had our lesson in the mornings and practised in the afternoons, skiing each day until the lifts closed down. After dinner the rest of the crowd gathered in the hotel bar for drinks but we took ourselves off to bed as soon as we could every evening. Our departure was always greeted with ribald comments from the others as we said our goodnights.

This was their chance to have a laugh at the inspector's expense and they relished it. In private Mike is funny, loving and uninhibited but at work he was seen by most of his colleagues and especially the junior officers as cold, introverted, stern and unbending so they were quick to take advantage of the relaxed après ski atmosphere to have some off duty fun.

As we left the bar hoots of laughter and remarks such as 'surprised you've still got the energy for it' and 'don't keep him up all night,' rang in our ears and we were greeted in similar vein in the mornings when we eventually appeared, bleary eyed, for breakfast.

They didn't realise, and we didn't tell them, that the real reason for our early nights was that we were exhausted by all the skiing. They wouldn't have believed us and anyway they weren't a million miles from the truth. But the last laugh was on us. We spent so much time skiing that we got on really well with our lessons and by the end of the week we were the best beginners in the group. I suppose Mike may even have won a bit of street cred for his stamina in the bedroom!

Once back from La Clusaz I made arrangements to let my house in Banbury. I considered selling it but Mike, ever prudent, suggested renting it out 'just in case us living together doesn't work out.'

Then I had another, painful, decision to make. I loved Mike, wanted to be with him. But he is not a cat person and I had three teenage cats. Min's sister, Demelza, was a sweet but timid, fragile little thing and I convinced myself, through my tears, it would be better to have her put to sleep than put her through the stress of moving house yet again. Following my divorce we'd already moved three times in two years and she was getting progressively more neurotic with every move. Snuff was Demelza's daughter and Mike found a new home for her with a family in High Wycombe. I kept Min – not entirely against Mike's wishes as he knew how upset and guilty I felt about the other two – and he lived with us for the remaining two years of his life.

By April we were still in a romantic haze. Mike bought me flowers, always lemon or white freesias, every Friday and I was still so starry-eyed over him that I even watched him playing squash twice a week.

Sailing was never far from our thoughts, though, and we spent a couple of chilly, late winter weekends on the harbour side at Porthmadog, working on Cevamp to get her ready for being craned back into the water for the summer. But our plans were shattered one Tuesday evening when we got a call from Mike Bicks, the harbour master at Porthmadog.

'I'm sorry to have to tell you this but we've had a really bad storm and Cevamp has been blown off her blocks. She's got a bad gash in her starboard hull and there's quite a bit of damage to the bilge keel on the same side. I don't think you'll be sailing her for a while. You'll need to arrange to get her transported to the yard at Pwhelli for repairs.'

We were devastated. All our plans for the summer revolved around Cevamp and we'd already booked a week's leave to go sailing.

We wondered what to do instead.

'Why don't you book a cheap flight to Spain?' suggested Vera, Mike's mum. 'You can have the use of our flat in Nerja for a week if you like. You can hire a car from Malaga airport and go exploring.'

But, as with everything Mike and I did, even a simple week in Spain proved eventful and we were glad to get back into our familiar routine. For our long weekend in June we went back to Porthmadog, where Vera owned another flat. It was a crumbling, semi derelict place but it overlooked the harbour and it was somewhere for us to camp out while Cevamp was out of action.

That summer, so we were told, was the best sailing weather the country had known for years. We spent our time off in June mooning around the harbour, trekking along Black Rock Sands to Criccieth and exploring the delights of Snowdonia while Cevamp remained high and dry in the Pwhelli boatyard. The weekend passed quickly and we set off for home.

'Look at that pipeline running down the side of that mountain,' I burbled from the passenger seat shortly afterwards. 'I haven't noticed that there before. Have you? I wonder what it is. D'you think it's a water pipe from one of the mountain reservoirs? Or what?'

By then we were driving through Penrhyndeudraeth, a grey village three or four miles out of Porthmadog. It was typical sailing weather, cold with low cloud, dismal visibility and a persistent, penetrating drizzle.

We were okay though, warm and snug in Mike's pride and joy. A new Ford Escort Ghia, bought a few months previously and even now showing fewer than five thousand miles on the clock. It had luxurious velvety seats, a dust-free dash and still retained that lovely new-car smell as you opened the doors.

Mike is careful to the point of obsessional with all his possessions and the Escort was no exception. With its gleaming paintwork, Windolene bright windows, shining alloy wheel trims and pristine interior it looked as though it had just left the showroom. On the day in question he was driving and I was nattering non-stop about the weekend's activities, the coming week and other, mainly inconsequential, matters.

'What pipeline?' asked Mike, peering through the windscreen wipers and out into the misty view ahead. 'I can't see anything.'

'Over there.' I pointed towards a distant mountainside, partially blocking his line of sight with my arm as I did so.

'Move your arm or I can't even see the road. What pipeline?' he repeated.

Mike is a fast driver and by now we were through the village and approaching a sweeping left hand bend. On the near-side of the road was a couple of pairs of semi-detached cottages. On the off-side was a crash barrier and on the other side of the crash barrier was a steep, twenty foot drop to the Glaslyn river, currently in spate after recent heavy rains.

I persisted. 'Look, over there. Two o'clock on that hillside.'

Mike looked up. 'Oh yes,' he said. 'Oh bugger,' he

added, as the car hit a patch of grease on the oily road. In slow motion it slid gracefully sideways across the road and bounced off the crash barrier. Then it drifted in slow motion back across the road, landing astride the boundary wall of the cottages and with its bonnet crunched firmly against the wall of the house.

We escaped unscathed but the car was a mess, with shattered windows, crumpled bonnet and twisted shell. A breakdown truck came to take it away, Mike's dad came to drive us back to High Wycombe and the local council sent us a bill for the damage to the crash barrier.

Once we were back at work, I decided to arrange a surprise to cheer Mike up. Just before I started my job with Thames Valley Police I'd written a feature for the Bucks Free Press about Nigel Lamb, the British National Aerobatic Champion. To write the feature I was obliged to fly a few stunts with him. Exhilarating, yes, but off the scale in terms of scariness. Mike enjoys flying and briefly flirted with the idea of becoming a pilot. A rugby ball whacking his left ear in his early twenties meant he failed the medical so he joined the police instead but he still sometimes toyed with the idea of learning to fly. I went to see Nigel at his base on Booker Airfield, just outside High Wycombe, and told him what had happened. He agreed to take Mike for a ride and do a few stunts with him. I can't say Mike enjoyed the experience any more than I did, but it was unforgettable and took his mind off his car for a few minutes while he concentrated on hanging on to his breakfast.

By the end of July the Escort was back on the road and Cevamp was ready to be craned back into the water. Mike and I made our way to Pwhelli ready to sail her back to Porthmadog. There were no apparent leaks but the gear knob had become corroded and was difficult to engage and disengage. The engine fired first time. It ran smoothly and although the fan belt was slipping we didn't think there were any major problems. Half an hour after we left Pwhelli the engine lost power and Cevamp slewed to a stop.

'You lower the anchor, Jack, and I'll go over the side to check the propeller. At least the sea is nice and warm at this time of year.'

He stripped off into his swimming trunks and jumped into the water. I leaned over the stern, watching but not offering to go in and help.

'Here's the problem,' Mike spluttered, hauling a heavy length of rope clear of the water. 'It had wrapped itself round the prop.'

He climbed back on board, I pulled up the anchor, Mike rubbed himself down with a towel and put his clothes back on. We were on our way again. Three hours later we were back in Porthmadog. I was standing up front, ready with the boat hook to pick up our mooring buoy but with less than fifty yards to go we ran aground on the ebbing tide. As we sat with mugs of tea and chunks of thickly buttered malt loaf and waited for the tide to come back in we passed the time by watching the oystercatchers along the water's edge. Calling noisily with their distinctive bleeping cry, they were smart in their striking black and white dinner suits and long red bills. They have a fascinating hunting technique in which they paddle rapidly with their pink feet on the wet sand, apparently to attract shellfish to the surface.

We eventually got back onto our mooring, where we made sure Cevamp was shipshape and secure before loading all our bags into the dinghy, rowing ashore and heading for home. We would be back in a month to begin our long awaited circumnavigation of the Isle of Man, and we couldn't wait.

24

Over the seas to Man

The light on chicken rock winked seductively at us through the deepening twilight as we sailed from day into night and on through the darkness towards the Isle of Man.

We'd arrived in Porthmadog five days earlier and taken our time harbour hopping around the coast to Holyhead, our jumping off point for the sixty mile crossing to Port St Mary.

Our first port of call after leaving Porthmadog was Abersoch. We enjoyed a leisurely day in light airs and very little swell, taking just over nine hours to cover the twenty six miles. During the summer we'd visited my parents in Wincanton and come home with their inflatable Tinker dinghy, which we were now trailing behind us. It was a pretty little thing and with its bright yellow tubes and orange cuddy it made an ideal tender for Cevamp. Once deflated it rolled up small enough to be tied down and carried on Cevamp's foredeck but on days such as this it created little drag and we were happy to tow it along behind us.

The following morning it was calm and cool with the promise of a fine day to come. Despite this, I made sure I was thoroughly prepared for whatever Bardsey Sound could throw at us and pulled on several layers of clothes under my oilskins, topped off with thermal balaclava, ski gloves and wellies. I was roasting and as it turned out I needn't have bothered. Bardsey Sound was flat calm for once and we sailed through at a good pace, with both sails up. By late afternoon there was a clear blue sky and warm sunshine. The helmsman stripped down to his shorts, the crew indulged in a spot of nude sunbathing, we put the cruising chute up and as we sailed along at around four knots we were enjoying ourselves immensely.

On arrival at Porth Dinllaen we paddled ashore for coffee in Ty Coch Inn, the red-painted pub on the beach.

'Sorry,' said Cliff Webley, the friendly landlord, known to locals and holidaymakers alike as Chris Ty Coch. 'The coffee machine's empty.'

So we made do with brandy instead. As I sipped my drink I gazed around the bar. We hadn't been in the pub before and I was fascinated by the collection of collections hanging from every nook and cranny. There was a tankard collection, a farming implements collection and a Toby jug collection. Instead of sawdust there was sand on the floor and the walls were littered with old seagoing prints and photographs. There was also a corner full of lifeboat memorabilia as well as myriad bits and pieces of fishing tackle, all adding their clutter to the relaxed and welcoming ambience.

The pub, which has been run by the Webley family since 1968, was built as a vicarage in 1823 although the cellar is much older. In 1828 the vicar moved into a new vicarage next to the church and his housekeeper, Catherine Ellis, opened up the house as an inn to serve the shipbuilders who worked on the beach. Apart from a three year closure in the late 1850s, it has provided a warm welcome to visitors and locals ever since. From its earliest days it has a tradition of being run mainly by landladies including the formidable Jane Jones, who was also the harbourmaster as well as running a school for mariners' children in the pub. The name Ty Coch translates in English to Red House, in recognition of the red bricks that were used in its construction. It is believed the bricks were originally used as ballast for a ship that came to Porth Dinllaen for a cargo of granite to take back to Holland.

We were sorry to learn of Cliff Ty Coch's death in August 2004 and not surprised to hear that more than 300 people and the local lifeboat attended the funeral service for this well-loved man on the beach at Porth Dinllaen.

These days the tradition of female landladies is still alive and well in the shape of Cliff's wife, Brione, who now runs the pub with the couple's son Stuart.

Our passage to Holyhead the following day was pleasant and, unusually for us, uneventful, apart from a little problem with the cruising chute. The chute is a colourful billowing sail, also known as a gennaker, made from a lightweight fabric similar to parachute silk. It's difficult to raise and lower as not only can the slightest puff of wind make it fly out of control but it also has to be 'poled out' into the wind if you don't want it to be blanked out by the mainsail. One end of the pole fits onto a bracket at the foot of the mast and the other end is attached to the ropes, or guys, that control the sail. We'd just got everything sorted and were sitting back to enjoy the view when suddenly the stainless steel u-bolt that held the pole to the foot of the mast snapped. Mike tried to make a temporary repair by tying the pole to the mast bracket with cord but this wasn't very effective so he sat on the coach roof holding it out himself. After a while he got fed up. Cevamp looked pretty sailing goose-winged but it was a bit of a strain so we brought the chute in and put the genoa back out.

The early forecast had been for south-westerly threes or fours, veering to northerly six later, but the six never materialised and we enjoyed easy sailing on a broad reach most of the way to Holyhead. As the tides started to turn against us on the approach to South Stack we brought the sails right down and switched the engine on.

It's always interesting approaching Holyhead harbour and we never tired of pointing things out to each other. We were well past South Stack rocks when we heard a heavy throbbing overhead. Mike squinted upwards.

'Look, it's an RAF helicopter. They must be practising search and rescue procedures. They're just hovering there, like giant yellow wasps. See the man hanging on that line – that must be their target underneath him, in the water.'

We watched for a while, as the dangling man rescued his 'casualty' and both were hoisted up into the big machine whirling noisily above, the downdraught from its rotors causing sheets of spray to rise from the surface of the sea and form rainbows in the mist.

A few minutes later I looked towards the shore, where I could see huge derricks lining the commercial jetty and towering above the harbour wall.

'They look just like massive dancing Daleks, stretching out their arms to take their partners for a stately waltz around the harbour,' I said.

Dancing Daleks and hovering helicopters aside, it's funny how even ordinary, unremarkable things floating on water get an inordinate amount of attention when you're sailing, probably because you have time to look at them properly. Or perhaps it was just an indication of how inane some of our conversations had become.

'Look,' I said. 'A floating cider bottle.'

'So it is. Shall we see if there's a message in it?'

'Oh, look. There's a little red balloon bobbing alongside us.'

'Mmmm. Fascinating. It's probably one of those that get let off at village fetes to see where they end up. You know the sort of thing – the one that goes furthest wins an I-spy book or some such thing.'

But as we got nearer to the harbour entrance Mike became more alert and the silly banter stopped. The big ferries to and from Dublin and Dun Laoghaire glide in and out of the port unbelievably quickly, appearing and disappearing over the horizon in no time. This wasn't the time for the skipper of a twenty six foot yacht to start insisting on rights of way and Mike wanted, naturally enough, to keep out of theirs.

We tied up to a visitors' buoy in the harbour, walked into town for cakes and bags of chips, enjoyed blissful showers in the yacht club and then returned to Cevamp for our staple dinner of beef stew and wine. After studying the tidal flow charts we decided to have an easy day in harbour the next day and prepare for a late evening sail to Man so that we would start off in the dark and sail with the current into daylight. It wasn't to be.

It was rare to have a bad night in Holyhead harbour but the weather deteriorated and that night was bad. It always takes a few nights of sleeping on board to get used to the thuds, bangs, groans, slaps and shrieks and convince yourself that the noise you can hear isn't footsteps on the roof or some fiendish visitation and that Thursday night was one of the noisiest we could remember.

We spent Friday pottering about the town –

launderette, food shopping and greasy fish and chips eaten on the railway bridge.

'I reckon Holyhead station must rate as British Rail's least attractive,' I said, wiping grease and vinegar from my chin with my sleeve. 'Just look at it. It's in a shocking state and they don't seem to be doing anything to smarten it up.'

Mike agreed. 'It can't give a very good impression of the place to people coming here for the first time and it wouldn't take much to make a big difference.'

When we got back to Cevamp we noticed the sail-training vessel Francis Drake in the harbour. A three masted schooner, she was built in 1917 and must have looked magnificent in full sail, although we never had the pleasure of seeing her underway. By the late 1990s, a decade after we saw her, she was berthed permanently in the Caribbean but came to an ignominious end in the last summer of the century when she was moored to a buoy in Marigot Bay on the island of Saint Martin and struck by Hurricane Lenny. She sank in four hundred metres of water and nothing was seen of her again, apart from one of her life rafts found floating in the aftermath of the storm by a patrolling coastguard vessel.

As it turned out we didn't leave for the Isle of Man that day after all. The weather worsened during the day, with steady rain and a gusting wind and even in the harbour the water was choppy. Instead, we went to bed at five o'clock and only got up to eat a late supper of beans on toast and gooseberry pie. All being well, we hoped to get away at midday on Saturday, making the most of a favourable tidal flow that would take us up round the Skerries and north to the Isle of Man.

In the morning, before we left Holyhead, Mike put both reefs in the main as we could see it was likely to be a lumpy crossing. There was already a vigorous wind and the forecast was for north easterlies so we needed to be prepared for an uncomfortable crossing. I made a big pot of chilli con carne for later and got things ready for bacon and egg rolls to cook once we were under sail. This way, I figured, we'd have something hot, easy to reheat and straightforward to dish up regardless of sea conditions. I decided against soup in a flask as it would probably be cold by night time and instead I made sure the tin, tin opener and saucepan were handy but securely stowed. We also had a plentiful supply of instant comfort in the form of cakes, Mars bars and sweets and I decided that with all this it was pointless to make up sandwiches as well.

That was my first mistake. Once we were out of the shelter of the harbour the north easterlies were already nudging thirty miles an hour, producing big rolling seas and an uncomfortable side to side heaving of the boat. It was impossible to do anything except wedge ourselves in. We were nauseous and miserable and the last thing I wanted to do was go inside and start frying bacon. At about three in the afternoon I could no longer ignore the pressing call of nature brought on by the countless cups of tea before we left and I went below to wee in the bucket and put on some extra clothes. The whole operation took about forty minutes and by the time I came out I was on the point of being sick. Mike felt as bad.

'It's one of those days,' I muttered.

'One of those what days?'

'One of those days when you wonder what you're doing here. Why are we here anyway? What on earth made us think we'd enjoy this? It's horrible and we've still got another ten or eleven hours to go.'

'Yes, if we're lucky.'

Eventually I started to feel a bit better and decided to have a go at heating up the tomato soup, my second mistake and an attempt that was doomed from the start. I managed to open the can, heat the soup and fill one mug, which I handed to Mike. I went back below to do mine. Cevamp lurched. I was flung backwards, throwing the second mug of soup over bedding, floor, ceiling, worktop and my hand and cracking the back of my head on the bulkhead as I went. I did my best to clean up the mess but the vivid tomato stain on the white ceiling remained a permanent reminder of the perils of combining hot liquids and bucking boats.

Shortly before six things started looking up. I took over the tiller and Mike rested in the saloon. To my surprise I really enjoyed the next four hours. There was plenty to look at, even when it got dark and that, combined with the concentration needed to keep the boat on course, shrank the hours. As it grew dark Anglesey became a silhouette that slowly merged with the night so that by nightfall the lighthouse on The Skerries was all that was left of land.

Soon after the Skerries light disappeared behind us, Chicken Rock light appeared straight ahead to the north. Although there were still several hours to go I found it comforting and it also gave me something to aim for. Looking like a candle on a birthday cake, Chicken Rock lighthouse took four summers to build, with the winters being used to cut the stone in Port St Mary. It shone its first beam on New Year's Day in 1875. The lighthouse is built from Scottish granite and towers thirty eight metres above the Isle of Man's most southerly island.

It was pretty hard work, keeping steady in such big seas but despite the heavy cloud cover it hadn't rained and I was grateful for that. Although there weren't many stars in the sky the water was full of them, thanks to the phosphorescence that sparkled in the light cast by the yacht's navigation lights: red and green to the front and sides and white to the rear. Phosphorescence occurs under certain condition in sea water and sometimes you can also see it on a beach in wet sand. A magical phenomenon with a scientific explanation, it consists of tiny sea-creatures that, thanks to an enzyme-catalysed chemical reaction, produce a heatless light and glow in the dark.

By ten o'clock the wind had changed direction slightly and it was impossible to sail without tacking. Mike reappeared, fresh from his sleep, started the engine, brought the sails down and took over the helm while I had a nap. Now the engine was running the boat's wild bucking had lessened, making it easier to keep our balance, so after my rest I made us something to eat. I was feeling guilty about my bad planning, especially as a couple of days earlier I'd boasted about how good the food was on board and how well organised it always was. After losing bread rolls on the floor and struggling to catch the butter and tomato sauce as they tumbled out of the cupboards I finally managed bacon and egg rolls with mugs of coffee, a hot feast that warmed us up and lifted our spirits no end.

Even so, it was still hard going against wind and tide and it was a relief when, at half past one in the morning, we reached Port St Mary harbour wall, tangling with a fishing line as we did so. As we entered the inner harbour the water was lower than we realised and there was a loud bang as Cevamp's iron centre keel struck a rock. Thanks to the forward gear stubbornly refusing to engage while we were manoeuvring in the cramped harbour, it took us three attempts and three quarters of an hour to pick up a mooring buoy and it was after three in the morning before we were able to tidy up the boat, have a quick wash and tumble into bed. It had been a thirteen hour sailing day and we embraced the stillness of the harbour after the turmoil of the open water. Snug under our duvet we heaved twin sighs of relief that we'd finally made it back to this jewel in the Irish Sea. The Isle of Man at last. We knew it would be worth waiting for.

25

Circumnavigation

Our circumnavigation of the Isle of Man didn't actually get underway for another couple of days as we spent the day after our arrival sorting out the boat. We didn't get up until ten o'clock and then Mike spent two hours working on the gear box and trying to sort out the problems with the forward gear. As with most yacht engines, Cevamp's Yanmar only had two gears. Forward and reverse. If they went wrong we had nothing else to fall back on – you can't give the boat a shove to get it moving then slip it straight into second as you do with a car! While Mike was poking around with screwdrivers and clenched knuckles, a scuba diver swam over.

'Need any help under the boat?' he called out. 'It'll give me something to do on my dive.'

Mike stood up and stretched his back.

'You must be psychic. We scraped the keel as we came in last night and I was wondering how I could check it for damage.'

'No problem,' said the diver and with a thrust of his fins he was gone. I sat on deck and watched his bubbles glooping eerily as they rose to the surface of the water. A few minutes later he popped up again.

'Yeah, you're okay. I had a good look but I can't see any signs of damage.' He waved aside Mike's proffered payment with a gloved hand.

'No, put that away. I do this for fun.' And with that he was off, presumably in search of more yachts to have some fun with.

It turned into a beautiful day and we walked into town for newspapers, Telegraph for him, Mail for me.

'Now I know the answer to last night's question,' I said.

'What question?'

'You know, the one about why are we doing this?'

'Doing what?'

'Sailing. I know it was horrible yesterday but it's so pretty here that it's worth it.'

For lunch we polished off the chilli con carne that we hadn't managed to eat at sea and followed it with apple crumble and custard. During the afternoon the wind picked up a bit so we moved into the inner harbour to be sure of a quiet night. Then we spent the rest of the day pottering happily around the boat and collecting fresh supplies of food before visiting the yacht club for showers and settling down for an early night.

As the boat left the harbour next morning we were pleased to see the Ocean Youth Trust's seventy-six foot steel ketch Greater Manchester Challenge. The yacht sails in the Irish Sea and is crewed, under supervision, by young people in their teens and early twenties. Some are from schools or youth groups and some have disabilities or come from disadvantaged backgrounds. Others may simply be a mix of people who have never met before. During their week or so on board they not only share the responsibility of running the boat but also learn about their personal strengths and weaknesses, develop teamwork skills and experience the satisfaction of rising to a challenge.

Mike decided to have a day off and handed sailing duties to me but he still kept a close eye on my ham-fisted efforts and issued instructions by the minute, tweaking the sails whenever he thought I wasn't looking. It was overcast and hazy but mild and we sailed goose winged to the entrance of Calf Sound, on a reach through the sound and then close-hauled up the coast.

Port Erin is even more beautiful than Port St Mary and as Cevamp made her way regally into the bay we were overtaken by a gleaming new catamaran as it flew through the shallows and grounded on the beach.

Mike was openly impressed by her speed and stability.

'If ever I had a cat that's what I'd like to do – whoosh onto the beach like that.'

But I wasn't quite so taken by this brash young upstart.

'Huh. I wouldn't want a catamaran. I wouldn't feel like a real member of the yachting fraternity in a cat. To me they're not real yachts. Where's the excitement of sailing a boat that doesn't heel over? It's like driving a Rover when you could be driving a Ferrari. Not counting the speed factor, of course.'

Mike knew what I meant.

'I'd miss the exhilaration of a tippy boat too,' he agreed. 'But cats do have their advantages. They're a lot more stable and depending on the design there's a lot more room inside too.'

We followed the cat into the bay and carefully ran Cevamp aground on the gently sloping sandy beach. Although it was low water and we were high and dry Mike put anchors out front and rear to make sure she stayed put when the tide came in. Then we set off to explore the town before settling ourselves on deck to eat lunch, luxuriating in the warmth of the hazy autumn sun.

During the evening we walked around the bay. Coloured fairy lights strung along the road round the bay reflected in the water in columns of shimmering red, green and yellow. The sea was tourmaline green and incredibly clear and even though it was dark we could still see big shoals of small fish swimming in its shallow depths. Behind a low wall bordering the beach we came across St Catherine's Well, which is believed to have been the site of an ancient hermitage. It was only when we read the words on a plaque under the stone arch above the well that we realised its significance. 'This source of fresh water inspired fishermen centuries ago to settle hereabouts. Port Erin began here.'

In the morning we paid a quick visit to Port Erin Aquarium, which is part of the University of Liverpool's Marine Biological Station, and then set off for Peel just before midday. We played around with the cruising chute for a while and I helmed while Mike circled in the dinghy taking photos of Cevamp under sail, but then the wind died and we motored in to Peel in time for tea.

The first thing to catch our eye was the large number of fish leaping around at the end of the harbour wall, being plucked out almost willy-nilly by at least a dozen anglers of all ages.

The second was a big old bull seal. He was obviously a familiar character to local people as we were virtually the only ones paying him any attention.

We'd already switched on the engine and lowered the sails ready to go into the harbour and weren't really surprised when the forward gear failed, yet again, to engage.

'There's nothing else for it,' Mike grumbled. 'We'll just

have to go in backwards. You steer and I'll put the fenders out.'

'I can't do that,' I squawked. 'Look at all these boats. You know what I'm like at reversing. Especially with a tiller. I can't co-ordinate. And there's loads of people watching. I'll panic. I'll crash the boat. I'll ram the bowsprit into the wall. I'll ...'

He sighed.

'Okay, there's no need to be theatrical. You do the fenders. I'll steer.'

Cevamp reversed her way unceremoniously to a berth against the harbour wall but a small fleet of fishing boats, followed by a fisheries protection vessel, soon crowded us out and Mike decided to move to the inner harbour, again backwards.

An Irishman, who had arrived on a yacht called Ulster Lady shortly before we did, followed us.

'You're good at reversing,' he called to Mike. 'It's a grand way of getting onto a mooring. I'll have to give it a try sometime.'

Mike laughed. 'I don't make a habit of it. I'm only doing it this way because the gear box is knackered and we can't go forwards.'

Once both yachts were safely tied against the wall the Irishman suggested Mike disconnected the linkage and push the gear into position by hand. He was a friendly soul, full of the craic, and before long we knew his life history. A civil servant from Carrickfergus, he was suffering from stress and was following his doctor's advice to take a year off work.

'I'm spending all my time sailing. When I first got this yacht I'd only sailed dinghies before and I was wondering why it was so hard to haul the sail up. Then someone told me what the winches were for.

'And if you think that's bad, you should hear about my pal. He's no time for the theory of navigation. He used to sail across the Irish Sea by following the ferries. When they changed the ferries to these big fast ones, he just got a boat with a bigger engine.'

We all laughed at this. True or not, it was a good story.

A young chap poked his head over the top of the wall to tell us to make use of the yacht club facilities and a bit later a returning fisherman did the same. We remembered the kindness we'd been shown during our first visit to the island and decided to accept their invitations.

'It would be churlish of us not to go after they've been so friendly. We'll just go for a shower and a quick drink then come back for an early night.'

The changing rooms were damp and mildewy and smelt faintly of shampoo, stale perfume and bleach but the water was hot and the welcome we received in the bar was warm. The fisherman we'd spoken to earlier was there with his wife, daughter and son-in-law. They told us they'd moved to Peel from Manchester two years ago and were full of praise for island life.

'We love it here. There's low taxation, low car taxes, low cost of living and a better quality of life altogether.' Everyone else nodded in solemn agreement, all chipping in with their own reasons for not wanting to live anywhere else.

They told us the seal in the harbour was one of a family of four that had been in the bay for a number of years. They also told us the big attraction over the previous few weeks was a shoal of basking shark that had come within a few yards of the shore.

In the spring and summer the Isle of Man is a basking shark feeding and mating ground and its waters are visited by more of these amazing animals than any other place in the British Isles. Second in size only to the tropical whale shark, basking sharks are plankton feeders that often feed on the surface of the sea, their huge mouths agape as they filter tiny planktonic shrimp out of enough water to fill a fifty metre swimming pool every hour. They have been known to reach nearly fourteen metres in length and can weigh as much as two elephants and yet they are harmless to humans. Manx Gaelic has its own names for them – Gobbag vooar (big mouth), Sharkagh souree (summer shark) or Sharkagh greinney (sun shark).

It was nearly midnight when we staggered out of the clubhouse but that didn't stop us from pausing for a few minutes to gaze up at Peel Castle, lit by spotlights and glowing golden against the dark sky. The castle, which has strong historical links with Man's Nordic past, dates from the eleventh century and dominates the harbour from its position at the top of the grassy slopes of St Patrick's Isle.

After a peaceful night on Cevamp we went into town to top up our store cupboards. I thought Peel looked a bit run down but it was unspoilt and uncommercialised, with tight narrow streets and simple stone terraced cottages. Then we had a walk round the castle ruins and admired a vertical sundial on the wall of the keep by the entrance. A notice explained that it is noon when the shadow from the corner of the keep falls on a line on the sundial, the time for the changing of the guard in the days when the castle formed an important defence for the island.

'What happens on days when the sun isn't shining

and there aren't any shadows?' I wondered. 'Does the guard have to stay put until the sun comes out?'

We waited for the shadow to fall on the sundial before motoring out of Peel for Ramsey, with plenty of food in hand for what we expected to be a long trip. Although the wind and tides were right behind us the weather wasn't that great but it was still exhilarating sailing. We only had the main up, with one reefing line in, but six knots became the norm and we once touched 7.6 knots, which was very fast for Cevamp. The desolate Point of Ayre with its ancient shingle banked beaches on the northern tip of the island marked the turning point of our holiday. The weather turned too. It was appalling, with dark skies, cold winds and torrential rain.

Mike summed it up in four words. 'The weather's bloody awful.'

We dropped anchor off Ramsey just after six o'clock – seven and a half hours to travel twenty eight miles – but we couldn't get in because the harbour dries out and can only be used two hours either side of high water.

'That's a bit of waste,' I grumbled. 'What's the point of a harbour that's only usable for eight hours out of every twenty four?'

'Stop moaning,' said Mike. 'Let's paddle ashore in the Tinker and see if we can find a mooring for when the tide does come in.'

'I don't like paddling. Can't we use the outboard to look for a mooring? It's really choppy and the wind will be against us. It'll be hard going in this if we have to paddle.'

'Stop moaning. The tide will take us in and the wind'll blow us back out. It'll be easy.'

But it wasn't. It was jolly hard going and the little boat

seemed to take on a life of it's own as its nose spun first this way, then that, while we paddled furiously with one oar each over the sides. The coastguard, parked on the beach in his Land-Rover, denied laughing at our efforts, which was just as well because I didn't think it was funny at all. Especially when, having identified a mooring, we returned to the Tinker, lifted it up and began to crunch over the shingle towards the water's edge. Suddenly the Tinker jerked out of our clutches and landed on the pebbles between us. We'd forgotten to untie it. Some people never learn. We'd performed the same trick a couple of days earlier on the beach at Port Erin. Almost as bad as when we'd fixed bungees tightly around the mast to secure the halyards and stop their infernal tattoo as they rattled in the wind, then wondered why the mainsail wouldn't go up!

We'd identified a mooring buoy near the swing bridge on the south side of the harbour and as soon as there was enough water we moved the boat and went to explore our surroundings. The island's second largest and most northerly town, Ramsey had the usual collection of shops and fascinating historical connections with invading Vikings and Norsemen. But other than being the northern terminus for the Manx Electric Railway it wasn't memorable for anything in my opinion and we spent the rest of the evening on board Cevamp.

We left for Douglas a few minutes before eleven the following morning. It was mild but cloudy and Scotland was clearly visible on the northern horizon with the Cumbrian mountains on the east. We made slow progress, tacking steadily, and the weather was fine. Then the radio burst into life with a securité weather warning from Holyhead coastguards, quickly followed by a forecast of gales from the BBC. We were aware that it was now quite late in the season and didn't want to chance our luck so I left the sundeck, Mike switched on the engine and we ran for shelter, rafting up to the fishing boat Girl Mary on a floating pontoon on the Battery Pier at Douglas at about eight o'clock in the evening.

The forecast the next morning was for more gales and rain so we decided to visit the local lifeboat house. The boat, the Sir William Hillary, was named after the founder of the RNLI who came from Douglas and was also a lifeboatman.

The orange and blue boat was immaculate with gleaming brass propellers and fittings. Costing £600,000, it was launched in 1988 and is the second to bear the name. Assistant mechanic Dougie Davidson said we could walk round her. Then he came and switched on her lights and gave us a guided tour. We sat in the cox'n's chair and marvelled at all the safety gear and an instrument panel that would have done justice to a jumbo jet. All the seats had safety belts, the crew's helmets were wired up with radio receivers in internal earpieces and, in common with all lifeboats, there were two big diesel engines capable of speeds up to eighteen knots.

Dougie had a fund of fascinating tales and needed little prompting to relate them to us. We were flabber-gasted by one story, which left us wondering whether there ought to be some sort of mandatory test before people were allowed out on the water.

'We were called out to a yacht whose skipper and crew were panicking in a force five – the sort of blow most yachtsmen spend most of their sailing lives praying for. When the lifeboat arrived we saw the yacht had no sail up at all. The mainsail wasn't even on the boom. "Why aren't you using the sail?" we asked. "Oh, we don't like them, we don't know much about them," they said. "Well why haven't you got a motor cruiser then?" "We like yachts for their safety" came the reply.'

Despite the serious nature of their jobs, and perhaps because of it, lifeboatmen – and their wives it seems – still manage to retain a sense of humour. Dougie told us about another occasion when they answered a call from a woman about a yacht in distress, only to find when they arrived it was their own cox, out for a day's sailing. He wasn't in any difficulty at all and could hardly believe it when his crewmates said they'd come to rescue him.

'I thought you'd come to pick me up to go out on a shout,' he said.

It turned out the call had been made by his wife, as a leg-pull.

It was still pouring with rain as we said our farewells to Dougie but, with typical Manx hospitality, he lent us his brolly and told us to leave it outside the lifeboat station for him to pick up later.

We walked for miles around Douglas in the rain and wind, including a visit to Marks and Spencer's food counters and a look round the smoke houses where the famous Manx kippers are given their distinctive flavour. I love kippers and wanted to take some back to the boat. Mike was not enthusiastic. They'll make the boat stink for weeks he grumbled, so I demurred and ordered a box to be sent home instead. Then we went for a long trek with our laden bags of shopping to Nobles Park and the Manx Cattery, which was closed. By the time we got back to Cevamp we were too tired even to go for a shower. Instead we tucked into our M&S feast of chicken pie, potatoes, cauliflower, carrots, apple and blackberry pie, thick Greek yoghurt and a bottle of wine and flopped exhausted into bed just after nine o'clock.

Around midnight, with the tide coming in the swell became very strong. Cevamp was banging and jerking around, her starboard stanchion posts were being knocked loose from being hit by Girl Mary's gunnels and there was no way we could sleep. It was very noisy, the boat was rocking around and we were worried about her.

We listened to the midnight shipping forecast then radioed for permission to move up into the relatively calmer waters of the inner harbour, beyond the swing bridge and on the opposite side of the inlet to where we were. It was a black night and conditions were tricky as we left the pontoon. I released the bow ropes but because of the strength of the wind and the swell, Mike was struggling to drive the boat and release the stern line at the same time and was forced to jettison his mooring warp.

'Don't worry,' he shouted above the noise of the wind. 'We'll get moored up and walk back round for it.'

'It'll be gone by morning,' I called back.

'I didn't mean in the morning. We'll go straight away.'

That wouldn't have been so bad had we been able to moor the boat and then walk across the swing bridge to get back to our original mooring. But the swing bridge is unmanned and left in the raised position at night so we had to walk round the top of the harbour, back down the other side to search, fruitlessly as it turned out, for the rope and then turn round and retrace our steps back to Cevamp, in all a good three mile round trip. It was a real slog. Bent into the wind, we fought to make headway against it. Rain was dripping snottily off the end of my nose, sopping tendrils of hair whipped my face, my eyes were streaming and my waterproofs stuck cold and clammy to my bare arms and legs underneath. I wasn't a happy bunny and was on the verge of mutiny or possibly even murder by the time we eventually crawled into bed at two thirty in the morning. Who in their right mind, I wondered, gets up in the middle of the night and goes for a three mile walk in the rain in a howling gale? Go sailing with Mike and you're guaranteed a real laugh!

26

Gale lashed

Despite the awful weather we decided to make a dash for it the next morning. We abandoned our plan to call in to Castletown and headed straight for Port St Mary instead. The forecast was still for strong winds but it was a lovely day for sailing and we made the most of it.

As we motored out we watched the J-class yacht Velsheda, sail number JK7, sailing splendidly in the bay. According to the Isle of Man Examiner, the yacht was in Douglas for a floating party to celebrate the 50th birthday party of a local businessman. She'd attracted attention on her arrival the previous lunchtime as she has no engine and had to be brought into harbour by tug boat. The second of four British J Class yachts, Velsheda was built in Gosport in 1933 and was one of the great names in classic yacht racing for the next three years. Built in steel, she is one hundred and twenty eight feet long, fifteen feet wide has a draught of fifteen feet and carries seven thousand square feet of sail. Sadly, Velsheda proved too costly to run and was consigned to the mud flats in the Hamble for many years before being rescued in 1984, faithfully restored and now she was once again sailing in all her glory.

We spent what remained of the weekend in Port St Mary, sailing, walking and relaxing, ready for our long passage back to Holyhead on Monday. But late on

Sunday night a strong tidal swell caused Cevamp to start rocking heavily and we were bounced into wakefulness. The strain on the ropes tore the starboard fairlead from the yacht's stern and half the port one snapped off. Both mooring warps quickly became badly frayed so yet again we dressed for a midnight jaunt and motored round to the inner harbour where the water was a little steadier. The trip only took a few minutes but it was spent in driving rain, which of course switched itself off the second we finished tying Cevamp up. Conditions remained diabolical for the rest of the night and, with a forecast of southerly gales, we were forced to abandon our plan to head south the next day.

By morning it was raining hard, the sea was boiling and there was a screaming wind. We moved further up the wall to try and get a little more protection from the elements and Mike decided to get the bus into Douglas to buy new fairleads and mooring warps.

On his way to the bus stop he met David McKaig, the harbour master. 'What do you make of this weather,' he asked him.

The harbourmaster squinted up at the sky.

'It'll be like this for at least another day or two. Unless you can get away on Thursday I reckon you'll have to leave your boat here if you have to get back to work.'

'Here we go again,' I thought. 'We're making a bit of a habit of this.'

While Mike was in Douglas I made scones for tea and listened in on Channel 16 of the yacht's VHF radio to monitor the inshore waters shipping forecasts. They were all depressingly similar: south westerly six to gale force eight, occasional severe gale nine. The wind continued to howl, creating surreal music as it blew through the hollow boom, the rain continued to fall and beyond the harbour wall the sea was impressive.

Mike was gone two or three hours and as soon as he got back I played theatre nurse to his surgeon as he removed the remaining bits of cleat and fairlead and replaced them with new ones.

'Screwdriver. Pliers. Wire.' He barked his requirements and I obediently placed the tools, only slightly rusty from the inevitable ingress of seawater into the toolbox, into his outstretched hand.

We had another early night to try and catch up on our sleep but it was another horrendous one. We slept in the forward cabin to try to counteract the low-tide list as Cevamp settled on the mud and were certainly more comfortable. But we knew from the whistling and howling sound effects, not to mention the thudding and heavy rolling of the boat as the tide came back in, that the storm was far from abating. As twilight crept stealthily over the island and merged with the leaden sky, enormous spectacular seas crashed onto the breakwater, along the bay, over the rocks and as far out as you could see, with spume blowing around like yellow tinted balls of cotton wool.

Next morning as the tide roared in we lost the new starboard fairlead and port cleat so as we were fast running out of mooring points we transferred the mooring warp to the starboard winch.

David McKaig came by and we discussed the weather, and our options, with him.

'You can get ferries to Liverpool and Heysham on Friday and Saturday morning,' he told us. 'But the eye of the storm should pass at midmorning today and tomorrow's forecast is for winds three to four variable, so you may still be lucky enough to get away in time.

I did some more shopping then returned to Cevamp and made a spicy Armenian lamb casserole ready for a quick getaway the following morning should the weather improve. I needn't have bothered. By lunchtime the BBC shipping forecast was still warning of south westerly force seven winds, increasing to severe gale nine. But every cloud has a silver lining and in this case it appeared as an optimistic footnote at the end of the forecast: wind decreasing four to five in the next twenty four hours.

For the time being, though, there was no let up in the gale and it was no real surprise when, early in the afternoon, the straining ropes caused the winch cover to fly off over the side. We transferred the rope to the port cleat that was usually reserved for the genoa sheet. It was our only remaining fixing. It was only a matter of minutes before this too was wrenched loose so Mike spent the rest of the afternoon sitting in the cockpit in the rain hanging on tight to the stern mooring line and waiting for the tide to fall.

'I wonder whether we should move Cevamp to the other wall,' he said. 'The way the wind's blowing it will blow her towards the wall but at least there aren't so many boats over there for her to bang against.'

'Seems a sensible idea.' I didn't really have a clue but wanted to appear supportive. 'Just tell me what you want me to do.'

Mike rubbed the stubble on his chin with his free hand and debated the pros and cons with himself.

'I don't know. We'd probably be safer and more comfortable over there but the harbour is full of boats and in this wind we need to be able to rely on the forward gear working. You know how temperamental it is. We could be in trouble if it packs up half way over there. I think we'd better stay where we are after all.'

The rain kept up all afternoon and by four o'clock the sky was closing in again. At seven-thirty the tide was receding fast and as the sea drained out of the harbour we spotted the outer casing for the damaged winch nestling in the mud a few yards away. There was still no sign of the spring clip that held it in place, or the missing fairlead.

We spent the early evening in our damp and steaming cabin, sitting on the bed half-heartedly playing Scrabble. Neither of us really had the heart for it and eventually Mike lost interest altogether.

'I've had enough of this hanging about,' he said, tipping all the Scrabble pieces back into their little cloth bag and fashioning the drawstring into a tidy bow.

'I think we should prepare ourselves to leave here as soon as there's a forecast without an eight in it.'

I wasn't too sure about that. I wasn't exactly afraid of sailing back in tough conditions. I just didn't fancy it. In fact, I really-with-all-my-heart just plain didn't want to do it. Not only that, the drama queen in me rather liked the idea of being forced to abandon ship in a strange harbour and have to catch ferries and trains back to Porthmadog to pick up the car. It would make a good story.

Mike read my expression.

'Okay,' he relented. 'Before we decide for certain we'll go over to the yacht club for a shower. While we're there we'll make some enquiries about spare moorings and see if we can find a reliable yacht sitter until we can come back for her next spring.

By the time we'd braved the foul weather to walk the few hundred yards to the yacht club our oilskins were soaking again and it was sheer heaven to get out of the rain and stand under a hot shower for a change.

Later, perched on bar stools with our drinks, we got talking to a bearded lifeboatman called John.

'I reckon the storm will pass over tomorrow and you'll be able to go,' he told us. 'Mind you, it'll leave a big sea for a few days.'

He assured us that, if it came to it, we could leave Cevamp without worrying.

'As long as you leave your phone number at the club and make sure a few people know how to get in touch with you, we'll all look after her for you. We'll check ropes, pump her out and let you know if there are problems. You don't even need to worry about leaving valuables on board – they'll be all right here.'

The next day, Wednesday, the weather was no better. The shipping forecast was even worse and gave winds up to storm force ten. As we sat glumly on board we watched nature do her worse and were powerless to prevent another of the new fairleads being ripped out by the forces of wind and swell, followed shortly afterwards by a cleat and a winch.

'Oh no,' I gasped. 'They cost an absolute fortune.'

'Don't worry,' said Mike. 'I'll go and have a look for them when the tide goes out. I expect they'll still be there in the mud.'

I went ashore for newspapers and fresh supplies of food and found that Velsheda had made the pages of the local and national press. She'd run aground on Douglas beach and damaged her rudder on rocks during the same heavy overnight surges that had caused problems for us.

There was lots of talk in the shops about the big yacht and popular local opinion seemed to be 'serves her right for not having an engine'. I was inclined to agree. What's the point of having a beautiful and expensive yacht such as Velsheda if you aren't able to keep her safe in a bit of a blow?

The local butcher was a lifeboatman at Port St Mary and he laughed as he told me of a shout during the summer to a sail training vessel where one of the crew had run amok and was threatening everyone.

'We went out on the lifeboat and took the local police inspector, police sergeant, dog handler and almost every other available policeman with us. They were all dead keen to get a trip in the lifeboat.'

Nothing to do with Velsheda but the way he told it made me smile, especially as I found it difficult to tell whether the white-helmeted officers I'd seen on the island were police officers or Royal Marines. In the light of the butcher's story I wondered whether they doubled up as both.

Despite the gales it was a beautiful sunny day and once we'd secured Cevamp as well as we could we walked over the cliffs to Erin. We had coffee and scones in the station office coffee shop and bought some more screws for the new fairleads from the hardware shop. The shopkeeper was a frail elderly man in old fashioned brown overalls and wearing a brightly coloured badge claiming 'I'm ready, willing and able but feeble'.

Back on Cevamp we carried on tuning in to the local shipping forecasts. Mike was getting gloomier by the hour and had virtually given hope of sailing Cevamp home.

'I think we're going to have to think seriously about what we're going to do. This weather isn't going to get any better and we're running out of time, bearing in mind it's now Wednesday and we both have to be back at work next Monday.' he said.

'The very latest we can leave here is early Friday, either in Cevamp, which would be pushing it a bit, or by ferry to Liverpool. Even if we take Cevamp it would probably mean leaving her in Anglesey and getting a train back to Porthmadog to pick up the car.'

That, secretly, was what I still wanted to do, and by now it wasn't just to satisfy my inner drama-queen. The thought of sailing back in gales and mountainous seas really filled me with dread but there's no way I was going to admit it to Mike.

'Well that wouldn't be such a bad thing,' I said instead. 'Surely it's better to leave her here, where she's safe and where we know people will keep an eye on her, than to risk sailing home in such bad conditions.'

'Let's give it another day and see what happens before we make up our minds,' was all he said.

I let it go. It had to be his decision and whatever he decided I knew I would agree to it.

This was the third day we'd been forced to remain in harbour because of gales and the winds were now being designated severe gales on the shipping forecast. Mike galumphed around in the mud at low tide and found parts of the winch but there was no trace of the missing fairlead. We spent an interminable and miserable afternoon sitting in the cockpit, taking it in turns to hold on to the mooring warps to try and relieve the strain on the other fairlead and cleat. The never-ending rain poured off the hoods of our oilskins and ran in cold rivulets down our faces, stinging our eyes and soaking the towelling scarves around our necks. At last the tide went out. Cevamp settled on the ground again and we stretched out the aching muscles in our arms and shoulders.

In the evening we ambled over to the yacht club

where, yet again, local people displayed their kindness and friendship by offering to look after Cevamp if we had to leave her behind. Nothing, it seemed, would be too much trouble for these warm and generous people and we were grateful to them.

It was a pleasant evening both inside the club and, when we emerged, outside too. What a surprise. It had stopped raining, there was noticeably less wind and by the time we went to bed we were more or less certain of getting away in the morning.

After another damply cosy night in the forward cabin we were up by six and went to have a look at conditions on the other side of the harbour wall. It was a fine morning despite a slight mist and low visibility, with a steady wind from the south rather than the full-blown gales of the previous three days.

Mike was smiling. It doesn't take a lot to make him happy. 'We'll go,' he said.

Hasn't he seen the size of those waves, I wondered. They were huge and erratic, as predicted by our new friends in the yacht club, but I kept my doubts to myself and we motored out of Port St Mary just after seven. It was a real roller-coaster ride, only it was far more gut-wrenching than any white-knuckle experience a mere theme park could offer, and I became more convinced with every passing wave that we should have stayed put.

'Do you want to turn back?'

Mike asked me the same question several times. Yes, yes, yes. The words screamed in my head. Of course I did. Who wouldn't? But he obviously thought we'd be okay and, as always, I trusted his judgement. And in any case, I knew how much he wanted to get Cevamp home.

So, 'no, of course not,' I lied. He believed me – he wanted to – and we carried on.

He'd intended to put the second reef in the mainsail the previous day while we were still in the shelter of the harbour but with all the palaver over the mooring lines it didn't get done. Now we were out at sea it was probably too late. We managed to get the genoa out and then Mike decided to put the reefing line in so we could get a bit of mainsail up and turn the engine off. Twice he attempted it and twice had to abandon the task because I was too scared to take the helm. The seas were crashing over the starboard gunnels and knocking us over, and I couldn't seem to get the hang of driving us into the waves and straightening the boat up again before the next wave hit. I wasn't frightened of the sea – I was fine when Mike was driving – and I still had total faith in Cevamp. My fear was rooted in my own incompetence and the not unlikely possibility that my lack of control, combined with my panic, would cause the boat to roll. As it was there were times, too many times, when, to my eyes, the mast seemed horrifyingly close to the water. Each time Mike tried to put the line in he looked back at me and asked 'are you all right?'

'No, not really,' I admitted.

He said afterwards I looked petrified. Eventually, as conditions improved so did my confidence and he was able to get the reef in, the sail up and the engine off.

For much of the day visibility was poor, we lost sight of land almost straight away and the only other boat to be seen all day was the Fisheries Protection Vessel M1154. Because we were heading pretty much into the wind we had to put in several big tacks and weren't able to record them all in the log because of the tricky conditions. This meant that, as we relied totally on charts and our log for plotting our course, we were uncertain of our position. It was late afternoon before I managed to grab a pencil and make an entry in the deck log. 'Time, 17.25. Log: 298.70. Compass: 180°. Notes: No land in sight yet – Falklands here we come' and it was a relief when, an hour later, the Skerries light finally appeared over the starboard bow and we were able to adjust our course for Holyhead.

We'd been out in the fresh air all day and by now we were starving. I went below, wedged myself into the galley, heated the last of the Armenian lamb casserole and we tucked into it with great slices of crusty bread and huge amounts of gusto. An hour later we arrived in Holyhead harbour where we tied to the same buoy as before. We were both very tired and couldn't even be bothered to go for a shower. We just washed our faces, brushed our teeth and fell into bed just after ten o'clock..

'What are you grinning at,' Mike asked as he reached up to switch off the cabin lights.

I stifled a yawn and smiled at him through half closed eyes. 'Just thinking what a good day we've had. I'm really glad we decided to sail back today.'

27

September Friday

Friday morning. The matches were too damp to strike and, like Mother Hubbard, my cupboard was bare. We wanted to make an early start which, in this part of the world, means before the shops open. Mike got up first, rowed ashore in the dinghy and went off in search of rolls, milk and matches so at least we could grab a hot drink and a bite to eat before we left. The town was still and quiet but he found a corner shop that was open and came back to Cevamp with a carrier bag of provisions. It was just after eight o'clock when we left Holyhead, feeling relaxed and cheerful and enjoying the contrast in conditions that were the exact opposite to the horrors of yesterday, with very little wind, oily calm sea and just a barely discernable swell.

Our pleasure did not last. By the time we were off Porth Dinllaen several hours later the wind had died completely and the engine was refusing to engage gear. Again. We were becalmed.

Mike tweaked at the ropes for a while, trying to breathe life into the drooping sails but to no avail. He was getting bored and twitchy.

'I think I'll change the fan belt. It doesn't really need it yet but it'll give me something to do and it'll take my mind off this.'

He waved his arm in true John Cleese fashion at the

surrounding calm then opened the locker where he kept the spares and fished out the new belt.

The belt was not a Yanmar spare but one that Alex had previously assured us was identical and would do the job. Mike clonked around the engine with spanners for a while, muttering and grumbling to himself, then emerged into the cockpit, sucking the blood from his knuckle where he'd knocked it against the engine.

'All done,' he said, and pressed the starter.

The engine gave a pained screech and refused even to tick over.

'I might have known it,' Mike said, with a bad-tempered scowl. 'Dad's got the wrong belt. I'd better go back down and change it back to the original Yanmar one.'

Of course, by this time the wind had picked up. I managed to coax a little into the sails and we were cruising gently along at about two and a half knots. But I was beginning to get uneasy.

'Mike,' I called down into the engine compartment. 'Will you be long? The wind's getting up and the sky's a bit ominous over Nefyn way. I think I need you out here. I think we need to reef in the mainsail.'

'It's not coming our way.' He brushed my concerns casually aside and continued his struggles with the fan belt.

The wind picked up a bit more and was now coming from the north west. Mike was still clonking around in the engine. My unease grew.

'Mike,' I called again. I think the sails need some attention but I don't know what to do with them.'

Wordlessly he reset the sails, adjusted our course, handed the tiller back to me and returned to the engine. We took off at speed. I felt a rush of adrenalin and wished he would hurry up. The sky was darker than ever and I was scared of being left on my own.

'Bugger.' Curses from the engine compartment. I heard the squeak of rubber against wood as Mike shifted position in the cramped space and his wellies scraped against the cabin floor.

'What's up?'

'I've dropped a nut from the alternator adjustment arm and it's rolled away into the bilges. I should have left the bloody thing alone in the first place. Now we've got no engine at all.'

'So what,' I thought. 'He's always telling me we're here to sail and the sails are still working. So what's his problem?'

But I knew him well enough by now to keep my thoughts to myself and let him get on with it. On his own. There were creaks and thuds as floorboards were lifted and replaced.

'Found it?'

'No. It's vanished. This sort of thing really pisses me off.'

'Hmm,' I thought. 'It wouldn't have happened if you'd left well alone in the first place.' But as usual, I said nothing.

He silently finished what he was doing, put his tools away and then with an attitude of great superiority and without saying a word, took over the tiller. I was a bit peeved at this unspoken implication that he could do better than I could, especially as by now I'd calmed down and thought we were doing quite nicely thank you under my helmsmanship.

But I bit my tongue yet again and was soon glad Mike was back in control. He sat in his corner, squinting sourly at the leaden sky and the clouds scudding overhead.

'I wonder if we ought to put the reefing line back in the main.' This more to himself than a request for my opinion. Although I was exasperated at him for ignoring me earlier when I'd had the same thought, I stayed quiet. He stayed put. A clear case, we were about to discover, of 'if you think of it do it and do it when you think of it.'

The sky suddenly became very dark and in the same instant we were hit by a gale. No rain – for which I suppose we should have been grateful – but a definite gale eight or nine with big violent waves and spray and spume everywhere.

This time I had no choice. I had to take the helm while Mike got the mainsail in. But even with both sheets fully out we still couldn't spill the wind from the sail and turn the boat round. There was nothing for it. He had to get the mainsail down with the boom swung at a right angle across the port side and the boat bucking wildly. I had never before been so glad to have proper lifejackets and safety harnesses. I was very frightened for Mike's safety and terrified at the very real possibility that he would be tossed over the side. By the time he'd lowered the main, lashed it securely onto the boom and scrambled back down into the cockpit my knees were shaking like castanets on his behalf.

Even then, with the genoa furled in to the size of a handkerchief, we were zooming along at well over five knots – fast for Cevamp – and heading straight for the boiling overfalls of Bardsey Sound.

A brief discussion – through Bardsey or round it? – and in no time we had shot through the sound. In a gale, under sail and with no engine to fall back on!

Cevamp was magnificent and surged through the waves, climbing easily up one side and hurtling down the other, crashing and slamming into the troughs with great thunderclaps of sound. On the crests the view was magnificent but down in the troughs all we could see around us was glassy green sea, with the curling white tips of the looming waves breaking over the top of the mast, more than thirty feet above our heads. Occasionally one of these monsters would crash over Cevamp's bows, sounding for all the world as though we'd run into a brick wall.

As I clung on I remembered touching wood earlier in the day. 'We haven't really had an adventure this holiday', I'd said cheerfully. I should have known better than to tempt the gods at sea. This was that adventure. And there was more to come.

28

The broken compass

Once through Bardsey Sound Mike asked if I wanted to moor up for the night at Aberdaron, less than an hour's sailing time away. I was tired and tempted. But although we were both feeling drained after the gale I felt if we were going to stop anywhere it should be Pwllheli, about twenty miles or so across the bay. Even so, I knew how much Mike wanted to get Cevamp back to Porthmadog so I said I was happy to go the full distance if he was.

By this time we'd already been at sea for about ten hours and I really didn't relish the thought of struggling on through the night for at least another eight. But if I had my doubts, I kept them to myself as usual. Although the wind had dropped it was still hard going, with big lumpy seas, and there had been further gale warnings.

'The only thing is...' I hesitated. 'I am a bit anxious about going up the shallow channel into Porthmadog in these heavy seas. Don't you think there's a risk we'll bump the bottom over the bar?'

'I suppose there is but if it's low water when we arrive we'll drop anchor at the Fairway buoy.'

'Yes but you haven't forgotten it's dark and the anchor light isn't working, have you?'

'No, I haven't. But we can always use the steaming light as a substitute to see us through what will be left of the night once we get there.'

We trundled on and on and on. I got cold and we were both desperately tired. We could see the lights of Abersoch, Pwllheli, Butlins holiday camp and even Criccieth twinkling along the shore line, tantalisingly close. I went inside around midnight to get warm, and fell asleep. An hour and a half later I woke up.

'Where are we?'

'That's Pwllheli, that's the holiday camp, that's Criccieth and I think I can see the castle mound.'

My heart sank. All this time and still only at Pwllheli! That meant at least another four hours. I began to feel I'd had enough. Why weren't we sailing round the Greek islands instead? This was a holiday? A nightmare more like. I was fed up having nowhere comfortable to sit. I had a sore tail; I was cold, damp, tired, unwashed and had a headache. I was fed up banging my head and I was fed up banging my shins and I was fed up having to walk around with a tuck in my neck. I was sick of the way my bobble hat made my hair go flat and straight. I wanted a hot bath, some perfume, clothes that weren't scruffy soggy trousers and a warm bed with dry pillows that didn't smell of wet anchor rope.

I sat huddled in misery and time dragged interminably on. Neither of us spoke much. Mike felt just the same, I know, and probably even worse because he hadn't slept at all. From time to time I saw his head nod and his chin drop onto his chest, before he jerked back upright and carried on peering into the black night around us. Neither of us spoke our thoughts but I think they were much the same.

At about two thirty, or maybe later, I roused myself enough to speak.

'If that's Criccieth, where's Harlech?'

Mike dismissed the question with a simple statement.

'Can't see Harlech.'

I accepted it.

'What are those lights over there then?' I asked.

'I think they're the lights of the main road that runs along behind Black Rock Sands.'

Again, I accepted it. It seemed the wrong place to me, for Black Rock Sands, but he knew the coastline better than I did and I'm wrong so often that he must have been right. Just the same, the contours didn't look right to me. And there was no sign of the flashing light of the Porthmadog Fairway buoy.

'Have a look at the chart on the Harlech side for a beacon with red lights.' It was an order more than a request. I did. It wasn't there.

'I'm not happy with the compass. It says we're going south when we're actually going north' Mike grumbled.

'That's funny,' I thought. 'Compasses aren't usually wrong.'

I took a deep breath.

'You don't think perhaps we've taken a wrong turning and we're not where we think we are – too far over, perhaps?' I ventured tentatively.

'We're on a boat, dear, not a road. You don't take wrong turnings at sea.'

Wounded, I kept quiet.

We still couldn't spot the Fairway buoy and still hadn't identified the beacon that Mike had seen on the land ahead. Eventually, at 3 am, he made a decision.

'The compass must be broken. I think the best thing we can do is put the anchor down and try and get some sleep till it gets light.'

'But compasses don't just break. I'll check with the hand-held one.'

The little blue hand-held compass put us on the same bearing.

'Well that one must be broken too.'

'But …'

'That's the only explanation.'

He was adamant

So we dropped the anchor and fell into bed, in all our clothes, still unwashed and still not having even cleaned our teeth. I could feel Mike lying tense beside me. It was a rough night and despite our fatigue we got little sleep. The boat was banging around and at one point Mike leapt out of bed and started lifting the floorboards.

'What's up now?' I groaned.

'We're in serious trouble. I think we might be sinking. That last bump sounded like a bilge keel hitting the bottom. I think it's been ripped off and now we're flooding.'

Of course it hadn't and we weren't. It was just exhaustion playing tricks with his mind. Once he was thoroughly satisfied we weren't about to be consigned to a watery grave he climbed wearily back into bed but I know he didn't sleep and by quarter to six he was up again. I heard him put the sails up and bring the anchor in and, selfishly leaving him to it, I slept soundly for another two hours, waking only at the insistent sound of the kettle whistling and Mike rattling around with mugs and teapot.

Rubbing my eyes in the sunlight and yawning loudly, I scrambled out into the cockpit and gazed around.

'Where are we?' I asked.

'On our way to Porthmadog,' he said, vague and imprecise. Not like Mike at all. I tried again.

'But where were we, then, last night, when we put the anchor down?'

'Erm…you aren't going to believe this. We were lucky not to run aground on Sarn Badrig, the causeway. We managed to cross it during the night without realising where we were and by the time we dropped anchor we were well south of Barmouth, not far from Aberdovey. Those red lights you couldn't find on the chart came from the navigation beacon at Llanbedr airfield. I must have nodded off when you were down below asleep and that's why we missed Porthmadog.'

Ah. So it was my fault then.

29

Proposal

Saturday morning in the garden room. This was just a posh name for the half brick, half glazed extension Mike had built onto the back of his 1950s semi in High Wycombe. I was wearing a grey towelling dressing gown. It started life as pink but was now very old, very shapeless and very...well...grey.

My face was partially concealed by large sunglasses – my hay fever always started in March and my itchy early morning eyes were swollen to golf ball proportions. We were eating breakfast. Weak Earl Grey tea, hot buttered toast and blackcurrant jam. The heat of the toast had caused the butter and jam to melt and slide over the edges. Some was trickling down my chin; more was clinging to the drab fibres of the unspeakable dressing gown. To be honest, I looked a mess. Pale face, scarecrow hair, stubbly shins and big, bare, bony feet.

Mike was wearing his old brown dressing gown that I hated. It was a relic from his first marriage. He wiped the last of the toast crumbs from his plate with his finger, which he then licked. He coughed. Then he cleared his throat.

'What would you think about getting married?' he said.

We'd been together for three years, living together for

a year. The M-word had never been mentioned between us.

I choked on my toast. Regurgitated tea bubbled from my mouth and nostrils and ran down my chin.

'You do say some funny things,' I spluttered.

'Well,' he said, 'I've had a couple of accidents lately and I'd hate for something to happen to me and you not get the police widow's pension.'

That was Mike. Practical as they come. But it was true. He had had a few lucky escapes. We were less than a quarter of the way through the year and he'd already had three potentially serious accidents. The first two happened when we returned from our skiing holiday at the end of January to find corrugated asbestos sheets from the garage roof lying in pieces on the back lawn, the result of a gale while we were away.

'I'll build a new one,' declared Action Man. 'This is a good opportunity to put a ridge roof on the garage. I never did like that old flat one.' But it isn't easy putting heavy roof trusses up single-handed and he fell off, twice in one day, each time suffering nothing worse than a few bruises and serious loss of dignity. But his most recent mishap was the most frightening and it was only the previous afternoon that I'd brought him home from spending three days lying motionless in a hospital bed. He'd been playing squash on the Tuesday night and got whacked in the eye by a squash ball. They can travel at well over a hundred and fifty miles an hour and in the past I'd occasionally seen bruises on Mike's arms and thighs where he'd been caught by one during a game. The night the ball got him in the eye the pain was intense enough to knock him to the ground. As we sat wordlessly gripping each other's hands in the hospital corridor while we waited for the eye specialist to arrive, we were both convinced he would be blinded. Thankfully, his eye was only bruised and he made a full recovery. It didn't stop him, playing squash, though.

Not wanting to risk any rights to the police widow's pension either, I sensibly accepted his unconventional proposal.

Later that morning he spoke to the registrar.

'I'd like to get married next Saturday. Can you book me in?' he asked.

'Sorry,' came the reply. 'We're fully booked that day. I've got a space the following week, though, if that would suit you.'

'Okay,' said Mike. 'I'll take that one. But could you let me know if you get a cancellation in the meantime?'

The wedding, at High Wycombe register office, was a quiet affair, which was just how we wanted it. My twenty-four year old daughter Sarah, who lived in London, and my old colleague Maureen were witnesses, my son Alex had a weekend home from school to be best man at the age of sixteen and the only other guest was my best friend, Lesley, whom I had known since our children were babies. She arrived out of the blue and I was delighted to see her. We'd always enjoyed a near-telepathic friendship so I wasn't surprised that we'd chosen similar outfits for my wedding.

After the ceremony we went home with our guests, drank champagne, ate chocolate cake and laughed at my memories of the day we met. Especially at the bit about 'I'm Inspector Williamson and it's my job to get rid of you lot as quickly as possible.' Our wedding was exactly three years after the day we met, on the weekend of poll tax riots in London and an earthquake in other parts of the country, and he hasn't got rid of me yet!

Two days later I was back at work and Mike was back

in Kent for the second week of a two week public order training course.

We delayed our honeymoon until the middle of May, when we drove to Poole in Dorset. Once there, we joined three strangers and an instructor on board a thirty four foot Sadler yacht, Sea Hawk of Rockley, for a Royal Yachting Association practical sailing course. We sailed in Poole harbour, Lyme Bay and over to Alderney in the Channel Islands, where we treated ourselves to Guernsey sweaters, and at the end of the week Mike was signed up as a coastal skipper. I, to my everlasting astonishment, was now officially a day skipper. And I had the certificate to prove it.

We enjoyed the company of the other sailors on the Sadler, but I wasn't so keen on the boat itself. I was seasick for the first and only time in my sailing career as we crossed Lyme Bay in a headwind. I blamed the yacht, and vowed never to set foot on a Sadler again. After all, I was never sick in Cevamp. It had to be the yacht's fault.

For the second week of our honeymoon we went back to Wales, visited Mike's parents and sisters and enjoyed a few precious days in our own company. We sailed round to Barmouth and Aberdovey in glorious weather, were visited by at least seven dolphins, gave lots of custom to all the bakers and gorged ourselves on fish and chips. What more could a pair of newlyweds wish for?

30

'Of course you'll enjoy sailing'

Question. How do you convince a reluctant, hitherto land-bound adolescent that a long weekend sailing with his mother and step-father will be more fun, more exciting and, above all, more cool than a weekend hanging around street corners with his mates?

Answer. You don't. You don't even try. You know you're on to a loser even before you frame the words. Words such as 'character forming' and 'challenging' and 'pitting yourself against the elements' have no place in the vocabulary or lifestyle of the average 14-year-old boy. It's a situation that demands positive action on your part. It's time to be assertive. You know that however logical you are he'll never understand or agree with your reasons for not letting him stay at home on his own. You'd be wasting your breath to try. It's one of those times when a brisk 'because I say so – pack your bag' saves you time and energy and, with a bit of luck, puts paid to one of those long-winded arguments that usually ends with you giving in because you're too exhausted to fight on. The sort of situation that any parent can tell you is never better exploited than when the chief protagonist is a teenager.

'Of course you'll enjoy sailing,' we told him.

'Of course you will,' we repeated. We'd almost convinced ourselves.

And so the three of us arrived at Porthmadog on a mild and muggy Thursday evening: my son Alex, less than enthusiastic about being there; Mike less than enthusiastic about having him there and me, hoping against hope that we'd all have a brilliant weekend, that Alex would turn into a committed yachtie overnight and that he and Mike would actually find they had something, other than me, in common. Ever the optimist.

After spending a couple of hours ferrying stores and luggage over the sand and fast rising water, followed by a vigorous pumping out of Cevamp's bilges, Alex was decidedly under-impressed with his first night as a sailor. It didn't help that he had to sleep in the slightly cramped and stuffy forecabin, where he hadn't the headroom to sit up in bed or stand up out of it.

'Where's the toilet?' he wanted to know.

'There it is.' We pointed to our trusty bucket.

'Hmph.'

Alex was at that stage in his life where much of his spoken communication was in the form of monosyllabic grunts. It worried me a little. It worried him not at all. All his mates could, apparently, understand him. Most of them communicated in Neanderthal grunts, too. On this occasion, I took the grunt to mean that he was not too impressed with our sanitary fitments. He was none too impressed, either, at the sound of rain beating on the cabin roof all night. Or at being told it was time to get up at what to him, on a weekend break from his Hertfordshire boarding school, was life-threateningly early.

'You'll enjoy it once we get going,' I told him. 'But can you just give Mike a hand fetching the diesel and fresh water, please, while I get on with making this stew and getting our sandwiches ready for lunch?'

Another grunt, but he helped out good-naturedly enough and we finally slipped our mooring shortly before noon. By then it had stopped raining. There was a gentle breeze and it was quite mild but the sky was still overcast and heavy.

We were heading for Porth Dinllaen and expected to arrive in the late afternoon or early evening. But before he committed himself, Mike wanted to be sure of the sea and weather conditions.

'Let's just motor out for a while and see what it's like. We won't put any sail up until we get clear of land."

Just over an hour later we had covered four miles and were barely making two knots. What with the wind blowing straight into our faces, the tide running against us and short lumpy seas, the hoped for day's sail to Porth Dinllaen was looking less and less likely. We rounded the fairway buoy, pointed Cevamp's nose back the way we'd come, put up a bit of genoa to help her on her way and she surged gratefully and speedily back to her mooring. We packed up and went home.

'Well,' I said to Alex brightly, 'what did you think of that?'

His reply was short and unequivocal. 'Not a lot.'

It was another two years before we were able to coax him back on board. A school trip to Scotland had introduced him to the Monroes, mountains in Scotland higher than 2,000 feet, and he was now keen on outdoor life. I know sailing wasn't quite the same as striding over the Scottish hillsides, but it had its similarities. Fresh air, for one. Changeable weather, for another. There the similarities stopped, but nonetheless Alex seemed happy enough to join us for a weekend in mid July and this time he didn't complain when we cast off from our mooring before seven on the first morning. I was so proud of my big, handsome son with his dark eyes and brooding good looks and desperately wanted him to enjoy his weekend.

Despite the very light airs we soon had both sails up and switched the engine off. It was already blisteringly hot and hazy and by the time we were ready to tuck into our bacon rolls we'd all stripped down to shorts and swimming costumes. We were on our second cup of coffee when we heard a sound alongside. A slight splash and a gentle puff of air. Dolphins. Three of them. We knocked the coffee cups over in our excitement as we rushed to the side of the boat, watching as they rose from the water, fixed us with their gentle eyes and smiled at us before submerging again.

I defy anyone not to be moved by the sight of these entrancing, mercurial creatures and even as I rushed for the camera I found myself on the brink of tears. They were so friendly, so intelligent, and there was almost a tangible sense of communication between us. They stayed for a while, swimming alongside and under Cevamp, arching from the water, each in perfect time with the other two. We watched, mesmerised, silent. Then they were gone.

The morning grew hotter and ever more still. Cevamp was wallowing. Her sails were drooping and we were going nowhere. Alex set himself adrift in the dinghy, Mike went for a swim and I lazed on cushions in the sun. Then we spotted five more dolphins, this time a little further off. Mike and I watched from Cevamp's decks. Alex paddled out into the heat haze towards them but the animals had lost interest in us and vanished. He paddled moodily back to the boat and spent the rest of the day in the cabin, reading.

'You'd think he'd want to do something,' grumbled Mike. 'I've been trying to get him interested but he just doesn't want to know.'

I smouldered at Mike's criticism of my son and heir. Not everyone wants to be Chay Blyth, I thought. Alex had other things he was interested in. Why did Mike assume that just because he liked doing something, everyone else would like it too? But I kept my thoughts to myself. With one notable exception, when I lost my temper with him on an American ski slope, we didn't have arguments and I wasn't sure I could conduct one without saying something I would regret, or, worse, risking Mike saying something horrible to me.

That evening saw us tied against the harbour wall at Barmouth, a popular holiday destination nestling between a mountain range and the sea on the mouth of the river Mawddach. One of Barmouth's claims to fame is that the town is the starting point for the Barmouth to Fort William Three Peaks Race, in which super-fit competitors sail the three hundred and eighty nine miles from Wales to England and then on to Scotland, climbing the UK's three highest mountains en route. Snowdon, Scafell Pike and Ben Nevis total more than eleven thousand feet of climbing and seventy two miles running so it's not a task for the faint-hearted.

It's other, generally less well known but equally as interesting attraction was the unofficial nudist beach at Morfa Dyffryn. I prudishly deemed this inappropriate for the eyes of a young adolescent male and although we didn't grace it with our presence on this occasion I did wonder whether it lay behind the RAF's continuing use of its single-runway airfield at nearby Llanbedr as a re-fuelling station.

Barmouth is also the home of the two-mile Fairbourne

and Barmouth Railway track. Originally laid in 1895 by Arthur McDougall, a member of the flour milling family, it was built to carry building materials for the nearby village of Fairbourne but these days it just carries visitors, holiday makers and railway buffs.

The evening was still warm and Alex decided to go for a walk up the mountains at the back of the town. My earlier annoyance with Mike forgotten, I suggested we went for a stroll around the attractive old town and over Barmouth Bridge. It was a lovely evening and we took our time, watching the oystercatchers in the mud at the water's edge and taking photographs of the final embers of the setting sun.

We returned to Cevamp before it got dark and went to bed. There was still no sign of Alex. I was getting worried.

'What if he's had an accident and broken his leg or ankle or something? No-one knows where he is. How would we find him?'

'Oh stop panicking you old mother hen. He's a big boy now. He'll come back when he's ready.'

'It's all right for you to say don't worry. You've never had children. You don't know what it's like.'

I lay there fretting and getting annoyed with Mike again. Then, through the open cabin door, in the failing light, I saw a figure scrambling up a cliff face high above Barmouth. Alex. Reassured, I fell asleep and never even heard him climb back on board when he eventually returned to Cevamp, both legs and ankles fully intact. The rest of that hot, airless weekend passed uneventfully. We sailed and motor sailed in blazing sunshine from Barmouth to Abersoch and back again, with Mike still grumpy at Alex's lack of enthusiasm and me still pretending with brittle cheerfulness that everyone was having a lovely time. I felt like Jennifer Aldridge in The

Archers, who spends most of her time brightly papering over the cracks of her dysfunctional family.

Four weeks later the three of us were back in Wales, a little older and much wiser. This time we all had a wonderful couple of days. Mike and I sailed goose-winged in perfect conditions to Abersoch, St Tudwals Islands and Pwhelli while Alex spent a wild weekend mountain biking, drinking beer and watching movies at an outdoor activity centre in Snowdonia.

Life was perfect again.

31

Troubled waters

We'd never had a good night's sleep in Abersoch and this was no exception. Cevamp was on a swinging mooring in the bay but she refused to swing and we spent the night with the wind battering against her sides. This was probably caused by the wind blowing against a strong tidal stream but knowing the reason did little to alleviate the misery of a very long night. Waves slapped noisily against Cevamp's stout hull as she heaved herself over them, and a cracked egg rolled irritatingly around the worktop until Mike could stand it no longer and trapped it in a cup.

We both slept intermittently and my discomfort was exacerbated by excruciating pain in my lower back. It flared up for no apparent reason the previous day and did not, I thought miserably, bode well for our summer holiday.

It was August Bank Holiday weekend and we were on our way to Ireland, our first long trip on Cevamp as husband and wife. We had nearly three weeks ahead of us and, as we'd told friends, family and colleagues, we were planning to 'sail the Atlantic and do the Fastnet'.

Not the race, of course. I don't think a handicap exists that would enable the workmanlike Cevamp to take a meaningful part in the six hundred mile biennial dash from Cowes, round the rock and back to Plymouth via the Scillies. We were just going to have a leisurely cruise. Nevertheless, Mike is quite a target-driven sort of person. We had to have something to aim for. What, we thought, could be better than the notorious Fastnet Rock?

'But that's quite dangerous isn't it,' said my sister when she heard our plans. 'Wasn't there a really bad disaster there a few years ago?'

'You're thinking of the Fastnet Race in 1979,' I told her. 'But that was mainly because of a terrible storm that blew in from America and created freak conditions. We're just going for a bit of gentle cruising and to visit a part of Ireland that we haven't seen before.'

Nonetheless, it gave me pause for thought and reminded me that however carefully we made our plans, however knowledgeable and experienced we liked to think we were becoming, nature still calls all the shots.

The race for the 1979 Fastnet Challenge Cup started in near perfect conditions on August 13. With three hundred and three yachts taking part, it was the biggest entry in the fifty-four year history of the race. But conditions worsened dramatically. Over the next three days the fleet battled against the worst storm ever to hit a British yacht race. One hundred and thirty six crew members were rescued, only eighty-five yachts finished the race and twenty-three vessels were lost or abandoned. Fifteen sailors lost their lives.

So perhaps my sister was right to be concerned. But as we prepared to leave Abersoch on a sunny Bank Holiday Monday, nothing was further from our thoughts. Mike was feeling especially pleased with himself and was in the love phase of his love-hate relationship with Cevamp. He'd set up her Autohelm for the first time and fixed the throttle cable, which had been causing problems ever since we left Porthmadog two days earlier.

I was in high spirits too, despite the stabbing pain in my back every time I moved. We cast off from our mooring and were soon sailing among Abersoch's racing fleet. Mike concentrated on putting on as much of a show as possible as we wove our way through the other boats and I settled myself gingerly on some cushions to admire the view.

A blue haze hung over the distant mountains but the light in the bay had a startling clarity and made the houses on the shoreline appear to be much closer than they were. The sea was a kaleidoscope of colour as the racing crews raised and lowered filmy spinnakers in garish blues, reds and yellows. Everywhere I looked there were people enjoying the water. Jet skiers, speedboats, water skiers, fishing smacks and all types of sailboats were making the most of the weather and the holiday.

'It's lovely to see people enjoying the sea,' I said. 'And it's lovely to be part of it, too. It's as though Cardigan Bay is a big watery playground and this is just the sort of weather to make the most of it.'

I watched for a while longer. 'Thing is though, although it's good to see people enjoying themselves you wonder if they're all really aware of the possible danger, especially when they go so far out from shore. What would happen to those jet skiers round the headland or out on the islands if anything happened to them? And I'm not too keen on the noise they make, either, impinging on our silence.'

As usual, Mike didn't answer. He didn't need to really. He was focused on getting us safely through all the traffic and not really listening to me thinking aloud to myself.

It was mid-afternoon when we dropped anchor eleven sea-miles further on at Aberdaron and after paddling ashore on the windsurfer for an ice cream we returned to

Cevamp, prepared a stew for dinner and sat on deck for a while.

'It's like Brands Hatch out here.' Mike reflected my earlier observations. Again, there were water skiers, jet skis and speedboats towing fat inner tubes. Their passengers, wedged into the rubber doughnuts with their legs flopping disjointedly over the sides and arms waving uncontrollably in the air, screamed and laughed in exhilaration as they bounced over the waves. Not far away, some Neoprene-clad people were chugging around in a rigid inflatable boat and flying the A-flag to indicate they had divers down.

'I wonder how many of those whiz-bangers know what that flag means? How many of them actually slow down and look for the divers' bubbles or watch out for their surface buoys?' I asked. 'Not many, I bet. This bay's an accident waiting to happen.'

But there were no accidents that day, as far as we were aware at least, and by early evening all the jet skis had returned safely to shore. We were in bed by seven-thirty, planning to get up at around three the following morning to make the most of slack water through Bardsey Sound. Mike had been dogged by a headache all day and was apprehensive about going through the sound in the dark but I had less to worry about than he did, apart from my back, and was hoping to see phosphorescence in the water.

'The other reason for leaving in the early hours is that it's better to leave familiar waters in the dark and sail into strange ones in daylight,' said Mike. 'It's about fifty miles from Bardsey to Arklow. If we average, say, three knots, it will take sixteen or seventeen hours. So even if we leave at three, it'll still be early evening before we get there.'

'I know,' I said. 'And I'm not looking forward to it. It's going to be a long day and we're going to be shattered by the time we arrive. But if we want to go to Ireland, which we do, there's not really any alternative. We can hardly pull up in a lay-by for a rest.'

Another grim night. We slept fitfully until the alarm went off at three. However uncomfortable it was in bed, neither of us relished getting up and having to face the cold, damp, drizzly and pitch-dark morning.

We scalded our mouths on a mug of tea each and gave our teeth a perfunctory scrub. Then it was into warm clothes and oilies. Time to go. We motored out and I helmed while Mike kept a look out with a torch for pot buoys and shouted left a bit, right a bit to me. By the time we reached the entrance to the sound it was clear that whatever else it was, it was not slack water. Ghostly sheets of grey topped with sparkling silver and white crests rose up in front of the boat, glowing weirdly with phosphorescence and the light cast on them by the boat's navigation lights. We could see the beam of the lighthouse on Bardsey Island but the island itself was lost in darkness and it was impossible to judge how far out we were from the rocky headland.

'I'm sorry love, but I'm not happy to continue in these conditions,' said Mike. 'And I'm still not happy with the alternator. We're going back to Aberdaron.'

The alternator had been giving problems all summer, despite Mike's best efforts to sort it out, and I agreed with his decision. We turned Cevamp round and returned to Aberdaron, where we dropped the anchor and went back to bed. Mike was up again before six to catch the shipping forecast, which was predicting force six winds in Irish Sea and gales in Shannon.

'Well that's it then,' he declared firmly. 'We'll just have to give Ireland a miss for today. We're both tired; it's a long way and means arriving in a strange harbour at night. Let's spend the day in Porth Dinllaen then go on to Dickies at Bangor tomorrow to stock up on parts.'

Very sensible.

Half an hour later we were on our way to Ireland.

He'd had a sudden change of heart, reasoning that if the wind did freshen we might be stuck at Aberdaron for days.

It was, as we knew it would be, a long, tedious and, for me, painful day and we were both afflicted with an appalling lethargy that, despite piles of bacon sandwiches and frequent hot drinks, we were unable to shake off. The only good thing was the Autohelm. It had always been on the boat but this was the first time Mike had enough faith in it to allow it to take over the helm. It was a real boon, especially at meal times, as it meant that neither of us had to struggle with eating irons and tiller while we ate. For most of the day we were out of sight of land and had to rely on the compass and log to plot our estimated course on the chart. By late afternoon the lowering sun was dead ahead, confirming that we were at least heading west, and we calculated that, unless wind and tide had put us considerably off course, Arklow was lurking somewhere beneath it.

'People boast about channel crossings,' I said. 'We do the Irish Sea and it's twice as far.'

Mike was never as cocky as I was. 'I still find it daunting,' he admitted. 'If I hadn't already been across to Ireland and the Isle of Man with Dad I don't think I would do it.'

'Yes you would. The day would have been bound to come when pottering around in the bay wasn't enough for you. It's like climbing mountains – it's there so you do it.'

It was a wonderful crossing for me, apart from my backache. I had a good two-hour sleep and before that enjoyed helming while Mike rested. It was great sailing weather, with interesting seas, the wind blowing just right and the boat going well – and fast. But it wasn't so good for Mike. He still hadn't shaken off his headache and took his responsibility for the boat and our safety very seriously. For most of the day he was silent and withdrawn and, apart from tucking in to his bowl of beef stew with his habitual gusto, he was nothing like his usual self. It was a relief to both of us when, at ten thirty that evening, we finally tied Cevamp to a wooden trawler in the peace of Arklow's small working harbour and went to bed.

It rained heavily during the night but it had eased off by morning and we enjoyed the feel of the soft Irish rain on our bare faces as we got ready to go shopping after breakfast. We walked into town – or at least Mike walked, I limped, bent in pain – and waited for the shops to open, a haphazard process that began at around nine. We sat in the garden of rest, which was edged with old headstones and had a lawn, seats, flowerbeds and a bandstand looking down on the river. A sign displayed the summer band fixtures for the previous year.

What the town lacked in architectural charm, it made up for in history. During the Irish Rebellion of 1798 a Roman Catholic priest, Father Michael Murphy, led an army of twenty-thousand United Irishmen in an ill-fated bid to free the town from British suppression. Seven hundred of his men died during the ensuing battle and when, on the evening of June 9, the survivors heard Father Murphy had been killed by a canon ball they were so disheartened that they gave up, abandoning their plans to march on to Dublin.

Arklow has always been renowned for boatbuilding and fishing. Gypsy Moth III, the yacht in which Sir Francis Chichester won the first solo transatlantic yacht race in 1960, was built at John Tyrrell's famous boatyard and even now the Arklow Shipping Company maintains a fleet of nearly forty vessels. Two centuries ago Arklow was one of the main fishing ports in Ireland and fishing is still a significant industry in the town.

Back on Cevamp we spread our two new Irish charts over the bed.

'If we want to do the Fastnet as planned in a week, we'll have to sail about thirty miles a day for seven days,' said Mike.

'Well I do want to do the Fastnet, but that sounds quite demanding. I'm not sure if my back is up to it. And a lot will depend on winds and tides being in our favour.' For once I was the pessimist.

Mike carefully folded the charts and put them back in the chart table and we set off for a look round the famous Noritake Pottery. We decided it was asking for trouble to buy china while we were living on a yacht, even thought the Lunceford dinner and tea service really took our fancy and we could have bought the lot for less than £300.

We spent the rest of the afternoon having a walk along the Avoca River, the longest in Wicklow and said to be one of the more polluted rivers in Ireland. Then we visited the beaches. South beach was sandy and glistened with mother of pearl shells while the north beach was nothing more than a building site for a massive and ambitious land reclamation programme. Lorries trundled constantly back and forth late into the evening from a quarry in a distant mountain, laden with huge rocks to build sea defences.

We sat and watched big waves breaking over newly placed boulders and, seeing how they drained the sea of its force, I wondered why they hadn't been put there before. It made much more sense than building smooth sea walls and then watching them wash away a few years later.

When we got back from our walk we found a sixty-foot steamer moored between Cevamp and the trawler, placing us six boats out from the wall. Undine was a rich man's pleasure boat used for cruising the Scottish islands and the Thames. The two crew members on board were delivering her from Scotland to the Albert embankment, having just come down from the Skerries.

'Yes, she's beautiful,' they agreed, 'but she's not much use in a roll. No sails, and very slim.'

I admired the highly varnished mahogany and gleaming brasswork. 'Yeah,' said one of the men. 'But we don't bother much with that unless the owner's on board. You'd never have time to do anything else.'

Everywhere we went in Arklow, people were willing to stop and talk, with us and with each other. On board the freshly painted fishing boat next to Cevamp a good-natured man was wielding a paint brush.

'This boat's French,' he told us. 'Twenty-five years old, so she is. My nephew bought her but he hasn't trawled her yet because he doesn't have a licence. In any case, he's been drinking all weekend and he's back in the bar drinking again today,' he added cheerfully, 'not that I'm criticising his lack of forward planning and excessive drinking habits. Just stating the facts.'

I enjoy peering into trawlers and admire the men who put out in them. It's not an easy way to make a living.

Many of the fishing boats in Arklow harbour were old and wooden but well cared for, clean and tidy and several were having their paintwork touched up. Others, though, were smelly rusting old hulks, littered with dead fish, desiccated starfish, decaying nets and weatherworn tackle, tired relics from better days.

'It comes in for six hours and goes out for six hours,' offered a knowledgeable redheaded man of Irish descent from Enfield, who had joined us on the sea wall to watch five local yachts take part in an evening's racing. They ranged from a humble twenty four footer to a flashy racing Sigma 38. But when you only have five boats you can't break them down into classes and Mike guessed they would be working a handicap system. Our new friend was anxious to impart every bit of wisdom he could, from sharing his knowledge of yacht racing techniques to telling us about the secret worship places of Arklow of old.

'Have you heard about the Ancient Romans?' he asked us seriously.

Earlier in the day we'd seen a big boat with tan sails, sailing some distance off. It turned out to be the Ocean Yacht Club's Greater Manchester Challenge, looking slightly more the worse for wear than when we'd last seen her a year ago in the Isle of Man. While we were watching the racing she motored out of the harbour.

'I hope she puts her sails up,' said Mike. 'It would be nice to see her under sail at close quarters.'

She continued motoring and was soon out of sight.

'It's too windy. That's why she isn't sailing,' said the knowledgeable redheaded man.

'Well all the other boats are sailing quite happily,' Mike pointed out.

For the first time that evening, the man was lost for words.

It was getting chilly so we scrambled back down the wall of the Roadstone Jetty, picked our way carefully across the five other boats, I eased myself gratefully back onto Cevamp and we had another early night, ready to leave after the early morning forecast.

But we didn't. We went back to sleep and finally left for Rosslare around nine, after dire warnings from a couple in a yacht rafted up to us – there was now a raft of eight – that it would be a difficult and long sail unless we had wind and tide with us. We had neither but set out undaunted.

'You be careful.' The man's tone was sombre. 'There'll be some big rollers out there.'

They'd already been waiting for three days for what the husband called the right conditions to sail to Wicklow so we didn't give a great deal of credence to what he said. And in any case, my backache was making me ratty, less tolerant of other people – totally unlike my usual easy-going self.

We sailed best part of the way there, almost straight into the wind so it was hard going, uncomfortable and every slam of the boat caused me to wince in pain. It was a flat and boring coastline with headland after headland after headland and when you got to them there was nothing worth seeing. There were no recognisable landmarks so I spent best part of the day wondering, and Mike worrying, where we were. The chart was littered with buoys and we spent a lot of time straining our eyes and peering at the horizon for them.

We were both tired and my back was getting worse by the hour. Every movement was agony and I couldn't get comfortable. Mike had the additional strain of navigating in unfamiliar waters in a very shoaly area and he was still quiet and withdrawn. We motor sailed the last twenty or so miles to Rosslare in reasonably good time and Mike surprised me by extolling the praises of motor sailing.

'Perhaps we'll have a look at motor-sailers at the boat show next year. There's something to be said for being sheltered while you're helming and having the engine take some of the strain.'

Now the engine was on Cevamp steadied up a bit and to try to take my mind off my back I decided to make some rock cakes for afternoon tea. Despite the engine being on, the boat was still heeled over and bouncing so I sat on the floor to do them. Every time I opened a locker plates and saucepans flew out and the vibration of the engine made the dial on the scales jiggle about to the point of being useless. The best that can be said of the resulting buns was that they were hot, sweet and fruity. Mike even managed a smile when he saw them.

By the time we reached Rosslare harbour we'd had enough and my back was worse than ever. We tied to the west wall, the other side from the ferries Munster and Felicity, and then poked our heads into the lorry drivers' rest room to get directions to the nearest fish and chip shop.

'You go through the customs shed, over the railway, up the embankment, over a fence, up a steep footpath and down the side of the hotel,' said a freckle faced Irish driver. By the time we got there my back was throbbing and I felt like a cripple. We sat on a seat and looked down on the harbour while we ate our supper.

'Isn't it amazing,' I pondered, 'that we arrived inside the custom area but no one bothered about us. You'd think they'd be really strict about security and want to check for arms and drugs and stuff.'

Back on Cevamp Mike made up the bed and I creaked my way into it. The most comfortable position, I found, was lying on my back with my feet on the ceiling, which wasn't quite as Karma Sutra as it sounds.

'If you're no better in the morning we're going home,' Mike said. 'You can't carry on like this.'

'Oh no,' I wailed. 'We've hardly started our holiday. I'm sure it'll settle down in a day or two.'

But he was in no mood to argue. 'We've got to be sensible. We've still got a long way to go and you're in no fit state for sailing. See how you are in the morning.'

'Oh yes,' I thought resentfully. 'We abandon the holiday and it'll be all my fault. I'm not enjoying this backache any more than he is. I'm beginning to wish we hadn't come away in the first place. '

Mike climbed into bed beside me and I pointedly turned my back on him. He did not attempt to snuggle up to me, as he usually did, and we lay there, maintaining the gap between us and an uncomfortable silence, until we fell asleep.

32

Sailing by

Even in daylight Rosslare Harbour hasn't got a lot going for it. Perhaps that's unfair as we didn't see much of it. But what we did see wasn't particularly scenic, just hotels on a hill overlooking the harbour, the terminal buildings and the daily comings and goings of the two big ferries.

I was dimly aware that I'd set the alarm far too early and dozed through snatches of Rule Britannia before falling asleep again and missing the shipping forecast for Lundy and Fastnet.

The first thing I did when I woke up was to test for pain. To my relief it was nowhere near as bad as it had been. Back on speaking terms again, we decided to carry on to Dunmore East, about thirty miles away.

'I'll do all the heavy work today and you rest your back,' Mike said. 'Give it another day and it should be stronger by tomorrow. In any case, this is our last long haul till we head for home, then we'll be able to relax a bit more.'

'Good,' I said. 'A bit of harbour hopping will be nice. It's what I like best, arriving in new harbours and soaking up the atmosphere.'

We motor-sailed along mile after mile of sweeping sandy beaches and celebrated the turn to west at about midday with bars of Marks and Spencer Irish coffee chocolate. Despite the niggling thought that perhaps the

Fastnet may have been a bit ambitious in the time we had available and wondering aloud whether we would make it after all, Mike had got over his moodiness of the previous few days and was back to normal, singing, whooping and talking to himself.

Not that I could hear him properly. I'd discovered a wonderful new place to sit, right out on the bowsprit, and all I could hear was the whoosh and splash of the waves.

'This is better than a funfair,' I called as Cevamp's bows climbed high out of the water to the top of the big rollers and then dropped in a stomach-leaping plunge down into the trough.

'Thought your back was hurting,' he called to me.

'It is, but it's heaps better now,' I shouted back. 'I'm on the mend.'

As we approached Hook Head I felt intuitively that it would be nice round the headland and it was. The wide estuary running the five miles or so into Waterford was the gateway to the Southern Ireland of my imagination. But we scarcely had a chance to admire the view before it was snatched away from us as the weather closed in, the mists swirled down and we couldn't even see the harbour wall, let alone the lighthouse on Hook Head or the twin towers on Brownstown Head over to the west.

We pulled on our oilskins just in time to prevent ourselves getting a soaking but then, to our shared relief, the downpour stopped as suddenly as it started, leaving the land ahead of us sparkling and fresh in the stark light that often follows rain.

We were entranced with Dunmore East and its tightly packed little harbour. It was crammed with yachts, a motley collection of fishing smacks with bright scraps of mizzen sails and big trawlers with wonderful names, such as Frederikja and the heroic Father Murphy. Once we'd rafted Cevamp up to five other yachts in varying states of decay we were able to look properly at our surroundings and our enchantment with the place deepened. A steep roadway led up from the harbour, lined with colourful terraced and walled gardens on the left and dropping steeply away to Stony Cove on the right. Two men with a donkey and cart walked down the hill towards us.

'Which way is the nearest shop?' Mike asked them.

'That way,' they said in unison, one pointing left, the other pointing right.

We laughed. We had to be in Ireland.

We found the village shop at the top of the hill, where we asked for directions to the town centre. We turned right as directed, down another lane lined with flowering shrubs, fuchsia, and privet and an almost indecent profusion of low roofed thatched cottages. We came to a huddle of pubs, hotels, restaurants, a health centre and another shop. Not exactly the town centre we were expecting.

The girl in the shop told us the town centre was back the way we'd come. We'd clearly misinterpreted the directions and should have turned left, not right. She was typically Irish looking and spoke in what we'd come to recognise as the soft, lilting Irish accent of these parts. She had dark, almost black hair curling into ringlets around her neck, large grey eyes fringed with dark lashes, ivory skin speckled with freckles, a delicately sculpted nose and a sweet Irish mouth. My immediate instinct was to get Mike away from her. Fast. I thanked the girl and rushed him out of the shop.

'What's the hurry?'

'Oh, nothing. It was a bit warm in there for me, that's all.'

We walked a bit further. 'She was pretty, wasn't she?' I said with as much nonchalance as I could muster.

'Who?'

'The girl in the shop.'

'Never noticed,' he claimed. That's my husband, Chivalrous to a fault. I said no more, just held more tightly onto his hand.

As we walked back the view over the sea was breath-taking. Red cliffs dropped into small sandy coves with yachts bobbing around on the still water, now a steely dark Atlantic grey and nothing like the limpid green of the Irish Sea.

Back in the harbour we came across two ice processing plants (one new, one old), the harbour master's office (he was out), the site of a unique nesting colony of kittiwakes (now deserted), a yacht club (closed) and spotless toilets (unlocked) with sparkling basins complete with plugs on chains, pristine mirrors and hot and cold water. At the lifeboat station we read the notices to mariners, posted by the magnificently named Fionan S. O'Muircheartaigh and were delighted to see a sign on the door offering showers at fifty pence a time.

The lifeboat St Patrick was moored on the water. It was, I thought, a fitting name for a lifeboat since the blessed saint obviously spent much of his time inventing ways of testing the faith of the sailors, what with his causeway off Barmouth and his bridge off Crossfarnoge Point.

Back on Cevamp we got talking to the owner of Shadana, one of the yachts in our raft. He told us he bought the thirty-one foot Nicholson the previous year and she'd previously sailed in an expedition to the Arctic.

By this time the sun was well over the yardarm so we enjoyed civilised gin and tonics on deck while the chilli con carne was cooking, and then went for a walk to work up an appetite. The harbour is an interesting structure and a wonderful playground. It doesn't dry and is built on concrete columns, which go right back under the road, forming dark caverns.

'Just the place for an adventure,' I said, thinking of Arthur Ransome and Enid Blyton as I watched a couple of dinghy-loads of small boys rowing around and shrieking in the darkness.

'Or a body,' said Mike, heading back for his chilli.

After dinner we sat on deck and watched the sun go down.

'It's so lovely,' I sighed. 'Why don't we stay here tomorrow? We could play in the bay, do some windsurfing, get our laundry done, maybe even get a bus to Waterford and visit the crystal factory.'

Mike thought about it. 'It's tempting. But I think we'd be better to press on, weather permitting, and spend time here on the way back. This is only one place to take our fancy. Who knows how many more there are, especially once we get further west?'

Just then a man called to us from the wall. 'Do you need diesel?' His cut-glass public school accent was strangely at odds with his scruffy appearance.

'Yes,' said Mike, pointing to our empty five gallon can. 'We do. I'd been wondering where we'd be able to get some.'

'Give me your can then, and I'll fill it up for you.'

Fifteen minutes later his battered old car pulled up in the harbour.

'That'll be £2.40,' he said. 'Don't worry if you haven't got the right change. Just give me the nearest you've got.'

Mike handed over a handful of coins, humped the now full fuel can back across the raft of boats and the man disappeared in a cloud of fumes.

'Two pounds forty for five gallons of diesel. That's incredibly cheap,' I said.

'Yes,' said Mike, suddenly all policeman. 'Suspiciously so. And what's more, I think it's the wrong colour. I think we may have been a bit too trusting there. I wonder where it's come from.'

'Well there's not much you can do about it now,' I said. 'Let's go to bed and worry about it later.'

Once the night time sounds of the harbour had died away we slept well. We were up, dressed and breakfasted by six and ready to go. Cevamp had other ideas.

'Bloody alternator belt's slipping again,' grumbled Mike, hauling his tool box out of the cockpit locker. He made yet more adjustments to the offending belt. Nothing happened. He tried crank starting the engine. Still nothing. Re-adjusted the belt. Cranked the engine again. Success.

We were all set. Just as I was about to release the final rope, four men on a Benettau in the next raft down asked for a tow out of the harbour as they had no engine at all. Of course, we obliged and I felt quite proud of our chunky little boat going to the rescue of the fancy yacht. Once we were clear of the harbour we set her free, raised the main and motor sailed into the wind towards Youghal.

The further west we went, the more picturesque the scenery became, with mountains silhouetted above the land, wide estuaries sweeping out into the sea and even the occasional castle. There was more wildlife to watch, too, including a big seal with a fish writhing in his mouth and his audience of seagulls, hanging around for easy pickings.

'How's your back today,' asked Mike.

'A bit fragile but much better, thanks,' I said.

'Well take it easy again today. You don't want to take any chances with it.'

I took him at his word, and lounged around the cockpit eating chocolate while he fitted the Autohelm, controlled the sails and kept watch. The only thing to rouse me from my sun induced stupor was his shout of 'dolphins.' We rushed onto the bows, lay on our stomachs with our arms over the sides and watched as five, possibly six dolphins flashed through the silky water of our bow wave and gave a brief display before slipping astern and disappearing. A flock of gulls was hovering nearby so we guessed the dolphins just saw us a momentary distraction from the important business of feeding.

We knew the tidal stream would be with us but were still staggered at the difference it made to our passage time. We covered an unbelievable thirty plus miles in the first four and a half hours and although we always say we're not interested in racing or speed we recognised that an extra couple of knots is the difference between making a harbour or not, and arriving somewhere fresh rather than exhausted.

Mid-afternoon saw us motoring into Youghal, but not before an Irish fisherman in yellow oilskins waved and shouted a warning to us from his boat. At first we couldn't work out what he was on about. Then we realised. There were miles of long-line nets on the approaches to Youghal and we were obliged to make a two mile detour to get round them.

Youghal was nice, just as the man on the Nicholson had said it would be. Lying in the mouth of the estuary to the Blackwater River, it's an ancient walled town with buildings dating back to the early thirteenth century. As we motored gently around looking for a mooring, a small man with sunshades protruding from his spectacles appeared on the wall. He said he was once a member of the harbour committee and advised us to tie up in Mall Dock, a tiny harbour with walls on three sides and a sandy beach. Children were squealing and splashing around at the water's edge and as we secured our mooring warps to a ladder against the harbour wall we realised Cevamp was turning into something of an attraction. At least half a dozen people came over to talk and to warn us the harbour dried out.

In the town an eighteenth century clock tower straddled the narrow street, which was lined on each side with small, individually owned shops. We bought meat and vegetables then as we headed back to the boat we heard whoops and cheers and car horns blaring. People stopped and lined the street then a long stream of cars drove merrily through. It was a wedding procession. The bridal limo was unsubtly decked out in ribbons and flowers and the newly-weds were obviously enjoying it all, leaning out of the windows, laughing and waving.

Back on Cevamp we sat on deck and watched the tide go out. As the water got shallower it turned black with literally millions of sprats. It was impossible to see a space between them. They flashed silver from time to time, flicking over and out of the water in a wide swathe that seemed to be following a definite path around the boat and the harbour wall.

We'd seen a garage in town and Mike decided to take a sample of the dodgy diesel for them to have a look at.

'Oh that's nothing to worry about.' The garage man was reassuring. 'It's agricultural diesel. You can use that no problem.' We took his word for it and topped up Cevamp's tank before refilling the can. This time it was £6 for the five gallons, reinforcing Mike's doubts about the legitimacy of the Dunmore diesel. ''I think the origins of that diesel were distinctly dubious,' he said. 'Do you remember that programme on television about the customs men and the fuel scam? This is a mirror image of that episode.'

I couldn't understand his anxiety. As far as I could tell the origins of the diesel were no more dubious than the origins of our Tinker dinghy, and he'd never had any obvious qualms about that.

We had a bottle of wine, polished off the last of the chilli and were in bed by nine, relieved the beach and harbour-side was gradually beginning to quieten down and the three lads on jet skis had packed up in the face of gathering gloom. We'd noticed that many of the pubs and bars were advertising live music and wondered how much of it would float down to Mall Dock, but we had a peaceful night, other than a couple who came to exercise their yellow Labrador on the beach at two in the morning.

We liked Youghal. It was a big town compared with Dunmore East but was still a community and it had a nice feel to it. I found it easy to imagine a young Irish man or woman moving from there to London, say, and being totally bewildered. Even so, it didn't have the appeal of Dunmore East for me and I wouldn't have been too bothered if we didn't call in on our way back.

We woke up in time for the shipping forecast, for once, and by six-thirty we were motor sailing into a mild, damp, misty and windless morning. We were hoping to make Kinsale in time for Sunday dinner but were making such good progress, despite another detour to avoid half a mile of fishing nets, that we decided to carry on to Glandore, said to be one of the prettiest villages in Cork.

By mid-morning the sun had broken through and we were sailing cheerfully past headland after headland. Many of them were topped with castles, churches, towers and forts, bearing silent witness to centuries of troubled history. It was a rocky coastline and there were lots of lighthouses, too, including a black-painted one.

I was fascinated, as ever, by the sea. 'This Atlantic changes colour hour by hour, day by day,' I observed. 'Look how it's gone from a dark, steely grey a week ago to a deep bottle green last week and now today it's navy blue. It's not as cold as you might expect either. I suppose that's thanks to the Gulf Stream. Where does it flow, anyway?'

'Dunno,' said Mike. 'Round here somewhere. Or is it Scotland?'

It was a pleasant, lazy day. I sat around reading, writing, heating soup for lunch and preparing our Sunday roast for later. Once again, Mike made the most of the Autohelm and spent most of his time picking out and identifying every ship, boat, buoy and charted feature he could. The binoculars were in constant use. At one point he saw a brief flash of two dolphins but this time they kept their distance.

With its wooded, steep sided estuary, big houses, castles, church and still harbour, Glandore, was a beautiful place to moor for the night. We hooked up to a buoy just outside the tiny enclosed harbour and sat down to a dinner of roast beef, Yorkshire pudding, cabbage, carrots, roast potatoes and gravy followed by apple crumble and custard, before rowing ashore to have a look for a shop. Glandore, or Cuan Dor in Irish, means 'harbour of the oaks' and when we looked at the majestic trees towering above the grand houses and castles of the village we could see why. Glandore may be beautiful but if there was a shop we didn't see it and the last of the milk went in the York pud.

33

Fastnet

When we woke just before five-thirty it was still very dark but the sky was clear and full of stars. As it became lighter it was clearly going to be a beautiful day for the climax to our holiday. Despite all our doubts and difficulties, we'd made it. Today was the day we were going round the Fastnet Rock and the weather pulled out all the stops for us. Sunshine, blue sky and at last, a real sailors' breeze, even though it was still blowing in the wrong direction. We motor-sailed out of Glandore into a sapphire sea and marvelled at the spellbinding coastal scenery. Secret coves, misty hills, islands, crags, rocky headlands. All topped with towers, forts and castles in various states of decay.

We got our first glimpse of the Fastnet lighthouse at nine-twenty-five, when we were off Baltimore. Constructed from Cornish granite, it was completed in 1906 and was the second lighthouse to be built on the rock. At around ninety-one feet high it took ten years to build and is the tallest lighthouse in Ireland. Its cast-iron predecessor only survived eleven years before the rock upon which it was built was partially swept away by waves, whipped up by the fierce gales that storm unimpeded across three thousand miles of Atlantic Ocean.

Two hours later we were close enough to take

photographs and as we drew nearer to the jagged reef the sea built up from a steady rolling swell into big boiling breakers with white crests that crashed in noisy lathers of foam over the rocks.

We were as excited as schoolchildren on an outing to be going round the rock and the lively sea added to our exhilaration. Once we were on the eastern turn the wind was blowing us towards the rock, which was a bit hairy, but at least we could have given rescuers a precise location: 51°23′3″N, 9°36′1″W, and we enjoyed the exhilarating ride.

The Fastnet Rock, at the southernmost tip of the Republic of Ireland, is a small island that rises to nearly a hundred feet above the low water mark. Known in Irish as Carraig Aonair, or Lonely Rock, it is also described as Ireland's Teardrop because, in the days before air travel was common-place, it gave Irish migrants their last view of their homeland when they sailed off to their new lives in America. According to legend the islet appeared after a giant seized a huge rock from Mount Gabriel near Ballydehob in County Cork and hurled it into the sea.

Before we knew it, the rock, wind and sea were behind us and at last we could sail. We had a mug of chicken soup to celebrate then concentrated on getting past Clear Island and into Baltimore. It was a tricky bit of seamanship. All around these parts the coastline is littered with rocks, islands and islets. They are all too obvious on the chart but very difficult to pick out from offshore because you lose the three dimensional effect and it becomes impossible to distinguish islands from mainland. All this means you have to have a strong belief in your interpretation of the chart, something that Mike's very good at and I never mastered. I'd read somewhere that men have better spatial awareness than women, which is why they are supposed to be better at reading maps and the reason they are so confident of their abilities behind the wheel of a car. I guess it also explained Mike's talent for marrying objects on land with the symbols on the charts.

'Listen to this,' I said later, as I studied the guidebook I'd bought in Youghal. 'It says Baltimore is a popular centre for yachtsmen.'

'Well I'm at a loss to know why.' Mike was considerably less than enamoured with Baltimore, where we'd tied up to an old fishing boat against the harbour wall. 'It's impossible to find a mooring, this old trawler smells disgusting and that lad on board couldn't be less friendly if he tried. The harbour toilets are the worst ever and this harbour is a mess. We'll get whatever we need from the shop and then as far as I'm concerned, the sooner we get away from here the better.'

'I know what you mean,' I agreed. 'Look at all these heaps of junk and rusty old bits of ships all over the place. And the supermarket needs a good tidy-up too.' In the chandlery section of the muddled store we'd had to step on or over heaps of boxes on the floor to get to the clutter of marine bits and pieces on the shelves. I walked past one cardboard carton overflowing with fishing paraphernalia and ended up with a fish hook stuck in the toe of my trainer. Still, we managed to get fresh milk, a new cleat for the genoa furling line and another canfull of agricultural diesel for less than £3 from a huge cylindrical tank beside the harbour. We had a cup of tea and a Swiss roll in a cafe and then left this Irish yachting Mecca to those yachtsman who reckoned they liked it.

The rest of the day was our best sailing so far. I was completely free of pain in my back and helmed from Baltimore to our next port of call, Castletownshend. The weather was idyllic and Cevamp went like a dream. As we left Baltimore we noticed a ketch on our port bow and decided, unknown to her crew, to race her but we lost speed as we went round the headland and we ended up following them in.

Castletownshend is a perfect haven. Perfectly sheltered and perfectly still. The ketch moored up to the quay wall and we rafted to the ketch. The owners were a recently retired couple from Fishguard and had bought the twenty-five year-old ketch the previous year to replace their Westerly Centaur as they wanted something bigger for cruising in. They were a friendly couple and I guessed he was ex-navy as his sweater bore the RNSA logo. The village itself was quiet and peaceful, with just one shop at the top of a precipitously steep hill, where the shopkeeper was happy to sell us a pint of milk even though he was closed. As in Dunmore East and Youghal there were standpipes in the street, which made us think that some homes were still without running water. At the end of the twentieth century this seemed incredible and improbable, but unless they provided access to water for fire fighting we could think of no other explanation.

We had rarely been in a place so thoroughly steeped in history and legend as this region of Ireland and Castletownshend was no exception, with roots going back to the Battle of Kinsale in 1601. The present village grew up around the seventeenth century castles built in the area by the Townshend family, whose descendants still live there.

Back on board we caught the early evening forecast: winds westerly backing south westerly three or four and increasing six to eight; weather fair with occasional rain; visibility good becoming moderate with fog patches. It could have been better but we didn't let it spoil our evening. We halved the cold beef left over from the previous day's roast and ate it with baked beans and fried potatoes followed by apple crumble and yoghurt, all washed down with the last of our Rioja.

As we settled down for the night a heron flew over with an unlovely screech and began his patrol of the shoreline, alert to the slightest sign of supper in the clear shallow water. Otherwise the only sound was silence. We slept.

34

Is this marriage a big mistake?

I got up very early and went out to watch the sun rise.
The heron watched me solemnly from his perch on a
nearby dinghy. I watched him back. Then he gave
another unmelodic squawk and flew off into the gloom
of early dawn. It was millpond calm, but quite cool and
it was cloudier than the previous day. We motored gently
out of Castlehaven, where we'd been moored, and
watched the rocks slide into place behind us, concealing
their secrets. After half an hour you'd never believe there
was a way through them to such an oasis.

My back problem had returned with a vengeance. It
was as though it wasn't strong enough to hold itself up
and every movement of my legs or upper body caused a
jagged pain to tear through my spine and lumbar region.
I dozed for a while on the cabin roof but it didn't help
and to take my mind off my discomfort I went inside to
make some scones, something that I can usually
accomplish in twenty minutes. On this particular
morning it took an hour from start to finish and they
weren't really worth the effort. I only had plain flour on
the boat and they turned out more like biscuits than
scones. What's more, I was now in agony from the effort
of making them and feeling very sorry for myself. My
self pity was not helped by the fact that Mike seemed
totally unaware of my sorry state and still expected me

to be able to carry out my usual crewing duties of pulling on ropes, pumping out the bilges and hanging on to the tiller.

We carried on with full main and cruising chute – sometimes boomed out, sometimes not. We noticed the ketch making good time behind us until her chute went up then she fell back. Off the Old Head of Kinsale the wind picked up and it was a little rippy. Mike reefed the main and only swapped the chute for the genoa after we'd rounded the Old Head, but then said he should have done it sooner to minimize the strain on the light fabric of the sail. I thought so too, but had kept my thoughts to myself. He's the skipper and I'd thought I was just being puny.

The ketch followed us into the marina at Kinsale and despite the gear failing to engage in reverse we moored Cevamp neatly to a pontoon then went ashore to explore. Mike set off at his usual brisk pace and I hobbled painfully and crookedly a few paces behind. Irritating though it must have been for Mike, it was the best I could manage. Despite my discomfort, I was curious about the town. I remembered from school history lessons that it was the site of the Battle of Kinsale when two Irish princes, Hugh O'Donnell and Hugh O'Neill, led an ill-fated attempt to drive the English out of Ireland. Their defeat on Christmas Eve 1601 led to what became known as the Flight of the Earls, when the two Hughs and many Irish aristocrats fled their homeland and became exiles in Europe.

The last of the day's sunshine bounced heat off the walls of the whitewashed buildings as we passed and window boxes of geraniums and late blooming nasturtiums all added to Kinsale's continental and cosmopolitan atmosphere. The town was bustling and lively. Even though it was now after six o'clock in the evening people were milling around and shops were still open. There were lots of French tourists and the medieval town clearly had strong links with France, possibly dating back several centuries to the days when French prisoners were captured at sea and held in Desmond Castle, popularly known as the French prison. Later, during the American War of Independence in the mid-eighteenth century, the crews of American vessels were also held prisoner in Kinsale. These days the castle is Kinsale's International Museum of Wine and its exhibits tell how the town used to be a designated wine port and supplied wine to the ships of the fleet.

I hadn't realised before that Kinsale was the centre of the rescue operation when the luxury cruise liner Lusitania was torpedoed by a German U-boat on May 7, 1915 with the loss of nearly two thousand lives. The pride of Cunard's fleet, the huge ship sank in just eighteen minutes when she was eight miles off the Old Head of Kinsale.

According to our guide books the town had a circle of a dozen or so restaurants advertised on blackboards dotted around the town and was famed as the gourmet capital of Ireland.

As I breathed in the mouthwatering smells of garlicky food that wafted through the restaurant windows, I knew what they meant.

'Mmmm. Doesn't it smell gorgeous here? The smell of all that food is making me hungry.

'It does smell good,' Mike agreed, 'but I'm not so sure about the garlic. D'you fancy a night off cooking? We'll have a wander round all the restaurants and make choice about where to go.'

'Well I won't argue with that.'

I perked up, my back temporarily forgotten, as we peered at menus and compared prices before deciding which eating house to grace with our presence that evening.

Kinsale is a fishing centre and many of the restaurants specialised in seafood, which neither of us is mad about. We finally decided on Seasons, a picturesque place on the site of a former milk market. It was an excellent choice. Mike had quail in sauce followed by fillet steak and I had chicken quenelles in nettle leaves and sauce, followed by délice of salmon in lemon pancake, all served with lots of beautifully cooked vegetables. For pudding we had fresh pineapple and orange wedges in vodka, followed by coffee with a choice of milk or cream.

'Let's have a day in Cork tomorrow.' Mike stretched languorously in his chair as we finished our meal. 'They're forecasting gales and a day of rest will probably do us good anyway. We'll catch the bus and go in after breakfast.'

Next morning I woke up early. My back was as bad as ever, if not worse but, determined not to let it get the better of me, I hobbled to the bus stop. The bus was a dilapidated coach with holes and dents in the bodywork at the front. We jammed ourselves into our seats and sat back for a real boneshaker of a journey. There were no obvious bus stops and the driver simply stopped to pick up passengers near their houses or at the end of lanes leading to isolated buildings.

We sat near the front, on a seat with worn upholstery and twin dents put there by years of traveling bottoms.

'Don't think much of his driving technique,' I whispered in Mike's ear. 'He pulls out, and then checks his mirror.' I thought of myself as something of an expert on safe driving practices, having spent a good deal of my time at work in the company of traffic officers who were only too happy to give me the benefit of their experience. 'Mirror, signal, manoeuvre,' was their daily mantra.

The bus tore along the bumpy roads and twenty or so miles later we arrived in Cork. We needed some new rope and were looking for a chandlery called Union Marine. Mike asked a man standing in a pub doorway for directions.

'Union Marine?' He rubbed his chin thoughtfully. 'Never heard of it? What is it? A pub?'

'No,' said Mike. 'A chandlery.'

The man shook his head. 'No. Don't know what you mean.'

Mike tried again. 'A chandlery. A place where you buy bits and pieces for boats.'

A big smile as light dawned. 'Oh, Ringacoltig. You mean the boat shop.'

Ringacoltig, it turned out, comes from the Irish Rinn-an-Cobhlach and means 'the point of the fleet'. Once he knew what we were talking about the man had little trouble in telling us where to go. Our next stop was a chemist for pain killers, Marks and Spencer for food treats and then it was on to the centuries-old English Market which had countless butchery stalls with good, low priced meat. There was also plenty of traditional Irish fare, including tripe and drisheen – black pudding made from pig or sheep blood, milk, salt, fat and breadcrumbs, flavoured with tansy and cooked as a sausage using animal intestine as sausage skin – but we didn't really have the stomach for them. I liked the English Market, so named because originally only English incomers were allowed to trade there, and I especially admired the centrepiece, an ornate fountain rising out of a grey marble bowl. The fountain itself grew out of a sculpture of bulrushes and birds and was cast in iron.

The sight of all that food made us hungry so we stopped for lunch but we still had an hour to kill before we caught the bus back to Kinsale. While we waited we sat on a park bench beside the River Lee, near the city hall. Although the painkillers had taken the edge off my backache I badly needed to sit down and Mike was glad of the rest too. As he flexed his arms to ease the aches from carrying all the shopping he said he was disappointed with Cork.

'We may as well have stayed in Kinsale,' he grumbled.

'I think if I'd remembered to bring the guidebook we'd have enjoyed Cork more,' I said. 'St Finbar's Cathedral is very pretty and I've never seen so many pubs. I saw six in a row at one point.'

Back in Kinsale we bought bolts and nuts for Cevamp's problematic alternator and sat outside Seasons to listen to the early evening shipping forecast on our little green transistor radio. It gave the wind as westerly, veering north westerly five to seven and we decided that unless it was really awful we would leave in the morning.

That evening I found I was more comfortable lying down and dragged myself off to bed right after dinner.

'I'll be with you in a minute,' said Mike. 'Just want to make the most of the pontoon tap and top up the fresh water tank first. It's so much easier than having to carry it on board in bottles and it'll be one thing less to do in the morning.'

Unfortunately, the tank was half full before Mike spotted the slimy algae floating around in the water. Just then Giles, the marina manager, strolled by.

'Don't worry, there's nothing wrong with the water,' he explained. 'The algae grow in the hoses.'

I spent most of the next day lying on the bed resting my back while Mike sailed us back to Youghal at high speeds in a brisk breeze. At one point we were doing well over eight knots with just a scrap of genoa to power us along and he was having a great day. I, on the other hand, was bored, frustrated and irritable and thought miserably that my back pain had really blighted the holiday. I just hoped a day of doing very little would mean I could start being active again the following day.

We reached Youghal at lunchtime and I crawled out onto the cockpit to lend a hand. There wasn't enough depth of water for us to get into Mall Dock straight away so I stood up front with the boat hook, ready to pick up a buoy on a swinging mooring.

Mike drove Cevamp slowly towards the buoy then, as it drew nearer, he cut the engine so we would drift onto and I could hook it up. I managed to get the hook under the line from the buoy, but it wouldn't come up. The effort of holding onto it against the not inconsiderable force exerted by the ongoing movement of the boat caused enormous strain on my back and I called to Mike to come and take it. He grabbed the line impatiently and after a struggle managed to make it fast to the stern post.

'That one's not good – it's not been used for two years,' said a man chugging past in a little fishing boat. He pointed. 'You'd be better off moving to that one over there.'

Mike restarted the engine, untied the ropes and handed the boat hook back to me. We motored very slowly over to the other buoy. I missed it on the first pass.

Mike was growing ever more impatient. 'This time, you drive and I'll get it,' he said, with an air of patronising superiority that annoyed me. It was, after all, only the second time I'd missed in three years. I took the tiller and stood in the cockpit, aiming carefully for the buoy.

'Stand on the seat so you can see it. I want it to come up on the starboard side,' he ordered.

'I can see it from here,' I insisted.

'You won't be able to when it comes into the bow,' he snapped back. Stubborn and mutinous, I stayed where I was. I could see the bloody buoy perfectly well. To start with. When Cevamp's bow swung round towards it, it disappeared. I scrambled, too late, onto the seat as the buoy passed majestically to port. I pulled hard on the tiller to correct my course and jerked my back agonisingly at the same time.

'That side,' Mike screamed at me furiously.

'She won't go over,' I yelled back, equally as furious.

Somehow he managed to hook the buoy from the other side and make it fast. I was in tears of pain and frustration and couldn't bring myself to speak. Eventually the tide came in and we moved over to Mall Dock. This time my knots were all wrong, naturally, and Mike silently unscrambled them and retied the lines.

By now I was really fed up and wouldn't have cared if he could read my thoughts.

'Is this marriage a big mistake?' I wondered, as my resentment mounted. 'He's an impatient, intolerant, perfectionist. He doesn't like it if I can't do things exactly his way and won't even give me a chance to try them my way.'

Of course, I didn't say any of this to him. Just muttered something about never doing things right. By now, of course, with his precious yacht safe and secure, he'd relaxed and just laughed at me. I hated him even more. Nevertheless, we went shopping in Youghal together and I made Armenian lamb casserole for dinner. Martyr or what? Although we were pleasant enough to each other for the rest of the evening, I still felt resentful and hurt and waited until he was in bed and asleep before creaking my way in beside him. I sat propped up on my pillows still simmering, determined to enjoy my misery to the full and to stay awake all night. I made a decision. In the morning I would tell him I was leaving. For good.

35

Green grass of home

The last thing I remembered was looking at the clock at eight forty-five. I slept like a log and never even heard the alarm. We had a silent cup of tea. I got dressed in bed to avoid the morning chill while Mike tried to start the stubborn, silent engine. It was back to its old tricks and he made yet another adjustment to the drive belt. We were, if not wordless, certainly monosyllabic. We ate our cereal in near silence, munched on some toast and were away before eight.

Before long the sun started to warm us up. Suddenly everything was all right again and my resolve to leave him dissipated along with the mist. We were back to our usual cheerful, affectionate and companionable selves, all my dark thoughts of the night before forgotten.

'How's your back today?' Mike asked.

'Funnily enough, it's loads better. I don't know what I did yesterday, but I think something must have clicked back into place. Pity it's waited until we're on our way home.'

'Yes, it has put a bit of a dampener on things. But have you enjoyed the trip otherwise?'

'Well,' I said, 'I'm glad we achieved our target of going round the Fastnet but to be honest I think it was at a cost. I've been reading through the log and although I've enjoyed what we've done I think it was a bit optimistic to set such an ambitious target in such a limited time. We've hardly done any exploring, you know. Next year I think we should take it more steadily.'

By this time we'd covered more than four hundred miles and still had to get back to Porthmadog. Apart from one day in Arklow and one in Kinsale we'd been up at six every morning, sailed for at least eight hours each day, eaten our dinner and fallen into bed, ready for a repeat performance the following day.

'You're probably right,' said Mike. 'Perhaps we should consider a different sort of holiday next year. How do you fancy going on a flotilla holiday in the Med?'

'Mmmm. Sounds good. Cheap wine, sunshine, calm sea, easy sailing ...'

'Don't know about that,' he interrupted. 'There might not be any sailing in the Med, if there's no wind.'

But by now I was cherishing secret visions of days of calm blue seas and hot sunshine with me slim and tanned in a stringy bikini, lazing on cushions on a pristine deck, sipping a long cool drink and letting him do all the work. I soon had to get back to reality. The wind blew a good force six for best part of the day, the sea was a mass of white capped steely grey rollers and although there were hundreds of sea birds hanging around a small trawler they were mostly hidden by the spray.

Back in Dunmore East we headed straight for the showers.

'I'm just about to lock up for the day,' said the man in charge. He must have taken pity at our downhearted expressions. 'But I'll tell you what. I'll lock youse two in there and you can let yourselves out when you've finished.'

It was blissful. It was only our third shower since

leaving Wales and it felt so good to wash my hair I did it three times.

'If it's a nice sunny day tomorrow, we'll stay here for the day. If it isn't we'll press on, but leave it a bit later so we have a leisurely start and late finish for a change.'

Mike must have been paying more attention to my earlier remarks than I'd given him credit for and I was pleased.

But Cevamp had other ideas. I prepared a casserole for dinner and put it on to cook. The gas spluttered then died.

'Oops. No dinner. We've run out of gas. Do they sell Calor in Ireland?'

'I don't know,' said Mike. I'll go and find out.'

An hour later the news wasn't good. He'd walked all over Dunmore East with a heavy gas bottle, with no luck. We abandoned our plan for a restful day on the basis that the sooner we got back to Wales and bought some gas the better, and got ready to leave for Rosslare early in the morning to make the most of a favourable tidal stream.

'Don't worry about dinner,' I said. 'We'll go to the take-away for tonight and heat the casserole on the disposable barbecue tomorrow.'

The take-away restaurant didn't open until nine in the evening so as the engine was getting a bit low on fuel we sat and waited for the diesel man to come. He didn't show up.

A big blue yacht from Fremantle was in the harbour, loading with provisions ready to leave for the Canaries the next day before carrying on to South Africa. The skipper told us to borrow his BMW to go and look for diesel and gas. Mike thanked him but with typical true-Brit reserve declined the offer.

A small red and green sailing boat called Pegarty was tied alongside Cevamp, with a couple on board. He was young and amiable with matted, curly, long blond hair and a ginger beard. She was quiet and slim with long, dark hair. They told us they left Cumbria at the beginning of July, had already been to the Isle of Man and were now planning to travel upriver from Dunmore East into the canal and leave the boat there for the winter. They had a bike lashed to the back of the boat and were towing a dinghy with a second bike strapped across it. They'd removed the yacht's guard rails to give themselves more room and were very impressed with Cevamp's big roomy cockpit.

The boat behind us was a Westerly Konsort from Shell Island, near Harlech. The couple on board said they had been away for three months and had also been to the Isle of Man but they were now on their way home and were leaving for Milford Haven in the morning.

Of course, with our current run of luck, by the time we'd found all this out it was after nine and the shop was shut, meaning we were now not only out of gas but also without any supplies of cold food to see us through the next couple of days without gas. We consoled ourselves with fish and chips from Jenny's Fast Food Emporium, which we ate sitting on the harbour wall, followed by apricots and cream back on the boat.

We were in bed by ten, surprisingly cheerful despite our problems, and confident of getting a replacement bottle of Calor once we got to Fishguard.

We had a good night and were up and about early next morning, grimacing at our glasses of cold orange juice, a poor substitute for hot tea. The girl from Pegarty joined us.

'I was talking to the people on Paddy last night,' she

said, indicating the boat next to hers. 'They said they have a spare gas bottle that you can have.'

'That's nice of them,' said Mike. 'But it might not be the right size. If we hang around waiting for them to wake up and then find it's a different fitting it means we'll be late getting away for no good reason. Tell them thanks for the offer, but I think we'll get going as soon as we're ready. We'll manage somehow'

We were on our way by six-fifty. With a full genoa and a single reef in the main we enjoyed a good morning's sailing and arrived at Rosslare in warm sunshine in time for lunch. We tied Cevamp to a fishing boat and walked to the ferry terminal for sausages and chips and, at last, a cup of tea, before heading off to the village to top up our food supplies and search, fruitlessly, for gas.

Back on the boat we stripped off into our swimwear and sat on cushions on the coachroof watching the boats come in.

After a while another trawler arrived at our stretch of the harbour wall and we moved out to let her inside. She had a genial, friendly skipper and two crew. They'd been out for two or three days fishing but had suffered a bit of bad luck when one of their nets got damaged.

'What do you catch,' I asked the skipper.

'Mainly plaice. Here, have a couple for your tea.'

'Thanks. I'd love them, but we've nothing to cook them on.'

I asked him what it was like to be a trawler man. 'There must be easier ways to make a living, what with all the rules and regulations, not to mention the wind and weather.'

'Yes,' he said. 'It's hard and it's dangerous, but I wouldn't do anything else. In the summer I like to have every Sunday off but in winter you go out when you can.'

He told us about the gales that had ravaged the mainland that January. 'The waves came over the harbour wall, to be sure, and you can see how high that is, to shelter the ferries. I tied the boat up with double mooring ropes, as thick as my wrist, and they just snapped. All I could do was sit and watch my boat get damaged and wait for the storm to pass over.'

One of the crew picked his way across the deck to where the skipper was sitting and handed him a small sole. He showed it to us. It was tagged with a small red disc studded right through the fish, with letters and numbers on it.

'I've never seen a red one before. It's probably come from your side, from Cardigan. The tagging is done by fishery protection boats so the Government's fisheries people can monitor fish movements. They try and encourage us to return the tags by paying us £1 a time. I'll probably send them the whole fish.'

He roared with laughter and we joined in, all of us highly delighted at the thought of the person at the other end opening a parcel of fish after it had been in transit for several days.

After he left Mike and I shared a can of lager and watched the activity around us. There was a pair of seals in the harbour and every so often their little round whiskered heads popped up, swiveled round to gaze at us with soulful eyes, then silently slid back under the surface, leaving barely a ripple. Greedy gulls hung around the trawlers as they came in, to see what they could scavenge.

'Did you see that?' said Mike. 'That seagull just swallowed a whole fish.'

I untangled another fish from the nets on the boat alongside us and threw it into the water beside Cevamp, where it landed near to a big herring gull. The bird eyed the dead fish for ages but was reluctant to come any closer. I wondered if its fear of us would be overcome by greed. After a minute or two of weighing up its chances, the gull grabbed the fish and tried to crush it with its beak. I was sure the fish was too big and he'd have to abandon it but to my amazement he managed to swallow it, head first, in three gulps. You could see it bulging in the gull's throat. The bird stretched and twisted its neck and we watched as the fish travelled in bulges down its gullet. Ugh.

The evening grew cooler and I pondered what to do about our own dinner. I found a bit of marine ply on the harbour wall and Mike stood it on four tins from our food store and used them as a base for the disposable barbecue. We always kept one or two on board, just in case we were ever moored on a suitable beach in just the weather for a barbecue. A rare event. This time it made a good substitute cooker. It smoked a bit but we heated the casserole on it and followed with Pears Belle Cevamp: in other words hot tinned rice pudding with cold tinned pears. There was even enough heat left in the coals to boil a saucepan of water for the dishes and a kettle to wash ourselves.

Fishguard was a terrible disappointment. No showers, no cafeteria…and no gas. And to start with, we thought there was nowhere to moor either. The first buoy we tried, in the main harbour at Goodwick, was foul. It was covered in leathery seaweed harbouring crabs and other wildlife and with a rusty chain. The second was slightly better and Mike was confident it would hold Cevamp so we tied up and paddled ashore in the Tinker. The ferry terminal was deserted. A fisherman directed us to the customs hall. There was nobody there either, and no post box. Technically we'd arrived from a foreign country so we were legally obliged to complete a customs form and hand it in on arrival in the UK.

'What should we do now? I asked.

'There's not much we can do.' Mike shrugged. 'We'll just have to see if there's anyone around later on.

We trudged a good half mile or so further on and found two garages that sold Calor. But their bottles were the wrong size and didn't match the fittings on ours. Somebody said we might get some in town, a mile away. But it was Sunday night and we doubted it. One of the garages had a restaurant and we looked forward to getting a hot meal but it was closing, or at least, that's what they told us. Perhaps they just didn't like the look of two malodorous scruffs with a tatty gas bottle and I can't say I blame them. We bought a loaf, a couple of dried up sausage rolls and two mini apple pies from the garage shop and chewed on them as we walked back to the dinghy.

On the way we passed a sign near the waterfront telling how Fishguard had been the site of the last invasion of the United Kingdom in 1797. The French troops were a rowdy lot who were more interested in getting drunk than they were in conquering the natives. They soon took to their heels when a group of local women, led by the redoubtable Jemima Nicholls, appeared in the distance. Through their drunken haze the soldiers thought the women, clothed in the traditional Welsh dress of the day, were members of the Welsh infantry, and they fled in terror.

Back on Cevamp we had a glass of orange juice with bread and the last of the jam. A world removed from our usual Sunday dinners.

Mike went ashore again with the customs form. What we'd been told was the customs office turned out to be Sealink, the ferry company, and he had a silly conversation with a Sealink man who, naturally, didn't know what Mike was talking about. There was no-one in the customs hall so he returned to the boat and we went to bed.

'What are you so grumpy about?' said Mike when I woke up next morning.

'I'm not grumpy,' I muttered.

Mike raised his eyebrows.

'Well all right, I am grumpy,' I admitted with a scowl. 'I'm desperate for a cup of tea and I'm fed up at running out of gas'.

I could put up with things such as having to fetch water, no baths and having to make up the bed every night. But when you don't have electricity you really rely on the gas in a way you wouldn't have to at home. Then when it's gone it's a worse blow because of all the other primitive stuff. It makes every little thing such an effort.

Mike knew what I meant about effort. He'd already spent ages mopping the floorboards and pumping the bilges and he would have enjoyed a cup of tea too. Instead he got ready to go ashore to try and find a customs officer.

When he got back he was smiling.

'How did you get on?' I asked.

'I got arrested by a customs man. They take a dim view of yachtsmen like us, who don't hand in part one of the form before going foreign. He said they've relaxed the rules so much to make life easier for yachties that they expect them to be complied with. Apparently, whenever there's the slightest possibility you may go foreign you should drop in part one and if you don't go you just let them know. Anyway, he said it's not his decision. It'll have to be reported and I'll probably get a letter of advice. Then he gave me a flask of hot water to make tea with and told me where I'll probably be able to get Calor.'

The tea was nectar. Mike gulped his down then said that rather than wait for a bus he'd walk into town. He came back with a wide smile and not only gas but Alpen, milk, ham, cheese, bacon, tomatoes and Toffee Crisps. Fishguard, we decided, had redeemed itself with honours, even though it was a good mile uphill into town and a seven and a half kilogram gas bottle is a heavy object to carry. Mike said his arms were three inches longer by the time he got back.

We packed everything away and set sail for New Quay immediately. Mike started the engine to get us away from our mooring then got the sails up while I prepared a huge breakfast for us to eat en route.

Once out of Fishguard Harbour we were in a wide bay flanked with gentle green hills. We sailed past Dinas Head, across Newport Bay with its long sandy beach, round Cemaes Head and then, out of devilment, sailed through the shallow sound between Cardigan Island and the land. It was a perfect day, with sunshine, white fluffy clouds against a brilliant blue sky and for once the wind was in our favour.

Beautiful though Ireland was it was lovely to be back in our home waters, with their familiar jade sea, unique blue light and majestic rock formations at the water's edge.

Mike must have been thinking the same.

'Once when I was a child on bonfire night weekend my parents brought us all to Wales to look at a property they were thinking of buying. It rained all the time. It was really miserable. We missed bonfire night and I decided then I hated Wales. Strange how time changes your opinions of a place. These days I think I wouldn't mind retiring to here.'

36

Dancing dolphins

Just when we thought the day couldn't get better we spotted a pod of seven bottle-nosed dolphins, including two mothers and babies. They were quite a long way off but as we watched we realised they had seen us and were deliberately coming our way, arching out of the water with a casual fluidity that belied their speed.

They stayed with us for nearly an hour and were so close to Cevamp that they made the echo sounder bleep as they leapt and dived around us, flashing first out of the water then swooping smoothly under the boat, to reappear just ahead, beside or behind us. We could easily see individual markings and scars on their silvery bodies and were soon able to pick out one from another – one, with a ragged dorsal fin, was especially distinctive. It seemed to us, watching spellbound from the cockpit, that the biggest animal, almost slate-grey in colour, was not only the leader but also the senior choreographer.

I'd read that there was believed to be a special kind of symbiosis between dolphins and humans, that there was even some kind of telepathic communication between the species, and it certainly felt like it to Mike and me that day. We sensed strongly that the dolphins were putting on a show especially for us. Their strength and power is hugely impressive, yet they are so graceful and friendly, smiling all the time and always making eye-contact, as if seeking our friendship and approval. The mothers and their enchanting babies moved me to tears as they breached and dived, always perfectly synchronised and always with their pectoral flippers touching, just as a human mother and toddler hold hands on a shopping trip. We couldn't bear to take our eyes off them.

All of a sudden the mood changed. As one, they became very excited. The pace of the display quickened from relaxed to frenzied and they transmitted their excitement to us. It was a strong group feeling and we were part of it.

'Perhaps they're planning something special for us,' I said. We watched, mesmerised, as, with perfect timing, they leapt towards, over and under each other, always conscious of the speed and position of the boat and always just slightly ahead. Then, just as suddenly, they all calmed down. All, that is, except the big leader. He began to thrash violently around, his entire body twisting out of the water in a series of massive horizontal body flips and ending each move with a thrust of his tail, before crashing back under the surface.

Then came the finale. We could scarcely contain ourselves. 'What's he doing, what's he doing' was all I could say and Mike was breathing 'Magic, magic,' over and over again as the big dark leader rose beak first, vertically out of the water, just yards from our starboard bow. We were both holding our breath.

He rose up, up and up until he was about a metre clear of the water. He gave a great thrash of his tail and then flung himself sideways. There was a thundering crash that vibrated through the hull of the boat as he threw himself back into the sea. He gave a repeat performance and a final encore.

Suddenly they were all gone. The water was still again. It was as though they'd never been there.

Tears were streaming down our cheeks. It was such an emotional performance and we had to remind ourselves that these were wild animals. They hadn't been trained in some obscene dolphinarium, or bribed with fish to perform to order. They were doing it for the sheer joy of it and they were doing it for us.

I wondered whether their flamboyant behaviour meant this was the time of year they display, prior to mating but I found out later that play is an important part of dolphins' lives and they are well known for their willingness to approach humans and interact with them. Dolphins weren't the only wild creatures to charm and amuse us while we were sailing. There are always plenty of birds to watch when you're at sea, whether it's gulls of various sorts following fishing boats, shags and cormorants perched on rocky ridges, or terns, guillemots, razorbills and puffins whizzing past your boat. The only problem I had was in identifying them all.

Terns are relatively easy. Their forked tails and long streamers give them the appearance of sea swallows, although they are nearly twice the size of the swallows that are such an integral part of British summers. Constantly on the look out for fish, they fly low over the water with their beaks pointed down, ready to dive the instant they spot their prey. With their black caps, black-tipped red bills, red legs and soft grey wing feathers they are pretty birds and although we occasionally saw them alone they were usually in small groups.

But how do you tell the difference between shag and cormorant? And even when you know the bluish black cormorant has white on its face and sits on rocks holding its wings out to dry, how do you then remember it's usually the cormorant that does that, not the smaller, blackish green shag? We got round this particular dilemma by calling them all shagarants. Both varieties are excellent swimmers and as they bobbed around on the surface of the water they would wait until the very last moment before ducking their heads down and diving away from us to avoid a collision. I always feel that cormorants are the nearest thing we've got to penguins in this country, the way they swim with their bodies submerged and heads out and sit bolt upright on rocks.

Then there was still the problem of razor bills and guillemots. Similar in size and similarly marked they also proved difficult to identify and so, to make life easier for ourselves, we took the shagarant approach, lumped them together as one and labelled them flappalots in recognition of their distinctive flight pattern.

We were very pleased with ourselves for coming up with these simple solutions to our bird spotting problems and although it gave rise to some very silly conversations what did it matter? There was no-one else around to listen to us.

That afternoon, on our way back from Ireland, I watched a few flappalots skim by and felt inspired.

'I know how you can recognise a guillemot,' I said.

'Oh yeah. How?'

'Like this:

'It's easy to spot

a guillemot

because it flaps its wings, a lot.'

Mike looked at me with a pitying but nonetheless slightly soppy expression.

'That's all very well,' he said, 'but how do you tell the difference between a guillemot and a razorbill? They all look the same to me.'

As if to prove his point a flight of whirring black and white birds flapped madly over the surface of the sea, just yards from Cevamp's stern.

'That's easy,' I said. 'Razorbills are chunkier. Different beaks.'

'Go on then. I bet you can't do another rhyme.'

'Bet I can.' I thought for a minute.

'What about this?

A razorbill is flappier still

with blacker back and broader bill.'

'Yes. Very good. But what about puffins?'

'They're easy. Everyone knows what they look like.'

That's true. Cute little parrots with stripy beaks full of sand eels, they use their wings like miniature propellers to make their escape when they're floating on the water and boats comes too close. And I loved the way their little red feet stick out behind them like paddles when they fly.

'Yes,' said Mike. 'But that's not a poem.'

'Neither were the others. They were rhymes.'

'Okay then. What rhymes with puffin?'

'Errrm.' I was silent for a couple of seconds. 'I've got it:

When you're at sea

you ain't seen nuffin

until you've eyed a full-beaked puffin.'

I was triumphant. Mike was not particularly impressed with my skill as a poet but he was amused. Even so, I thought, enough's enough, and returned to my favourite occupation: watching gannets.

Most of the birds we saw were appealing in their own way but gannets were, and still are, my favourites. With their brilliant, whiter-than-white plumage, black tipped, scythe-shaped wings, yellow head and intelligent eyes, they are the largest sea-bird to breed in British waters and there is a thriving colony on Grassholm Island, a few miles off the Pembrokeshire coast. I can sit for hours watching them. Impressive divers, they circle round high above the waves, bodies, heads and tails a slim cylindrical shape, pointed at each end just like a cigar. Then their heads drop as though on hinges – in profile they look like Concorde aircraft – and they bank round by tipping their inside wing down. Suddenly they plunge head first straight into the sea, wings held stiffly like a trident, and enter the water with a plop and a splash, folding their wings partially back at the last possible moment. Hitting the water as they do at sixty miles an hour, it's one of Nature's miracles that their skulls are reinforced to withstand the impact. Another thing I noticed was the way adult gannets give the young birds flying lessons. The youngsters follow close on the tail of the adults, mimicking their every movement: when the adults glide the young glide, when adults flap the youngsters flap, when adults soar the young soar.

Sitting on the deck of a yacht for hours on end gives you a chance to study the wildlife at first hand, to observe things that you don't read about in books and I always think it's a great privilege to be able to do this. I'd never even seen a gannet until I started sailing and the closest I'd been to a dolphin was watching a wildlife programme on television.

On this special afternoon as I sat musing on nature, compiling silly rhymes and absorbing the beauty of the scenery on land and the power of the sea around our little boat, the last traces of our bad tempered few days had flown .

This was where I wanted to be.

37

Decision time

It was six thirty when we got to New Quay. Exposed only to the north (and guess where the wind was blowing from) it's a semi-circular bay with wooded hills up one side, terraces of houses and shops rising from a small central sandy beach and an unusual old terraced harbour wall on the third side, ending in a clump of big rocks and boulders at the end of the breakwater.

I was fascinated by the old notice boards on the side of the harbour building, listing 'tolls and tithes to be levied on the undermentioned goods imported into or exported from any place with the limits of the harbour'. These simple lists don't only tell how much it cost to import or export a wide variety of cargoes but, because they are so detailed, they also give a snapshot of local social history in the second half of the nineteenth century. Loads coming through the once busy port included foodstuffs such as potatoes, oranges, hops, herrings and hams, furniture, slate, bricks, culm – or coal dust – millstones, tombstones and fireplaces. The fee for a coffin was two shillings, a bath-chair one shilling, a four-wheeled closed carriage was charged at ten shillings and a barrel organ was five shillings. Livestock was also transported through the harbour for a tithe of two shillings and sixpence for a horse or mule, one shilling per head of horned cattle and fourpence for a fox. All tolls and dues were payable at the office of the harbour master, Thomas Davies, who had previously been master of the schooner Mary Hughes.

As far as I could see from the numerous information boards and posters, New Quay, or Cei Newydd, had two great claims to fame. One was its connection to Dylan Thomas, who lived there in 1944 and probably used it as a model for his 'cliff-perched town at the far end of Wales' in his play Under Milkwood. The other is its population of dolphins that, on most days, can easily be seen from the breakwater wall or from the trip boats that operate from the harbour.

We went off in search of showers and met three men taking a stroll along the harbour wall.

'Showers? You'll get them in the yacht club,' said one. 'It won't be open till Friday but Roger'll give you the key. See that house over there? Go and tell Roger you're visiting yachtsmen and he'll give you the key I'm sure.'

We followed directions. Roger had been gardening. He gave us a bunch of keys and told us to put them back 'under the cushion' on a chair in the porch when we'd finished, warning us that one of the men's showers was out of order and if I was going to wash my hair in the basin in the ladies to take care not to splash as the water ran into the 'fishermen's place' in the floor below. There was nothing to pay and we thought it was exceptionally trusting.

We had our showers and used the pay phone in the clubhouse to call my daughter, Sarah, and my mum. I used a left-over Irish fifty-pence piece to pay for one of my calls. It was only after the coin had dropped into the slot that I realised it was one of those private pay phones so I'd not only had a free shower but fiddled the club out of fifty pence into the bargain. I've been plagued with a guilty conscience ever since and one day, I promise, I will make it up to them.

That night we were forced to endure a gusty, onshore wind that meant we bumped, jolted and sloshed around all night, with Cevamp rocking from side to side. We tried to sleep, with me holding on to the rail on the edge of the table-cum-bed and Mike holding on to me. I snoozed a little and dreamt I was on a boat in a storm. Shortly after midnight Mike woke me up.

'Are you awake? We're not going to get any rest here. How d'you fancy trying for that buoy closer in to shore?'

I wasn't happy, but it was worth a try. I yawned dramatically, rubbed the sleep from my eyes and got dressed.

The engine wouldn't start. It just went click. On battery one, battery two and both together. Mike doesn't usually swear. He didn't, now. At least, not very much. We went back to bed. I went back to sleep.

'Are you awake?' said Mike again.

'Um,' I said.

'We're not going to get any sleep here. How about if we set sail now? Once we get going you can go back to bed till it gets light about half past six then you can take over and I'll get some sleep.'

'I can't think properly. I'm not awake,' I said, struggling into consciousness. I tried to think.

'What do you mean, I'll take over at half past six? We'll be at Aberystwyth by half past six,' I said.

'We won't get into Aberystwyth without an engine,' he said. 'I meant we'll go straight back to Porthmadog. I don't remember seeing a marine engineer here.'

I groaned silently.

'Oh. The engine. I'd forgotten about that. Let me think for a minute.'

I thought for a minute and I didn't think much of what I thought.

'It's an awful long way to Porthmadog without an engine and we've got two causeways to cross,' I said.

'That's why I want to go now. At least we know there's some wind now to get us clear of them. If the morning's anything like the last two it'll be flat calm.'

I tried to focus my brain into sensible thought. I know from past experience Mike has this stubborn determination to get the boat home, despite Alex telling us to leave her behind if there was the slightest risk. With the winds we'd been having, blowing from north-north east, I reckoned it could take us twenty-four hours to get back. We'd almost run out of food, apart from eggs, bacon and a little bread, butter and cheese. No milk, no soup and nothing for a hot dinner. If the wind died we'd have to wallow and even if it didn't we wouldn't be able to get into Aberystwyth or Barmouth without an engine. I thought Aberdovey was doubtful, too, because of the bar, and I knew how difficult the channel was into Porthmadog. Furthermore, if the weather turned really bad, which it could quite easily do at this time of year, we'd have no engine to help steady Cevamp or to run for shelter. I thought it was a very bad idea and was taking unnecessary risks. I thought we should stay put and ask around for a marine engineer in the morning. That was what I thought.

What I said was, 'I think we'd be foolish to go but if you really think we should then I'll go along with it. I just think that if it was the other way round, if we had total engine failure at sea, we'd run for the nearest port, for safety. I don't think we should go out without an engine but I will if that's what you want.'

Mike was silent for a while. I could feel him thinking. In the end he decided we'd stay for now and sail out in the morning. I went thankfully back to sleep.

Mike woke me with a cup of tea. It was still very early.

'I'm just popping ashore to see if there's anyone about who can give me some advice about the engine. If not, we'll set off when I get back. Stay in bed until I do,' he added.

After he'd gone I felt quite glum. I got the chart out and the dividers and found that Porthmadog is about fifty miles from New Quay. Still a long way but not anywhere near as far as I thought. I didn't think it was likely that anyone would be around at seven in the morning and resigned myself, not very happily, to the fact that we'd be going. Then I gave myself a mental shaking. I don't suppose Mike relishes it either, I thought. He's had even less sleep than I have and he has the boat to worry about too. It was a lovely morning and I decided to be as cheerful as possible, partly for my own sake but mainly for him. It was bad enough for him, without me sulking too.

When he got back I was up, washed, dressed and stowing the bedding.

He, too, was more optimistic than when he left.

'A man in the mackerel centre told me that Merv the lifeboatman knows about engines and he'll help us out. Apparently he drives a mauve Morris Marina and gets down here about eight o'clock, when he drops his wife off at the shop where she works.'

Then a fisherman came past in his boat. He confirmed Merv was our man.

'But it'll be more like nine before he gets down here.

He drives a mauve Marina and he's got a beard.'

He also told us that the owner of the mooring we were on used it for his pleasure boat, but he'd finished with it for the season and the boat had already been lifted out of the water.

'He's out fishing just now but he'll be back within the hour – that's the mooring for his fishing boat, over there.'

We had toast and marmalade and went ashore to wait for Merv in his mauve Marina. When he arrived he asked Mike a few questions and said it sounded like solenoid failure – or was it starter motor? Adams Garage was the place to go. Up the hill and turn left.

I went shopping while Mike went to the garage. Back on the boat he told me the garage man said he was a week behind, was very busy and couldn't help. But he wasn't too busy to give Mike loads of advice and even lent him some test apparatus to check the starter motor – or was it the solenoid? – and to test the batteries.

Mike spent some time with his head and arms in the engine compartment with the batteries. 'I think we need a new solenoid,' he finally declared, 'and number two battery's flat.'

Back into the dinghy with the battery and Mr Adams' testing apparatus. It was a long steep walk up the hill to the garage. Mike was carrying the battery, which was heavy. It was hot for September and he was dripping sweat when we got there.

'This battery's fully charged,' said Mr Adams, and fitted a new connector. He was a funny man. He tried hard to give the impression of being awkward and unhelpful then went out of his way to help, such as giving Mike a lift back down to the harbour with the battery.

He showed Mike how to short out the solenoid and start the engine by by-passing the solenoid or starter motor. Engines and electrics are mysteries to me and I still hadn't a clue what was the root of our problem. Mike did as he was told. We were filled with trepidation. Last time he shorted the engine electrics, they caught fire.

He tried starting it on battery one…nothing. He tried it on battery two…it fired.

We moved Cevamp closer in to shore and put the anchor down, hoping for a more peaceful night. Our arrival upset the owner of a boat doing bay trips and boat rides. We were in his way, he told us abruptly. We'd have to move. The harbour master would tell us where to go and would we do it straight away. We said the harbour master wasn't around and asked the surly man where he thought was the best place for us to move to, to be out of everyone's way.

'The harbour master's always around,' he said. 'See that house up there, with the red, white and blue awning? He lives there.'

Well. And to think we'd only tried his office.

The man was so unpleasant we uncharacteristically decided to eat our sandwich before we went. He came back.

'Are you going to move?'

'Yes. We're on our way up to the harbour master now.'

'Well can you move your boat before you go there? The tide's going out.'

We found the harbourmaster, a cheerful, bearded man, who pointed out a suitable mooring and refused to accept a mooring fee. 'Just mind you don't go barging into anything,' he said, as he waved us off.

That night we had a serious talk about our sailing

future, and Cevamp's. We'd had some wonderful holidays together over the years, but there was always something going wrong. It was clear to us that she now needed a lot of work over the winter on the engine, electrics and paintwork. What was more, one of the bilge keels urgently needed a repair.

'The trouble is,' said Mike, 'a lot of work means a lot of money. One option is to sell her and replace her with a fibreglass boat, perhaps even something a bit smaller.'

'But she's not our boat to sell,' I said. 'And how would your Dad feel about selling her? Cevamp's his dream come true.'

'Yes,' said Mike, 'She was. But I think the satisfaction for him was the actual building and knowing we get pleasure from her. I don't think he'll want to keep her just for sentimental reasons.'

What Mike said made sense. We'd done enough long trips by this time to know that we were capable of them. But we had to be realistic and recognise that while we were both working full-time we were too constrained by time to do them justice. For the next few years, we agreed, it would be better just to go harbour-hopping, giving ourselves time to linger, explore and stay a night or two. Ireland and Scotland would be long trips, once we retired.

'The other thing is that if we didn't have the financial upkeep of Cevamp we'd be able to afford to charter a boat abroad in the summer,' Mike added. 'What do you think?'

'I'll be sad if Cevamp goes,' I said. 'She's been such a big part of us and our lives together. But I think you're right.'

'I'll talk to Dad when we get back,' said Mike. 'I'm sure he'll agree.'

The next day was Wednesday and we had our longest lie-in of the holiday, getting up at nine twenty. It was a beautiful morning and after a quick trip ashore for milk and sticky buns we started the engine and left. We'd only travelled a few inches when we jolted to a halt. The mooring line, which was very short and impossible to throw clear, caught on the prop. Mike had an enforced swim to free it and we set off again. We had a wonderful day and we stripped off to make the most of the glorious weather. It was hazy but warm, the sea was gentle and green and the scenery was magnificent. We motor sailed into Aberystwyth and spent ten minutes motoring gently round the harbour. My eyes were drawn to an historic-looking old castle, interesting buildings forming the university, a trelliswork pier and a funicular railway up the hill.

We headed on to Barmouth, sailing, motor sailing and eating. We toyed with the idea of going on to Porthmadog but decided not to as it would have meant tackling the shallow channel in the dark, which we thought was unnecessary risk-taking so late in the holiday.

Once Cevamp was secure on a visitors' mooring buoy in Barmouth harbour Mike and I paddled ashore in the dinghy for a bottle of wine. The lights were on in the yacht club but we couldn't be bothered to go for showers. One more day wouldn't make much difference. As we drank our wine and ate our evening meal we laughed about the shocking decline in our standards of personal hygiene. We'd been away for nearly three weeks and in that time we'd had only four showers, compared with a bath or shower at least once and sometimes twice a day at home. I'd washed my hair five times. Usually it's every day. We'd done one load of laundry. At home it's every couple of days. Perhaps it's just as well we hadn't been in a single pub or yacht club bar. We clearly weren't fit for normal human company.

We were up bright and early for the final leg of the final day of our holiday. It was a fine, cool morning and we left Barmouth for Porthmadog on an ebbing tide just after eight thirty. We started off with full mainsail and genoa but as we approached St Patrick's Causeway the wind died right back and Mike switched the engine on. We saw a seal off Mochras Point, jets practising take-off and landing at Shell Island, lots of jellyfish and a dolphin between Harlech Castle and the Porthmadog Fairway buoy. Otherwise there was very little activity on the water and we realised it was actually quite late in the sailing season to be taking a summer holiday.

By lunchtime Cevamp was safely back on her own mooring. I packed my bag, tided up the cabin, polished the woodwork until it gleamed and Mike wrote his last entry in the log. Cevamp had taken us nearly six hundred and twenty miles in sixteen sailing days, an average of about thirty-nine miles a day, and despite all her problems had returned us safely back to Porthmadog.

We loaded up the car and returned to tuck Cevamp up under her covers. We gave her a long, final look as we drove away from Porthmadog and headed over the Berwyn Mountains to Llangynog, where Alex was waiting for us.

'Did you have a good trip,' he asked as he welcomed us back.

Mike drew a deep breath. 'Well actually Dad, there's something we want to tell you ...'

38

Cevamp's revenge

The temperature had dipped below zero and great flakes of snow dashed into our faces as a raw wind from the east gusted at forty knots or more.

All three of us were exhausted and tense. We'd been heading home since mid-afternoon, when we'd taken a chance on the weather and left Porthmadog harbour just as the light was failing. It was now late evening and the atrocious conditions were forcing us to make a one hundred and fifty mile detour to complete the forty mile journey.

The superstitious member of our party – me – was inwardly convinced that Cevamp had called up the gods and was now wreaking revenge in the way that only a spurned woman knows how. She had served us well, kept us safe through wind, waves and weather and in return we had rejected her. We'd sold our yacht.

We hadn't found it easy to tell Alex the decision we'd made on our way back from Ireland. We knew how much pleasure he got from hearing about our exploits, and we were painfully conscious of the pride he took in having built Cevamp. It was always a sadness to Mike and me that, because of Alex's ill health, he never really enjoyed the full fruits of his labour. And yet he'd accepted our news with good grace, agreed with our reasons and immediately set about advertising Cevamp.

And so it was, on a damp November day in 1990, the chilly quiet of Porthmadog harbour out of season was disturbed by the throb of a motorbike engine. The rider dismounted, removed his gloves and helmet and walked stiffly over to where Mike and I were sitting on a bench, hand outstretched.

'Mike Williamson? I'm Hugh Eaglesfield. Nice to meet you.'

Hugh had ridden the five hundred and twenty five miles to Porthmadog from his home in Rogart, Sutherland to take a look at Cevamp, a journey of about fourteen hours. He was the first person to respond to Alex's advertisement and we weren't sure whether to be pleased or sorry. But we took him over to Cevamp's winter's storage spot in the boatyard and showed him round. We pointed out all her foibles, right down to the crop of fungus growing up the bulkhead in the saloon. We were unable to put him off.

'I'll give you the asking price,' he said. He and Mike shook hands on the deal and made arrangements for the formal handover.

Now that had been done. We had said good-bye to a dream. And now, as Alex, Mike and I attempted to cross the bleak Berwyn Mountains in a snowstorm on a bitter winter's night, in a car with no chains on the wheels, Cevamp was paying us back.

The weather was already closing in as we began our drive back to Alex and Vera's pub in Llangynog but we were still enjoying the pleasant, rather desultory chit-chat common in people who know each other well and are comfortable in each other's company. Long before we reached the stage of wondering why on earth we hadn't brought flasks of hot soup and a supply of blankets, and blaming each other because we hadn't, I encouraged

Alex to reminisce for one last time on how Cevamp came to be built, starting from when she was nought but a twinkle in his eye and a set of plans gathering dust in a drawer.

'It's a long story. Are you sure you want to hear it all again?' he asked as he wrestled with the steering wheel on yet another icy patch of road.

'Well this looks like being a long night and there's nothing I'd like more,' I told him. 'I want to try and understand how it must have felt for you when you achieved your ambition and set sail for the first time in a yacht you'd built yourself.'

It was a fascinating tale, one that spanned many years and one that provided a welcome distraction from the demons of the wild night as it raged around us. Mike and I listened, captivated. Although we'd heard some of it before, neither of us was really aware of all the complications and difficulties that Alex surmounted to turn his dream into reality.

We never did make it over the mountains that night. It was a nightmare journey, and we ended up having to go a very long way, round Conwy and Oswestry. We pushed the car up every incline, slipping and stumbling as we went. Every few hundred yards we had to stop to dig ourselves out of the snow, shovelling it from beneath the wheels until our muscles ached. The final couple of miles were the worst. We could see the lights of the village ahead but our progress remained agonisingly slow and we finally reached the New Inn at Llangynog, mentally drained and physically exhausted, just before midnight.

Cevamp's revenge was complete.

Epilogue

Distant harbours

Once Cevamp was formally his, Hugh Eaglesfield made several more trips to Porthmadog, by car, and gradually Cevamp began to lose her identity for us. He replaced the port keel supports, carried out a few other repairs, painted her blue, changed her name to Gypsy and sailed her to her new home in the far north of Scotland.

Naturally, Mike and I were sad to see her go. She had, after all, been an important part of our lives – the third partner in our love triangle. Cevamp, Mike and me. The three of us had been inseparable for three years. I knew if I hadn't loved Cevamp, Mike would have quickly lost interest in me. And I have to admit, from my point of view, a man with a yacht was a pretty good catch!

But we soon dried our eyes. We knew our reasons for parting with Cevamp were sound and in any case, we had two new loves in our lives by now. The first was Beattie, an adorable eight week old beagle puppy. The second was Jayanems, our new yacht. A twenty-six foot Heavenly Twins catamaran, she was just a year old, in immaculate condition and, best of all, she didn't leak.

Over the next few years we gained another beagle, Bertie, and carried on sailing. Beattie and Bertie were our crew, dolphins our sometime companions and the yacht continued to be central to our lives together until the mid-1990s, when we sold Jayanems and took up scuba diving.

These days we enjoy the best of both worlds. We retired to a village on the north Pembrokeshire coast, joined a local scuba diving club and invested in a Westerly Tempest that we keep eight miles away in Fishguard harbour. Her name? The Jacqueline.

But what of Cevamp? Is she still afloat? We didn't know. In July 2006 I wrote to Hugh to ask whether he still had the boat and, if not, what happened to her. 'Where is she now?' I asked. 'Are you still sailing her, or does someone else now have that (dubious) pleasure? Or perhaps she has been scrapped after all this time?'

His reply had me smiling through tears.

'I sold the Eventide about ten years ago and I don't know if she is still afloat or not. Within three years of buying her she was leaking so badly along the keel I had to do a major repair, as the original build had not been good. During the repair I noticed blisters in the fibreglass and on inspection found the ply so rotten underneath I put my hand through it. To repair it I used two complete sheets of ply, making about twelve patches. I then re-skinned it.

'I sailed her for another couple of years but had not much confidence in her, so sold her for £1,500.

'I had some good sails around the West Coast of Scotland from Islay right round to the Inverness Firth, including of course most of the islands and the Outer Hebrides from Barra Head to Stornaway. I imagine she went round Cape Wrath and the Pentland Firth three or four times and to the Orkney Isles once. So as you can see, my memories of her are very varied.'

Good old Cevamp. Our memories of her are varied too. Some things never change.

Footnote: As this book was going to press I heard from Ron Billing, Cevamp's current owner. Now Gipsy Maiden, the yacht is still a feisty lady and still enjoying life in Scottish waters. Here are extracts from his letter:

'Hello Jackie,

I cannot tell you how delighted I am to hear from the builders of my beloved Gipsy Maiden.

I first bought her over five years ago (I have actually owned her twice!) from Victor Strong who had bought her from Hugh Eaglesfield. Initially when I first bought her she was wasn't in the best of order and had hardly been sailed, only motored. She is now in fine fettle although a new set of sails wouldn't come amiss as the mainsail ripped on a particularly boisterous trip up north.

I always knew this boat had something about her. When I sold her about a year after I'd bought her it was because of ill health. But I got better and the owner wasn't doing anything with her so I bought her back. She willed me to buy her back I'm convinced. I bought her originally for £3000, sold her for £4500 and bought her back for £4000. I think I'm in profit. So there's a story for your book: Gipsy Maiden neé Cevamp has magical powers!

The only problem I have with her is rain water leaks through the cockpit area. I had intended to sort it out but three major leaks on the deck had to be seen to first. The hull is as sound as a pound and the little engine which I'm sure is the original, still runs like a watch.

Grateful thanks for finding me.'

Appendix A
Cevamp facts and figures,
1986–1990

Total miles logged: 2,685
Total hours logged: 659
Total daylight hours logged: 584
Total night-time hours logged: 75

Average speed: 3.8 knots

Appendix B

Some recipes

Being of a certain age and somewhat old fashioned, I always use Imperial measures when cooking but have included what I believe to be workable metric equivalents for the following recipes. There may be some inconsistencies – trust me. If in doubt, use the Imperial!

Casseroles, stews and savouries

CEVAMP STEW

Prepare this versatile, hearty and warming stew before you leave harbour and leave it to cook gently while you're sailing. Good for eating from a bowl with a spoon while still at sea. Use as many or as few vegetables as you fancy!

Ingredients

Potatoes – as many as you think you will need for a couple of meals

1 or 2 onions

Selection of suitable vegetables of your choice: carrots, runner beans, swede, peas (tinned or frozen), sweetcorn (tinned or frozen), leeks, etc, etc

400g – 1kg / 1 or 2lbs of meat of your choice (braising beef, chicken breasts, pork steaks or casserole pork, lamb steaks or casserole lamb – be advised by the butcher)

1 or 2 tins of chopped tomatoes

1 or 2 appropriate stock cubes

3 tablespoons gravy granules

500ml / ¾ pint water, approx

Salt and pepper

To make

- Peel the potatoes and cut into ping-pong ball sized pieces, chop the onions and prepare the other vegetables in your usual way.

- Trim excess fat and gristle from the meat and cut the meat into bite sized pieces.
- Put the meat and all the vegetables into a large saucepan with a lockable lid – a pressure cooker is ideal for this (forget the pressure; just use it as a saucepan).
- Add the crumbled stock cubes, seasoning, tinned tomatoes and any other tinned vegetables.
- Sprinkle the gravy granules over the ingredients and mix well in. Bring to the boil and when it's bubbling add the water. Bring it back to the boil, secure the lid and cook on a very low heat for several hours. Adjust the seasoning and thickness (if too watery, add more gravy granules and bring back to the boil) before serving.

Middle Eastern Spiced lamb

Succulent chunks of lamb, lightly spiced with cumin and allspice and cooked gently in a rich sauce until tender. Very impressive and deceptively easy – ask the butcher to bone the meat for you. More filling than it looks, and serves four.

Ingredients

2 lb fillet end leg of lamb, cut from the bone
1 tablespoon cooking oil
25g / 1oz butter
2 medium onions
1 clove garlic
1 tablespoon plain flour
1 teaspoon ground cumin
½ teaspoon ground allspice (not the same thing as mixed spice)
2 tablespoons tomato puree
300 – 500ml / ½ – ¾ pint lamb stock (a stock cube is fine)
Salt and pepper

To make

- Cut the meat from the bone (or ask the butcher to do this for you), discarding fat and gristle, and cut it into bite sized pieces. Slice the onions fairly thinly and chop the garlic.
- Heat the oil in a thick-based saucepan (a pressure cooker saucepan is ideal), add the butter and when it foams brown the meat a few pieces at a time, transferring each batch onto a plate while the next lot browns.
- When all the meat is browned, add the onions and garlic to the pan and cook gently for five minutes, stirring to stop it sticking.

- Stir in the flour and spices and cook for another couple of minutes.
- Remove from heat and blend in the tomato puree with half the stock. Return to the heat, stirring, until it boils. Add the meat and cook gently for about an hour on top of the stove or in the oven on gas mark 4 / 180°C / 350°F. Stir from time to time and add the rest of the stock if necessary. Add salt and pepper to taste before serving.
- Serve with rice, crusty bread and butter and a green salad.

Mike's favourite sailing breakfast sandwich

A massive sandwich that keeps Mike going for at least a couple of hours! Can be made on a boat cooker with two burners and a grill. Serves one!

Ingredients

2 good quality, well-flavoured sausages

4 rashers thick back unsmoked bacon

2 eggs

2 slices thick sliced granary bread

Spray-on cooking oil

Butter

Tomato ketchup (optional)

To make

- Preheat the grill.
- Prick the sausages and grill on all sides.
- When the sausages are half cooked, spray some oil into a frying pan and heat the pan thoroughly. Add the bacon rashers and fry over a medium heat until almost done to your liking. Transfer the sausages to the pan with the bacon.
- Place the bread under the grill and toast lightly on both sides.
- While the bread is toasting, push the sausages and bacon to one side of the frying pan and break the eggs into the space, turning them when they are half cooked.
- Put the kettle on to boil, for tea or coffee (or other hot drink of your choice).

- Remove the toast from the grill, butter it generously and build the sandwich onto one slice with a layer of bacon, a layer of eggs and a layer of sausages (split in half lengthwise so they lie flat in the sandwich). Add tomato ketchup if wanted and top with the second slice of buttered toast.
- Serve with tea or coffee and await compliments!

JACKIE'S COW PIE

I've had people offering me a small fortune to make them a cow pie! Freezes well so you can make it well in advance and take it with you. This recipe is easily enough for four greedy people or six with normal appetites.

Ingredients

Short crust pastry made with 400g / 1lb flour, 200g / 8oz butter and sufficient cold water to bind (or equivalent amount of ready made pastry)

1kg / 2lbs of the best braising beef you can get
1 onion, peeled and sliced
1 stock cube
Gravy granules

To make

- Leave the pastry in a cool place while you prepare and cook the meat.
- Prepare the meat by removing and discarding excess fat, gristle etc. Cut the meat into bite sized pieces and place in an ovenproof casserole dish with the onion and crumbled stock cube. Make up 500ml / ¾ pt gravy granules, following the instructions on the carton. Pour the gravy over the meat. Cover the casserole dish with foil, shiny side down, and then put the lid on. Cook in the centre of the oven on a low temperature for two or three hours, until the meat is so tender it melts in your mouth. (Oven temperature of, say, gas mark 3 / 170° / 325° F – doesn't really matter how low it is, as long as you leave the meat to cook until it's really tender).

- When the meat is ready, remove it from the oven and raise the heat to gas mark 6 / 200°C / 400°F.
- Grease a large, deep pie dish or pie plate (minimum 23cm / 9˝). Cut the pastry into two and roll it out into two rounds. Use one round to line the pie dish / plate.
- Using a slotted spoon, transfer the meat from the casserole to the pie dish. Save the gravy to reheat and serve with the pie.
- Brush the pastry rim with water and then fit the other round of pastry over it. Press the edges down firmly, trim off the surplus pastry and make several crosses in the pie top using the point of a sharp knife.
- Place on a baking tray in the centre of the preheated oven and cook for half an hour, until the pastry looks cooked and golden.
- Serve the pie with its own gravy, mashed or new potatoes and a medley of vegetables such as carrots, broccoli, cabbage, cauliflower, runner beans etc.

YORKSHIRE PUD

My grandma was a Yorkshire-woman and made her puds instinctively. She taught me, so there are no precise weights and measures here. The important things to remember are to use plain flour and very hot fat. The secret ingredient? A splash of cold water! Traditionally served with roast beef but in our house it also comes with roast lamb, roast pork, roast chicken...

Ingredients

*One measure of plain flour
(eg, a small cupful)*
Pinch of salt
*Milk (Use one measure of
whatever you used for the
flour)*

Two eggs
Splash of cold water
*Dripping or fat from the
joint (vegetarians can use
sunflower oil)*

To make

- Heat the oven to gas mark 7 / 220°C / 425°F
- Sift the flour and salt into a small mixing bowl. Plop in the eggs and enough milk to beat to a thick sticky mixture, using an electric or hand whisk. Now add a splash of cold water and gradually, while still whisking, the rest of the milk. The mixture should be the consistency of smooth, thick cream.
- Heat a little fat in a sponge tin or individual patty tins and put near the top of the oven until the fat is smoking hot. Pour the pudding mixture into the tin or patties and return to the oven for about 10 minutes. Keep an eye on it as it changes from 'cooked' to 'burnt-round-the-edges' very quickly.

- If your first effort doesn't quite succeed – keep trying. They're never the same twice running and you'll get there in the end.

Soss Cass

Sausages with a difference, in a tomato-based sauce perked up with green peppers. Prepared in advance and served with crusty bread and butter, this makes another good cockpit meal and is enough for four or five people.

Ingredients

12 good quality pork sausages
2 x 400g tins chopped tomatoes
1 tablespoon cooking oil
2 onions
25g / 1oz plain flour
2 green peppers, seeded and sliced

Salt and pepper
1 tablespoon Worcestershire sauce (optional)
1 bay leaf (optional)

To make

- Heat the cooking oil in a thick-based saucepan (pressure cooker saucepan is ideal). Add the onion and cook gently for a few minutes until it softens. Blend in the flour. Add the tomatoes and peppers. Bring to the boil, stirring. Add salt, pepper, Worcestershire sauce and bay leaf. Simmer for about half an hour.
- In the meantime, parboils the sausages for ten minutes. Drain them, remove their skins and cut each one into three slanting slices. Add the sausages to the sauces and cook gently for another 30 minutes or so.

333

Puddings, cakes and sweet things

CHARLIE'S CHOCOLATE MARS BAR RICE KRISPIE CAKE

A real favourite in our family but be warned – it's very comforting, very more-ish and extremely fattening!

Ingredients

3 Mars bars (or two for a smaller one)

3 ounces butter (or two ditto)

3 tablespoons (15ml) golden syrup (or two ditto)

3 ounces Rice Krispies (or two ditto) (Supermarket own brand are fine)

2 large (200 gram) bars of milk chocolate

To make

- Use a little bit of extra butter to grease the sides and base of a 20cm / 8˝ cake tin with a removable bottom
- Cut the Mars bars into slices. Put them into the saucepan. Add the butter and the golden syrup. Heat them gently on the cooker, stirring all the time with a wooden or plastic spoon. When everything is melted and fairly smooth stir in the Rice Krispies. When they are well coated with the mixture, transfer it all into the cake tin. Smooth it over with the back of a metal spoon. Put it in the fridge for a while to cool down.

- While the cake is in the fridge break the chocolate into squares and put them into a pudding basin. Sit the pudding basin into a saucepan of near-boiling water so that the rim of the saucepan supports the basin. The bottom of the basin should not touch the water. Now heat the saucepan on the cooker but don't let the water boil. It should just simmer. Stir the chocolate with a clean metal spoon until it has melted and is nice and smooth.
- Take the cake out of the fridge and pour the melted chocolate over the cake. Use a knife if necessary, to spread it right over the cake. Leave in the fridge for a few hours until the chocolate has set.
- When it is ready, remove the cake from the tin by pushing it up from the bottom. Put it on a cutting board, cut it into pieces and enjoy.

FAYE'S MARMALADE CAKE

This is a lovely flavourful cake, with the advantage that it's easy to make and doesn't need eggs. Once cold, it keeps quite well, either wrapped in foil or in an airtight tin.

Vegetarians can substitute the lard with another 50g / 2oz butter or soft margarine.

Ingredients

225g / 8oz self raising flour (white or wholemeal)
50g / 2oz butter or soft margarine
50g / 2oz lard
110g / 4oz sugar (caster, soft brown or a mix)
Small pinch of salt
110g / 4oz mixed dried fruit
25g / chopped mixed peel (optional)

Grated rind of a lemon
Grated rind of an orange
1 teaspoon mixed spice (or more to suit your taste)
1 teaspoon cider or wine vinegar
175ml / 6 fluid oz milk (skimmed, semi skimmed or whole)
2 tbsp of strong flavoured marmalade

To make

- Heat the oven to gas mark 4 / 180°C / 350°F
- Grease a loaf tin and line the bottom with greased greaseproof paper (tin size approx 7″x3″ or 19cmx9cm)
- Rub the fat into the flour. Stir in the sugar, salt, mixed fruit, rinds, peel and spice. Slowly stir in the milk and mix it well in. Add the vinegar and stir until everything is well mixed. Now stir in the marmalade.

- Transfer the mixture into the tin and bake in the centre of the oven for about one and a quarter hours. When it's cooked, leave in the tin for a few minutes then transfer to a wire cooling rack.

QUICK AND EASY ROCKIES

Another great stand-by – but eat them while they're still warm to enjoy them at their best.

Ingredients

200g / 8oz self raising flour
1 teaspoon mixed spice (optional)
100g / 4oz butter or margarine
75g / 3oz caster sugar

100g / 4oz mixed dried fruit
25g / 1oz chopped peel (optional)
1 egg
3 teaspoons milk

To make

- Preheat oven to gas mark 6 / 200°C / 400°F
- Thoroughly grease a baking tray with butter or margarine
- Sift the flour and spice then rub in the butter or margarine. Add the sugar and fruit and stir them in. Beat the egg and milk and mix thoroughly into the mixture, which will be quite stiff. Dob eight to ten spoonfuls of the mixture onto the baking tray, leaving space between them to allow them to spread.
- Bake near the top of the oven for about 15 minutes.

Marianne's Easy-Going Apple Cake

An easy version of a traditional favourite. Serve hot with custard and/or cream (if you want to be really wicked) for pudding or cold as a cake. Delicious either way and doesn't last long! Use Bramley apples for the best flavour.

Ingredients

One very large, two large or three smaller cooking apples (peeled, cored and chopped into little dices)

75g / 3oz margarine, butter, Flora or Olive etc

175g / 6oz SR flour

75g / 3oz sugar (any type)

One or two eggs, lightly beaten (I usually use two but it works with one)

Optional: Add cinnamon and/or sultanas or anything else you fancy to ring the changes

To make

- Preheat oven to 180°C
- Grease a deepish 8" sandwich tin
- Rub the fat into the flour until it resembles breadcrumbs.
- Stir in the sugar and the apples.
- Stir in the egg. Keep stirring until everything is well mixed.
- Spread into the sandwich tin.
- Bake for 45 minutes.

Alternative method

- If you use a soft margarine (such as Flora, Olive etc) you can place all the ingredients except the apples in a mixing bowl, beat them with an electric mixer on a slow speed until they're all combined and fairly smooth, then stir in the apples before turning it all into the sandwich tin.

JACKIE'S SIMPLE SCONES

Brilliant for when there's nothing else – they can be on the table almost before the kettle has boiled.

Ingredients

200g / 8oz self raising flour, sifted

50g / 2oz soft margarine or butter

25g / 1oz caster sugar (optional)

50g / 2oz sultanas or raisins(optional)

150ml / ¼ pint fresh milk (skimmed, semi-skimmed or whole)

To make

- Preheat oven to gas mark 8 / 230°C / 450°F
- Thoroughly grease a baking tray with butter or margarine
- Sift the flour into a bowl and rub in the butter or margarine. Stir in the sugar, sultanas or raisins (if used). Add the milk and mix thoroughly. It will be a bit on the sticky side.
- Turn out onto a floured board or worktop. Using floured hands, knead lightly until smooth.
- Roll or pat lightly into a round, about 1 cm / ½ thick. Cut into rounds using a 7cm / 2½″ tart cutter or upturned wine glass and place on the baking tray. Bake near the top of the oven for about 10 minutes.
- If you prefer, you can bake it as one big scone round: Place the dough onto the greased baking tin, score into portions with a knife and bake as before, giving it a few extra minutes in the oven.

Fruity Banana Bread

Filling, energy-giving, full of flavour and not too heavy on the waistline!

Ingredients

½ teaspoon vegetable oil

120g / 4oz white or wholemeal SR flour

½ teaspoon ground mixed spice

60g / 2oz soft margarine or Olive spread

90g /3oz raisins

240g / 8oz bananas – weight when peeled

1 egg, beaten

½ tablespoon clear honey

To make

- Preheat the oven to gas mark 4 / 180°C / 350°F
- Brush a 480g / 1 lb loaf tin with the oil and line it with greased greaseproof paper.
- Mix the flour and spice in a bowl and rub in the margarine. Stir in the raisins.
- Mash the bananas with the egg and honey (I use a potato masher for this). Pour them into the flour and mix well.
- Transfer into the tin and bake on the middle shelf of the oven for 45 mins – one hour, until golden brown and firm.
- Leave in the tin for few minutes before turning out onto a cooling rack.
- This is okay to freeze, if you can stop people eating it before it cools down! A good way to use up very ripe bananas. When cool, wrap in greaseproof paper and store in an airtight tin for one day before slicing – if it lasts that long!

Sylve's Isley Bun

One from my mother's personal recipe archive – don't ask me where the name comes from. This is an excellent cake to take sailing – big and full bodied, it's a terrific stand-by on a miserable afternoon and easy to make too.

Ingredients

225g /8oz sugar
400ml / 1½ cups water
1½ teaspoons bicarbonate of soda
350g / 12oz raisins or mixed dried fruit

75g / 3oz butter or margarine
3 eggs
350g / 12oz self raising flour

To make

- Preheat oven to gas mark 3 / 170°C / 350°F
- Grease a 23cm / 9˝ cake tin and line it with greased greaseproof paper
- Bring sugar, water and bicarbonate of soda to the boil in a saucepan, reduce the heat and stir until the sugar has dissolved.
- Mix in the fruit and butter / margarine. Leave to cool.
- Beat the eggs and add them to the mixture, stirring them well in. Add the flour, stirring well until all the ingredients are combined.
- Transfer to the prepared cake tin and bake in the centre of the oven for 45 minutes – 1 hour 10 minutes. The cake will be done when a skewer inserted into the centre comes out clean.

Sylve's Famous Chocolate Cake

My mother is very proud of her recipe and makes these chocolate cakes-with-a-difference for Mike on a regular basis

Cake ingredients

175g / 6oz low fat natural yoghurt
275g / 10oz caster sugar
175g / 6oz soft margarine
3 eggs
1 tsp vanilla essence
225g / 8oz SR flour
50g / 2oz cocoa powder
1 tsp bicarbonate of soda

Icing

50g / 2oz soft margarine / Olive spread
3 tbsp milk
350g / 12oz icing sugar

To make the cake

- Preheat oven to gas mark 4 / 170°C / 325°F
- Grease a 23cm / 9˝ sprung tin. Line base with greased greaseproof paper, dust lightly with flour and tap out excess.
- Beat caster sugar and margarine in a mixing bowl until smooth. Beat in eggs, vanilla and yoghurt. Sift in flour, bi-carbonate of soda and cocoa powder. Pour into the tin and level the surface.
- Bake in the centre of the oven for 40–45 minutes or until skewer comes out clean. Leave tin on cooling rack for five minutes then turn the cake out and leave it to cool completely.

To make the icing
- Melt the margarine in a saucepan. Stir in the cocoa powder. Heat gently, stirring, until combined. Remove from heat. Stir in milk and icing sugar until everything is smooth.
- Spread icing smoothly over top and side of cake. Allow icing to set before serving.

Appendix C

What food to take on board?

If you're stuck for ideas, this list of food, taken on board for a recent two-and-a-bit week cruise around the southern and western coasts of Ireland may get you started. After nine days of sailing into the wind, heavy rolling seas, driving rain and next to no visibility we cut the trip short and came home again. This meant we were somewhat over-stocked and ended up bringing some of it home again. Despite that, it may be helpful as a guide for novice galley slaves who are still at the 'what on earth should we take with us?' stage. Please note: these days I take it a bit easier in the galley, and rely on quite a few ready made items, such as tinned puddings, crumble mix, sauce mixes, packet custard etc. And don't forget frozen oven-chips. They're great to bring back on board after a visit to local shops and just want to rustle up a quick meal. Serve them with anything you like!

There is a lot of stuff here but we are lucky in that we now live close to our home harbour. This means we can take non-perishable foods to the boat and get them stowed away on several trips in the days before we go. I'm not suggesting you would want to take this much with you if you have a long journey to your boat and plan to set sail the day you arrive! If this is the case, plan carefully, take with you just what you will need for the first couple of days and then shop locally for other items on an as-needed basis.

We never had a refrigerator on Cevamp but these days many yachts do have them. When considering quantities of food, it's important to remember yacht fridges are mainly powered by the engine or by shore power in marinas. Clearly, the more you sail the less you have the engine on so you can't keep food as cool and fresh for as long as you can at home. And you can't be sure you will be in a marina every night, either. Yes, I know, they can also run off the boat's service battery but it's wise not to rely on this form of power unless, of course, you want a flat battery and tantrums from the skipper.

And finally: We always take one ten-litre and 2 five-litre bottles of fresh drinking water with us at the start of a trip. We find five litres a day is sufficient for two people but we always take more as you never know when you will get to a tap.

This list is more than sufficient for two people for two weeks. You may want to adjust the quantities to suit your needs.

Bakery and cakes

Large, crusty, sliced granary loaf (for him)
Weight Watchers sliced granary loaf (for me. What a joke!)
Half-baked baguettes (vacuum packed, they last a couple of weeks)
Sylve's Famous Chocolate Cake (see Appendix B for recipe)
Sylve's Isley Bun (see Appendix B for recipe)

Fresh fruit
One bag of Braeburn apples (for him)
One bag of Pink Lady apples (for me)
Two large Bramley apples
One lemon
Bunch of bananas

Fresh veg and salad
Broccoli
Carrots
Leeks
Onions
Potatoes
Runner beans
Cucumber
Lettuce
Red onion
Red pepper
Tomatoes

Meat
Pack of eight sausages
Two packs of thick cut bacon
One pack of sliced ham
One pack of sliced chicken breast

Dairy
Two pints semi-skimmed milk (for him)
Two pints skimmed milk (for me)
Two pots of Elmlea (this cream substitute is almost as good as the real thing and keeps longer)
Four yoghurts (quick and easy puds when cooking is beyond you)
Packet of butter

Tub of easy-spread butter substitute (for cold days when the butter won't spread)
Slab of Cheddar cheese
Box of processed cheese triangles (as a change from butter on savoury sandwiches)
12 local free range eggs

Ready-made Items
Home-made beef casserole (sufficient for at least two main meals)
Frozen blackcurrant cheesecake (pudding for the above casserole)

Biscuits, snacks and sweets
Pack of individual orange and carrot cake slices
Two packs of individual cherry bakewells
One pack of chocolate digestive biscuits
One pack of chocolate orange wafer biscuits
Three packets of Jaffa cakes (comforting)
Packet of cream crackers
Large bag of salted peanuts
Two tubes of Pringles
Large bag of dried apricots
Pack of ten snack-sized Toffee Crisp
Pack of nine full-sized Mars bars
Bag of chocolate toffee éclairs
Bag of mint humbugs
Four tubes of fruit chews

Breakfast cereal
Plastic tubful of Bran Flakes with sultanas (for him)
Diet muesli (for me)

Cooking ingredients / sauces
Black pepper in grinder
Branston pickle (small chunks in plastic bottle)
Cooking oil (decanted into small plastic bottle) / spray-on cooking oil
Cumin and allspice (for Middle Eastern Spiced Lamb – see Appendix B for recipe)
Dried mixed veg for adding to casseroles in emergency
Easy-cook long grain rice
Garlic puree
Gravy granules
Mustard
Powdered milk substitute for emergencies (Coffee-mate is good)
Salt
Stock cubes: two each of vegetable, chicken, beef and lamb
Sugar: caster is the most versatile
Sugar-free jelly (sets quickly)
Tomato puree
Tomato ketchup
Vinegar
Makings, previously weighed, bagged and labeled for scones, rockies, apple cake and Yorkshire pud (see Appendix B for recipes)

Tins, packets, jars
Four cans baked beans
Four cans chopped tomatoes
Tinned spotted dick
Two packs of instant soup (warming and easy on days when the galley is impossible)
Jam
Marmalade

Mayonnaise
Schwartz packet mixes: chilli con carne, sausage casserole, spaghetti bolognaise, tuna & pasta bake
Tikka masala cook-in sauce
Tin of red salmon
Three tins of tuna
Two tins of grapefruit
Two tins of fruit (for quick and easy puddings)
Tin of fruit pie filling (for crumble)
Two packets of instant custard
Two packets of crumble mix

Drinks
Tea bags
Instant coffee
Instant drinking chocolate
Instant Ovaltine
Long-life orange juice in cartons
Ribena
Orange squash
Lemonade
Bottled fruit flavoured spring water
Four one-litre bottles of tonic
Six-pack of lager
Bottle of gin
Bottle of strawberry cream liqueur (seemed a good idea when we bought it in Spain)
Bottle of sherry
3-litre box red wine
3-litre box white wine